Felix Mendelssohn

A LIFE IN LETTERS

Felix Mendelssohn

A LIFE IN LETTERS

Edited by Rudolf Elvers

TRANSLATED FROM THE GERMAN BY

Craig Tomlinson

Fromm International Publishing Corporation

NEW YORK

The editor wishes to thank Frau Eveline Bartlitz,
Frau Corinna Fiedler, and Frau Dr. Cécile Lowenthal-Hensel for their
kind assistance in the preparation of this volume.

The translator wishes to thank Rudolf Elvers for his generous assistance,
and Raquel DaRosa for her many invaluable suggestions.

Translation copyright © 1986
Fromm International Publishing Corporation

Originally published in 1984 as
Felix Mendelssohn Bartholdy Briefe
Copyright © 1984, Fischer Taschenbuch Verlag GmbH,
Frankfurt/Main, West Germany

This edition published by arrangement with
Fischer Taschenbuch Verlag GmbH.

Designed by Constance Fogler
Printed in the United States of America
First U.S. Edition

Library of Congress Cataloging in Publication Data

Mendelssohn-Bartholdy, Felix, 1809–1847.
Felix Mendelssohn, a life in letters.

Translation of: Felix Mendelssohn Bartholdy Briefe.
Includes index.
1. Mendelssohn-Bartholdy, Felix, 1809–1847—
Correspondence. 2. Composers—Germany—Correspondence.
I. Elvers, Rudolf, 1924– . II. Tomlinson, Craig.
ML410.M5A4   1986   780'.92'4   [B]   86-12028
ISBN 0-88064-060-X

CONTENTS

house of Hermann Mendelssohn, the son of one of the composer's cousins. But the volume was put together by Paul Mendelssohn alone, without the assistance of Droysen. The book was a publishing success; three editions appeared within two years.

A continuation of the travel letters was likewise published by Hermann Mendelssohn in 1863, under the title *Briefe aus den Jahren 1833–1847* (Letters from the Years 1833–1847). The volume was assembled by Paul Mendelssohn and his nephew Karl, Felix Mendelssohn's eldest son. At that time both volumes were put under the series title of "Letters from the Years 1830–1847." They continued to appear in new editions until 1948, while a single-volume "inexpensive edition" was reprinted seven times before 1899.

The sensation caused by Felix Mendelssohn's letters, of which actually only a small selection had appeared, initiated a wave of publications of musical letters. The musical essayist Ludwig Nohl, who had published the first collections of the letters of Mozart and Beethoven in 1865, was particularly important in this regard; he also brought out a selection of letters by musicians in 1867, including several by Felix Mendelssohn which were missing in the two Leipzig volumes. An undiminished flood of publications of Mendelssohn's letters then followed, often accompanied by reminiscences of friends and contemporaries.

As the executor of the estate and guardian of Felix's children, Paul Mendelssohn for many years withheld publication of his brother's quite considerable musical *Nachlass*; the publication of the composer's posthumous works is a chapter in itself. But when Paul Mendelssohn died in 1874, Felix Mendelssohn's children quickly decided to make their father's musical estate, which had

INTRODUCTION

Berlin, February 1860.
Joh. Gust. Droysen.
Paul Mendelssohn Bartholdy.

To all persons in the possession of letters by Felix Mendelssohn Bartholdy: The undersigned believe that they may be certain of the approval of all who cherish the memory of Felix Mendelssohn Bartholdy in undertaking the publication of a series of letters particularly illustrative of his life and works, selected from among the many he wrote. They are already in possession of almost all of the letters written to people who could be found directly; but of many other letters there are no records.—Thus they take the liberty of humbly requesting that the unknown recipients of such letters, or those in whose possession they may be found, send either the originals—which will be gratefully returned afterward—or reliable copies, unfranked.

This notice appeared in Berlin and in newspapers in other German cities, as well as several music periodicals, in February and March of 1860. Mendelssohn's close friend Droysen and brother Paul were able to obtain a large number of letters in addition to the ones already available, and thus the *Reisebriefe von F.M.B. aus den Jahren 1830–1832* (Travel Letters of F.M.B. from 1830 to 1832) could have been published as early as the autumn of 1861, appearing in the Leipzig publishing

ILLUSTRATIONS

been carefully bound together in green volumes, available to the public. In exchange for the foundation of a "Mendelssohn Scholarship," they sold them to the Prussian treasury in Berlin, where they were placed in the Royal Libraries. The more than nine hundred letters which Mendelssohn had written "home" during his short life, however, to his parents and siblings—source material of incalculable value—still remained unavailable. They were to remain so until the present day.

II

Letter writing was carefully cultivated in the Mendelssohn household, and the family had long maintained the tradition. The letters of Felix's grandfather Moses are still striking in their elegance, and the next generation practically made a cult of letter writing, starting with Felix's aunt Dorothea Schlegel and continued by his mother Lea, of whose lengthy letters hundreds have survived. The family had a large number of relatives, in Vienna, Paris, and Stockholm, all with an insatiable appetite for news. It was a steadfast rule that the children should report home when traveling, regularly and in great detail, even down to awkward financial circumstances arising during the trips. Whenever regular reports were not provided, those left at home grew restive, and reproaches were heard, but usually everything was cleared up amicably. In his letters to Leipziger Strasse 3, the family's main headquarters, Felix Mendelssohn was completely unconstrained, and he was even more open when writing to his elder sister Fanny, who remained within the family even after her marriage to Wilhelm Hensel, since the two continued to live in the parents' house. After the death of his mother, Fanny remained his closest confidante. The two younger siblings, Rebecka and Paul, were neglected somewhat by comparison, although his brother was kept in complete confidence in all official dealings, such as those with various Berlin ministries; Paul was responsible for overseeing the family estate, and, together with his cousin Alexander Mendelssohn, for managing the renowned banking house of Mendelssohn and Company. But financial matters were written about as little as possible.

Mendelssohn found it difficult to write "these cursed diplomatic letters." Thus several rough drafts have survived which clearly show him struggling to find the proper form for his subject matter. Ministers, royalty, and "other potentates" had to be treated according to custom. The style is less formal when he writes to older colleagues such as Ludwig Spohr, or his much-beloved teacher Karl Friedrich Zelter. He was completely open when writing to his intimate friends; a good example is provided by his gradually evolving friendship with Heinrich Konrad Schleinitz in Leipzig, the last of his close friends.

There were no manifestos or public declarations by Mendelssohn. For him a letter was what it was always intended to be, a purely private communication shared with another person, for whom alone it was intended and comprehensible. For this reason some of his letters are difficult to interpret, in that only the addressee would have been able to understand various references and turns of phrase. And many quotations from unknown authors are worked into the letters, without any indications as to their source, and thus comprehensible only to their recipients; this is particularly apparent in the letters to his family.

III

Mendelssohn saved almost all of the letters he received, and a total of almost seven thousand; they were bound in green-colored volumes each year. These are now in the Bodleian Library in Oxford. He gave only a very few to friends who collected autographs, usually women, such as his friend Klingemann's wife and his sister-in-law Julie Schunck. Since he had been brought up to respond to the letters he received, he must have written about as many letters during his short life—for us it is an unimaginable number, especially when one looks at the thousands of pages of his musical manuscripts which survive. About five thousand letters are currently known; selecting from among them for this volume was a difficult task, and inevitably a subjective one. Since the letters to his family have all survived, and also make up almost a fifth of the total, these have been emphasized here. The others provide more of a framework, included to show Mendelssohn as a conductor and music director, how he evaluated an opera libretto, how he took an interest in his nephew Sebastian, wrote thanks for an honorary award or a gift, or procured a decent pianoforte for his cousin Benjamin (Mendelssohn was imposed upon to select more than two dozen pianos for his relatives and friends.)

Owing to limitations of space, it was necessary to omit many important letters—ones which would well have deserved inclusion (among them letters to Klingemann, Schubring, and David). But it may be hoped that this selection will allow the unique character of this musician to appear to the reader in all his subjectivity, this remarkable man who left nothing uncompleted, though his life was all too short.

The Mendelssohn letters which survive are spread throughout America and Europe in public institutions and private collections. Those printed in this volume are found in the following locations, and the editor wishes to thank all of them, as well as Frau Johanna Neis, Königswinter, for her kind and generous assistance in transcribing them: AMSTERDAM (Maatschappij tot Bevordering der Toonkunst); BERLIN (GDR: Deutsche Staatsbibliothek, Musikabteilung): WEST BERLIN (Staatsbibliothek Preussischer Kulturbesitz, Handschriftenabteilung, Musikabteilung, Mendelssohn-Archiv); DARMSTADT (Landes-und Hochschulbibliothek); DÜSSELDORF (Goethe-Museum A. and K. Kippenberg, Heinrich-Heine-Institut); HALLE (Handel-Haus); HANOVER (Kestner-Museum); LEIPZIG (Museum für Geschichte, Stadtarchiv); MERSEBURG (Deutsches Zentralarchiv); MUNICH (Bayerische Staatsbibliothek, Handschriftenabteilung); NEW YORK (Public Library, Otto Lobbenberg Collection); OXFORD (Bodleian Library, Department of Western Manuscripts); PRAGUE (National Museum, Music Division); WASHINGTON (Library of Congress); WEIMAR (Nationale Forschungs-und Gedenkstätten); VIENNA (Gesellschaft der Musikfreunde); and three anonymous European private collections.

YOUTH AND EARLY TRAVEL

The Mendelssohn children, Fanny, Felix, Rebecka, and Paul, were raised in an atmosphere which emulated the ideal classical education of mind and body; the children received instruction in ancient and modern languages, mathematics, drawing, gymnastics, and swimming—and, of course, above all in music. They traveled for the purpose of learning as well as for vacation, and they were constantly pressed to record their experiences in writing, by means of letters as well as drawings, so that those family members who were unable to come along could share as much as possible of the experience.

A brief glance at the surviving letters written by Felix Mendelssohn prior to his first great trip to England in 1829 is all that is required to convince us that these "letters home" are strikingly descriptive. When the whole family traveled together, as in Switzerland in 1822, Mendelssohn reported the trip in just as much detail to his teacher Karl Friedrich Zelter.

The early letters from Berlin—doubtless composed under the supervision of his mother Lea—display striking perceptiveness. The young Felix was quite candid when writing to his organ teacher, August Wilhelm Bach, and to Johann Ludwig Casper, who often frequented the household and later became a prominent Berlin physician; in contrast, he was poised and formal in his correspondence with Friedrich Voigts in Hanover, whom he did not know personally. Voigts provided the libretto for Mendelssohn's only (and unsuccessful) opera, The Marriage of Camacho (Die Hochzeit des Camacho).

When writing to other musicians the young Mendelssohn was quite frank in expressing his opinions; judgments as candid as the one about some of Herr Kelz's fugues were rarely to be found later in his life. Just how important his first performance of Johann Sebastian Bach's St. Matthew Passion in 1829 was to him was shown by a previously unknown letter inviting the conductor Johann Schneider from Dessau, whom he greatly admired, to attend. And, of course, Mendelssohn sent the only book he wrote, a translation of Terence's Woman of Andros, to His Excellency Johann Wolfgang von Goethe, accompanied by a carefully worded, confiding note. Other letters serve to cast light on everyday life: Mendelssohn borrowed a book from the librarian and curator of the Berlin Sing-Akademie, Georg Poelchau, invited the singer Eduard Devrient to a private family concert (naturally including compositions by Bach), sent an annotated score of Handel's Acis and Galatea to his composition teacher, Zelter, and consoled a distraught Swedish friend and classmate, A. F. Lindblad, in tones alternately humorous and warmhearted.

Felix Mendelssohn

A LIFE IN LETTERS

Berlin, August 2, 1820

Dear Herr Doctor,

How grateful I am to you for the lovely operetta! I will
do my best to compose it so as to do credit to the
translation. I already have the scheme in my head. But
I won't start until after our trip, so that I will be able
to devote all my spare time to it, and summon all of my
muses to do honor to the words. Zerbine and the duchess
will be sopranos, Felix and Victor tenors, and Tonio
and Ernst basses. I don't care for the portraits of Victor,
because they make him look like a dolt, and I had
pictured him as looking just like you during that strange
illness when you looked like a hussar.

I found Nos. 8 and 9 especially appealing. I am very
pleased that you inserted the first duet, for I would not
have been as happy if you had started off with a dialogue.

Of the first duet I can say: "C'est tout fait, il n'y a
qu'à l'écrire." For I have worked it all out in my head
already. I am especially pleased with Tonio's "Ha, ha,
I don't believe it" ["Hä, hä, glaub's nicht"], for example,
how he doesn't believe that he is crazy. I recently did a
new sonata, which Herr Berger liked. I am saving it in
order to play it for you myself. I hope I shall see you
again soon? Please do come again very soon. I hope

you are seeing lots of fascinating things, and remain yours as ever,

Felix Mendelssohn

The "lovely operetta" is the still-unpublished Singspiel Die Soldatenlieb-schaft (Soldiers' Loves.)

To August Wilhelm Bach

Berlin, the 3rd day of the lovely month of May, 1821

What does the sexton say, my dear Herr Bach? Can we play this afternoon? Or is there a wedding? or a confirmation? Please be so kind as to send answers to my many questions via the bearer of this letter. Unless we are thwarted by one of these things today, I'll be waiting at the tower punctually at four, with my sister (as you permitted). Greetings to the Prelude and Fugue in G Minor. I am presently sweating over an *organ fugue*, which will come forth into the world within the next few days. My heartfelt greetings to all of the principal pipes, yours faithful,

F. Mendelssohn

At the end of October 1821 Karl Friedrich Zelter visited Goethe in Weimar, together with his daughter Doris and pupil Felix; he thus renewed ties between the Mendelssohn family and the poet, whom Abraham Mendelssohn had met in Strasbourg as early as 1797 (likewise through Zelter).

The "motet" mentioned in the following letter is probably one of the six four- and five-voice motets on German religious texts written by Mendelssohn under Zelter's tutelage in 1820–21 as examples of vocal polyphonic writing (all still unpublished).

To Abraham Mendelssohn Bartholdy[1]

Leipzig, Tuesday, October 30, 1821

This time, dear Paul, I shall begin with you, and my heartfelt congratulations to you on your birthday. Indeed I have often thought of you today, and wished we could be having fun together. When Father writes me you can write me too, so that I may learn what nice presents you received. Casparis must have been at the house, and no doubt the blue room was turned upside down; and amid all the merriment I hope you haven't forgotten my Monk? Grow tall for me, both in mind and body, and may you soon be done with the pronouns. This is my wish, and also that *you* remember me to Grandmother. Are you listening?—But to continue.— First of all I must tell you, dear parents, that Professor Chladni lives in Kemberg, and came on foot from there to visit us on Sunday, and then returned on foot as well. We drove to Kemberg at three on Monday, after I worked on my opera in the morning from seven to twelve. I am already up to the finale, dear Fanny. At twelve we climbed up the towers of the Stadtkirche, and from the gallery or bridge which connects the towers there is a very pretty view. So, at three we rode to Kemberg, a tiny little spot, or village, where Dr. Chladni received us, telling us that we should be his guests. We retired immediately to his apartment, single small room,

1. The young Felix Mendelssohn's letters home, though usually addressed to his father and his mother, were most often intended for the whole family; consequently Felix alternates between the second-person singular (*du*) and plural (*ihr*) in these letters.

in which his instruments, three Klavicylinders and a Euphon, are kept.[2] (Ask Beckchen[3] what a glass harmonica is.) This room is his bedroom, his workshop, and his visiting room. All of his tools are there, and there is a newly begun Euphon in a small cabinet. He played all of his instruments for us. The clavier-cylinder's tone is like that of a very gentle oboe. The Euphon is made of glass rods, which are moistened and then stroked with wet fingers; the sound is like that obtained by rubbing glass chimes. So you can easily imagine, dear Fanny, what this instrument sounds like. We then retired to our *feather beds* and slept quite—poorly. Professor Zelter complained about the shortness of his bed, Doris about the bug population in hers, and I about the wretched feathers. Before daybreak I felt a hand being gently placed on me, drawing back the cover a bit. It was the professor. I asked if he wanted something, if I should get him some water, or anything else? He said: "Oh no, I dreamed that someone had stolen you from me, and then I wanted to see if you were still there!!!—?"

The next morning we rode to Düben; the cold was unbearable, and halfway along the bad sandy road we ordered a *Warmbier*.[4] When we arrived in Kransatz I saw the exact same spot and doorstep where a year ago we waited out that terrible thunderstorm. At half past seven we arrived in Leipzig, and checked into the Hôtel de Russie, which was a bit of a contrast to the Hôtel de Kemberg. I sat down to write this letter to all of you: but soon we were called to the table d'hôte. I hope I

2. Euphon, Klavicylinder: friction rod instruments invented in the 1790s by Ernst Friedrich Chladni; relatives of the glass harmonica.
3. "Beckchen" was a diminutive nickname for Felix's sister Rebecka.
4. *Warmbier*: a drink of warmed beer, sugar, and spices.

needn't ask about all of your health, and Father's? But how is Marianne?

The 31st

At eight-thirty. We slept well, and will go to the post office at nine, then to visit old Schicht. I'll have to present my motet. Forgive my poor handwriting, or rather my poor pen; it really is very bad. Tonight we'll be going to the theater, *Das Leben ein Traum*[5] is being performed. Remember me to all our dear friends, and pass along what I wrote about my opera to Dr. Casper. I have already read a bit of my Caesar, Herr Heyse, and send my *most courteous regards* to you. A kiss to all of you.

F. Mendelssohn

To Abraham Mendelssohn Bartholdy

Weimar, November 6, 1821

Men think,the pen guides.[1] Just as I was about to write you to scold you all for being so lazy about writing, look, along comes a nice, nice letter, which made the old *hen* very happy. Paul, your face is very pretty, and I could draw one of my *cheerful* faces for you, but I shall draw it for you *in natura* in Berlin instead. Now listen everybody, all of you! Today is Tuesday. Sunday, the Sun of Weimar, Goethe, arrived. In the morning we went to church, where half of the 100th Psalm by Handel was performed. The organ is large but weak, and the St. Mary organ is much more powerful, though

5. *La vida es sueño* (Life Is a Dream), by Calderón de la Barca (1600–1681).

1. *Der Mensch denkt's, die Feder lenkt's.* Play on words, from the German proverb "Der Mensch denkt's, Gott lenkt's."

smaller. The one here has fifty ranks, forty-four stops, and one thirty-two foot pedal. Afterward I wrote the short letter dated the 4th and went to the Elephant,[2] where I drew Lukas Cranach's house. Two hours later Professor Zelter came. Goethe is here, the old gentleman is here! In a flash we were at the bottom of the steps— in Goethe's house. He was in the garden, and was just coming around a hedge; isn't that odd, dear Father, just the way it happened when you met him? He is very friendly, but I don't think any of his portraits look at all like him. He then inspected his interesting collection of fossils, which his son organized, and kept saying: Hm, Hm, I am quite pleased; afterward I walked around the garden with him and Prof. Zelter for another half hour. Then we sat down to eat. One would think he was fifty years old, not seventy-three. After dinner Fräulein Ulrike, Goethe's wife's sister, requested a kiss, and I did likewise. Every morning I receive a kiss from the author of *Faust* and of *Werther*, and every afternoon two kisses from Goethe, friend and father. Fancy that!! (In Leipzig I went through the remarkable Auerbach courtyard several times, a large alley of the type which is common in Leipzig, packed with stores and people, and surrounded by houses six to seven stories tall. Facing the marketplace there is even one which is nine stories tall.) But how I have strayed! In the afternoon I played for Goethe for over two hours, in part fugues by Bach, and in part I improvised. In the evening they played whist, and Prof. Zelter, who played at first, said to me: Whist means that you should keep your mouth shut. Strong language! In the evening we all ate together, even Goethe, who usually never eats at night.

2. Renowned hotel in Leipzig.

Now, my dear coughing Fanny![3] Early yesterday I showed your songs to Frau von Goethe, who has a pretty voice. She is going to sing them for the old gentleman. I also told him already that you wrote them, and asked him if he would like to hear them. He said yes, yes, very much. Frau von Goethe is especially fond of them. A good omen. Today or tomorrow he will hear them. I am very sorry that I shall not see Lipinski anymore.

To Father. We will certainly stay here the rest of the week, perhaps longer. Last night there was a tragic accident. The younger Herr von Goethe was at the Schloss, and suddenly a loud shot was heard inside the Schloss itself. The archduke's gamekeeper was trying to pull a rifle from out of the case. The barrel was lodged against the trigger of another rifle, which was loaded, so that when he yanked at it the other one went off from the pressure on the trigger. The ball went through the case, through his clothes, through his hand, and right through his body into the wall. He was carried to the emergency station, and died at one o'clock in the morning. He was not married; but his mother is still alive. How sad!

To Mother. I thank you most humbly for your kind defense, I think you are right. Please be so kind as to thank Cousin Pereira for the libretto, and as soon as I am back home again I will certainly do so as well. Tuereine is very pretty. If you take me for *Klein-Zaches*, then Doris is *Rosabelwerde*, for she's the one who combs my unruly mane.[4]

3. Wilfred Blunt (*On Wings of Song*, p. 35) explains that "when Felix submitted his latest compositions to his sister, she used to mark any disapproval by coughing."

4. *Klein-Zaches, Rosabelwerde*: characters in *Klein Zaches Genannt Zinnober*, novel by E.T.A. Hoffmann (1819).

For Grandmother. Yesterday I went to see Frau von Henkel at ten, and there was music making; and in the evening Herr Prof. and Doris visited Frau von Heigendorf. I also went to the theater yesterday. And saw Mme. Hartknoch, who acted very nicely. What are the Freitags doing, and the aunts?

For the merry doctor: I have already worked diligently up through the finale, and am very much looking forward to hearing my two operas. I thank you for your letter, and assure you that I would gladly leap through fire for you, but that just then the work bells were calling; so just a couple more lines to little Roe-bucka— and this feast will have ceased.[5]

To Rebecka. Here is a riddle. In Leipzig we stayed for a while, with a man whom all thought vile, and yet his house was clean. What can this riddle mean?

I thank you, dear Marianne, for the lines you wrote. I end with you, since it is customary to conclude with what is beautiful and valuable.

F. Mendelssohn

To Karl Friedrich Zelter

Frankfurt, July 19, 1822

So, we have arrived in Frankfurt, and have also stopped in Magdeburg, Cassel, and the Harz. The weather was as favorable as we could have wished for, and only on the last day of the trip was the heat severe, so that Mother was slightly exhausted (though thank goodness not seriously) from the trip. Otherwise we are all fresh

5. *Rehböckchen*: a pun on the name of Rebecka and *Rehbock*, roe deer.

and healthy, and Paul and I both have terrible sunburns. I have already sketched some scenes from the Harz in my little book, but have had less time to compose so far, and have only been able to work on my fourth opera a little.

I am extraordinarily fond of the Harz, and had imagined it completely differently; I always pictured it wild and rough, but it is quite the opposite, peaceful and charming. We did not go up to the top of the Brocken because the weather there is seldom supposed to be good enough that one may enjoy a pretty view, and because the long Herr Philistine was making altogether too much wind, and brewing clouds. But we did climb to the Rosstrappe, and Baumannshöhle, and the Stubenberg, and admired them, as they indeed well deserve. On the Rosstrappe (a high cliff which is surrounded by even higher cliffs) a pistol was shot off. The shot had barely sounded when an echo came back from the closest cliff, and then about five seconds later there was a second distant echo, which sounded like rolling thunder. The Baumannshöhle is entirely different, though no less imposing. One dresses in miner's overalls and uses a miner's lantern to climb into the cave, which is made of pure stalactite, and soon one loses sight of the daylight, seeing endless abysses wherever one looks, where perhaps nobody has ever been. The path is wet and slippery, and the air in the cave is very cool. One climbs on ladders from one cave to the next, everything is absolutely still, the miner's lanterns light up only a small spot, and all around there is black darkness. One wanders among the strangest figures formed by the stalactites, here there is a monk, there a crucifix, here a baptismal font, there a Virgin Mary, here a flag— which is *transparent*—there an organ, a waterfall, a cow, and only God and the guide could know the huge multitude of forms which the unfathomable cave has created for itself. Forty caves are known, and God knows how many have not been discovered. Only seven of them are usually visited, and we saw just five, even though we stayed in this abyss for an hour. How refreshing it is to see the daylight after one has wandered through the darkness for so long.

Save for the fact that I was left behind in Potsdam and had to walk two miles, no adventures have come my way. In Magdeburg I went to visit Seebach, but didn't find him at home. I did see Wachsmann one evening.

In Cassel I made use of your kind letter to Spohr, he welcomed me in cordially, and in the evening a string quartet played at the house; he played two of his quartets, and I played mine. It was very kind of him to accompany me.

I remain, Herr Professor, your devoted pupil,

F. Mendelssohn

P.S. In Ballenstedt in the Harz I played the organ at the Schloss, which was quite a task—ten voices, six of which did not work at all—if you had been there, you would surely have taken the organist to task (as with Motschiedler) and said: Quos ego!—but I was happy that at least four were functioning and played the miserable thing until I was exhausted.

Mendelssohn met Spohr through a letter of recommendation from Zelter, and remained respectfully devoted to him throughout his entire life. The quartet which was played in Spohr's house was probably the Piano Quartet, op. 1.

To Karl Friedrich Zelter

Interlaken, August 22, 1822

So, we are now in Interlaken, right in the middle of Switzerland, whose beauty cannot be expressed in words, as every guidebook in the world has already stated. We didn't "spare" the mountains, as you put it, and it cannot be denied that we visited the Albis, Rigi, and Teufelsbrücke, and were in the Unserene-Tal at the foot of the Gotthard. Father hopes he will lose weight in the mountains, Mother, that she in turn will gain some; Fanny is also climbing up, and where she cannot travel on her *own* feet, her horse's or porter's seem to be adequate; Paul is walking his legs off; and Beckchen too climbed quite a ways up the Rigi; and the gallant Fräulein has also been riding a few times, which was no harder on her than some of the Wednesday or Saturday afternoon rides. In short, we are all cheerful, healthy, and in good humor; were it possible, though, I would ask them to just sit in the blue sofa and have it carried here.

And now, my dear Herr Professor, I shall tell you all about our trip from Zürich, since that will probably interest you most of all.

In Zürich I was introduced to Herr Liste, who sends his regards, via a letter from Spohr, who always praised him as a good musician, and even more as an outstanding hiker who had traveled through all of Switzerland, which he indeed proved to be. As chance would have it, we did not get together until four hours before our departure; the discussion turned to his hikes, and how he next hoped to climb the Rigi, one thing led to another, and in short, he promised to take us up to the Rigi.—From Zürich we climbed to the Albis-Hochwacht, then down the Albis, around Lake Türler, and to Zug. But Liste, in order to demonstrate his knowledge of the footpaths (since we had already had ample opportunity to observe his long legs, which made all paths into shortcuts), came down from the Albis with Herr Heyse on foot, on footpaths, across fields, over hedges and fences, and over cemeteries, appearing now in front of us, now in back of us, and finally arrived in Zug a half hour ahead of us; there we were taken in by very friendly and well-bred innkeepers, and since the elder Mlle. Saling's illness, which wasn't serious, kept us another day in Zug, we went to see the paintings by Annibale and Ludovico Carracci in the church, and I myself played the organ, which is missing a few things— here it sputters on G-sharp, there on B-flat, etc. At the home of a certain Professor Kaiser I played on a rather good fortepiano. That same day we went across the charming Zuger See, departing from Immisen, where Gessler wanted to go, through the gorge, which isn't as awful as Schiller must have imagined it.[1] It is a beautiful and rather wide ravine lined with slender beech trees, and the chapel is quite pretty, standing in the middle of a fresh green meadow. The others went to Küssnacht, but I remained on the hallowed grounds, drawing this attractive and yet somehow ghastly ravine. We then returned to Zug, but Liste continued on up the Rigi.

The next day we drove to Arth and Goldau, and then left Goldau to climb the Rigi with a caravan of porters and guides, thirty-four in all. When we had put about

1. Gessler, Schiller: references to Friedrich Schiller's drama *Wilhelm Tell.*

half the distance behind us, we ran into a sudden
downpour, which we waited out in a hut. When the
rain had abated somewhat, we continued climbing along
the slippery paths, first to a cloister named Maria vom
Schnee, then to Rigistoffen, and finally arrived at the
summit; we all quickly crawled into the inn, as the air
at the summit was raw and cutting, and the whole area
was blanketed by a thick fog. Only occasionally did a
break in the clouds afford us enough of a view of the
region to show its beauty, and everyone regretted
the bad weather. Hoping we might look forward to the
sound of the alpenhorn, which is sounded when the
weather improves, we then went to bed. The next
morning no alpenhorns sounded, sullen faces emerged
from every room, and Liste went back down;—the
summit was covered with a thick fog, one could see
nothing but rapidly moving clouds. Father was at the
point of abandoning the summit, but since we wouldn't
have been able to make it to Lucerne anyway, it was
decided to leave the following morning. In the evening
there were pretty views, but we couldn't see the snow-
capped peaks. Dejectedly, everyone returned to their
little cells.—Then I heard some little bells ringing during
the night, shortly before dawn, and after this had
continued for several minutes an alpenhorn suddenly
boomed forth, everything awakened, and it seemed to
me I was dreaming—the brightest of mornings had
begun to dawn, the moon was shining brightly and lit
up the snowy peaks; the Schreckhorn, Jungfrau, and
Finsteraarhorn were clearly visible, there wasn't a cloud
in the sky, and hordes of people were streaming toward
the summit. The sun came up, turning the snow-covered
mountains red, but in the valley it was still night; little
by little day broke over the Rigi and Pilatus, and finally

in the heights over the valley and then the valley itself, and an old guide opined: Dawn can easily be this beautiful on the Rigi, but more beautiful it cannot be.

We still plan to go to Lauterbrunnen today, and we won't omit the Grindelwald glacier and valley. So I'll close for now, the day after tomorrow we'll be back here again, and I won't fail to write you about our further adventures.

Your devoted pupil,

F. Mendelssohn

To Lea Mendelssohn Bartholdy

Breslau, August 9, 1823

So we have arrived in Breslau, quite healthy, happy, and hungry. Father and Heinz have gone to see the girl from Marienburg. Paul is thinking on the sofa (he is thinking of falling asleep), and I am writing this little note. Our inn here is nice, except for a few flaws, i.e.: It looks bad from the outside, and is no better on the inside, the rooms are tiny, damp, hot, high up, the people are unfriendly, the courtyard very dirty, the location is quite ugly, etc., etc. Otherwise it's an outstanding place.

Now I will turn to the obligatory details; thank goodness we arrived without accident, peril, misadventure, or breakdowns; so where am I to find some? I would have to tell the story of how we got only a little wine in Müncheberg, lousy wine in Crossen, and none at all in Parchwitz, otherwise I'd soon run out of things to tell. Meanwhile I know you are all interested in hearing about all of our trip, ergo, I will begin describing our various adventures, even though we didn't have any whatsoever.

After we had refreshed ourselves with the beautiful view from Vogelsdorf, which really is "delightfully pretty," we arrived in Müncheberg, and here (*for Beckchen*) I found to my great surprise the much-admired, highly praised—Fesca! What do you have to say now, *Fleschinn?*[1]—From there the road goes to Frankfurt, with stops every 5 miles; for there is no such thing as a stop every 2 miles here in the country, it always has to be 4½, 4¾, 3¾, 3½, or at least 2½ miles. After arriving in Frankfurt we visited Uncle Itzig, whom we found robust, cheerful, and healthy. We were grateful for the pleasant surroundings and delicious supper to be had in Frankfurt, and went to bed stretching and yawning.

The following day we traveled past the cemetery where the battle of Kunersdorf once raged, to you, O noble Ziebingen, to you, on whose steppes Tieck once lingered a while! Here we found a young sweetheart resting in the shade, who on account of a quite ugly countenance was quite precious. From there we went to Crossen, where the area is quite charming; it lies on the Oder, amid hills on which bounteous quantities of *Viermännerwein* are ripening in the sun. Here we ate quite a lot, drank a lot, ate, drank, and paid.

Felix has gone to church, not realizing that the mail is leaving, so I'm finishing this for him.

[Abraham Mendelssohn Bartholdy]

1. Nickname for Rebecka.

To Karl Friedrich Zelter

Berlin, December 9, 1823

I'm sure it is wise for you to remain as long as possible with Goethe, Herr Professor; but in the meantime do give some thought to the great many people here who long for your return, when they find fifths here or cross-relations there. Please don't let them languish too long, and return soon.

Our Sunday concerts are not doing so well at the moment. Poor Rietz hasn't been able to touch a violin since you left, because the pains in his fingers haven't subsided at all, and no one knows how long they'll last. Lindenau has to lead us as concertmaster, and since he isn't yet familiar with our orchestra, nor it with him, the loss of Rietz is quite noticeable.

My opera is completed, and our parents are being so gracious as to have it sung at our house—but I do hope that you will be there to help me rehearse it.

My double concerto is also finished, and last Sunday Fanny and I played it.

In addition, I have started a quartet for piano, violin, viola, and bass, and have also written several little pieces, which with your permission I shall show you.

Please give my regards to the honorable Herr Geheimrat,[1] Herr Kammerrath, his esteemed wife, Ulrike, Walter, Schopenhauers, Hummel, and to anyone who remembers me fondly.

I remain, Herr Professor, your devoted pupil,
Felix Mendelssohn Bartholdy

1. Goethe's official title, "privy councillor."

The household music making which started in the Markgrafenstrasse apart-
ment in Berlin developed into the "Sunday concerts" at the Mendelssohn
house, which featured new compositions by Felix and his sister Fanny,
and were performed by musician friends and paid members of the royal
orchestra.

The works mentioned here are the Singspiel Der Onkel aus Boston,
oder die beiden Neffen (The Uncle from Boston, or The Two
Nephews *(here referred to as an opera), the Concerto for Two Pianos and*
Orchestra in E Major, and the Piano Quartet, op. 2.

To Johann Ludwig Casper

Berlin, Sunday, February 8, 1824

I was here, dearest Doctor, in order to ask your forgiveness for my hasty words. They were all the more
inappropriate for having come on the occasion of
yesterday's celebration, which after all you organized,
though would have preferred not to. But please, "Let
what is past be forgotten." I also hope that no one in
the orchestra repeated your remarks.

Yours as ever,

Felix Mendelssohn Bartholdy

To Friedrich Voigts

Berlin, March 13, 1824

Forgive me, esteemed Sir, that my thanks for your
splendid first act come so late;[1] but I didn't want to pay
my compliments until I had at least looked at some of
its beauties myself and admired them, and now that I
have, I think no amount of thanks could suffice for such

1. This letter refers to the libretto for *Die Hochzeit des Camacho (The*
Wedding of Camacho), based on an episode from *Don Quixote.*

a masterpiece. I will take pains to *emulate* your words; if my music cannot *express* all that anyone would *feel* at the first reading of your text, then it will not be for lack of good intentions, and I will strive to do the best that I can. But the more beautiful the first act, the stronger my wish to see the second. Please grant my wish as soon as possible!

Permit me to make a few observations.

As regards the choice of verses and the overall language in the musical episodes, I have seldom or never seen verses that inspired my own musical ideas, even at first glance, the way these did. They are harmonious, well suited for music, not overly long, and in short they have all the qualities of a good opera libretto.

There might perhaps be a few too many musical episodes. So meanwhile I will take the liberty of invoking your permission to omit several of them, possibly Vivaldo's "Yes my sword, my lute, etc." aria, Lucinda's "Wealth is a curse" aria, and the Carrasco aria following it, "This is a race, etc."; otherwise, there would be *seven* musical episodes in a row, which would be a bit tiring for the audience. In contrast to Carrasco's monologues, however, I like the Weather and Cousin Choruses[1] beyond all description, and the few words you said to me about them made it very clear to me how they ought to be composed.

Above all, I urge you most strongly not to divide the opera into three acts, but rather to leave it in two acts as planned. I recently went to a *Hamlet*, saw the priest appear and talk, and overcame all the difficulties the prohibition against clerical vestments in the theater should have caused us. *Veni, vidi, vici.* So the priest will be allowed to

---

1. *Wetter- und Vetterchöre.*

remain a priest (but he probably still won't be permitted to *sing*), and the opera can remain an opera in two acts. Amen. Vivaldo is a splendid fellow, and a good tenor, and since you want to spare Basilio from having to fly through the air, this role can easily be taken over by a good singer. "And may St. Peter grant to each his own," says the bass Sancho to his horror.

My only request, as I said, is to send me the second act as soon as possible—I am extraordinarily curious to see it. Please don't let me languish any longer, and send it very soon; you will give me the greatest pleasure in so doing. With heartfelt thanks I remain your most faithful

Felix Mendelssohn Bartholdy

P.S. I am all the more eager to receive the second act in that I can't begin composing until I have it, in order to have a good idea of the whole.

Felix Mendelssohn Bartholdy

To Lea Mendelssohn Bartholdy

Doberan, July 3, 1824

So, we arrived here in good health, and since we hear that the mail leaves at six o'clock we are seizing the opportunity to write you at once. The weather was not very good today, and several times it was even abominable, so that we were forced to put down the windows. But the few clear views were sufficient to show us a charming, bountiful countryside and the most beautiful wildflowers, so that when we had to post six miles today it didn't seem unreasonably long. Yesterday, on the other hand, we were in a not terribly interesting area, with poor weather, an awful coach, miserable horses, and a detestable postilion, and took almost *nine* hours to post six and a half miles—we almost lost patience altogether; it really was a bit vexing. Meanwhile we did arrive, are comfortably lodged, and with friendly people, have a decent piano, pretty view, what *more* could one ask for? *I* have a great desire to go to the *sea*, soon this wish too will be fulfilled, and then we can really be content.[1]—Now we have just eaten our midday meal, and quite a good one at that; but in order to show you all that I am nothing if not a little sweet tooth, I would like to tell you about the splendid strawberries and cream, which we devoured hungrily and without saying a single word.

So far I have yet to write a note, but am thinking of starting this evening. Nor have I rendered any odes from Latin into German, but instead have rendered a large number of roasted almonds, chocolates, and bonbons from the bag into my stomach. But I am not such a sweet tooth after all, for more than half of them have yet to be unwrapped.

And so far, there is nothing really to gripe about, the coach has held up well, nothing was left behind; but as soon as some such thing does occur, I will send you a dispatch rider, O Paphel!—[2]

Now you, young lady, I would like to tell you a Schüppenstädt-Güstrow joke.[3] You probably know of the Borghese Warrior? (Judging by your erudition, this may be assumed.) A man from Güstrow had this stony-

---

1. *more . . . sea: mehr . . . Meer*
2. Paphel: a nickname.
3. *Schüppenstädt*: here, a fictive town whose inhabitants are known for their lack of education. *Güstrow*: a real town en route to Bad Doberan, where someone had placed a sculpture resembling the Borghese Warrior on top of his house.

hearted fellow mounted on top of his three-story house. Whenever anyone walked by, they thought that the fellow would jump off, he was making such a mighty charge. Usually it's just a gathering place for ravens, who would eat, drink, and be merry if left to their own devices.

Please give my regards to Herr Professor Zelter, I shall write him in the next several days, as soon as I can write about something more important than strawberry cream.

Do tell Rietz that I visited Knuth in Gransee, and found him and his two sisters in good health. I also took careful notice of the lake, but the mountains, which are of no small height, could not be seen clearly even with the strongest glasses. Do convey to him also: *that I send my regards!*

Please do give my regards to Herr Lindenau as well, I think of him every time I hear someone saying *eine Mile, um negen, Adjüs,*[4] etc., and then give my warm regards to all of our acquaintances, friends, and relatives.

Apropos! The cake that Mother so generously gave me has made it all the way through the mountains, but I am *not* a sweet tooth, but rather yours

Felix Mendelssohn Bartholdy

To Paul Mendelssohn Bartholdy

Doberan, July 7, 1824

I thank you, my dear Paul, for your lovely little letter; it is short and good; but do write often; you surely have

4. Low German dialect: "a mile, at nine, adieu."

nothing better to do than write your very learned brother. But you did make a few huge mistakes. I shall list them for you:

I. Who told you that I sleep in the coach? I have never slept in the coach, for when the scenery is dull I think. This is how it works: I close my eyes, sprawl out, open my mouth from time to time, to take in fresh ideas from the air, as it were, and to sing out, though it's rather through the nose. So anyone who says I sleep is lying.

II. Who told you that I am bored in Doberan? If you were here, you would be talking differently. Just have Fanny read to you about all of the work we have here; the worst will come later today, when the theater is opened. So anyone who says that I am bored is lying.

III. Who told you that I like to eat pastries? This is really too much. I may do this at home, just for everyone's amusement, but otherwise I am quite indifferent to them; a good soup and hearty meat are all I need. But pastries mean nothing whatsoever to me. Without them I am as ravenously happy as five hundred bunnies. *Vide* Goethe's *Faust*. So whoever says that I like to eat pastries is lying.

There are about twenty-two such errors in your letter, and where would I find the time to enumerate all of them for you? And I also wanted to tell you all about a great swimming party we had. But today is the first nice day we have had, and I hope you won't take it amiss if I go to draw now and write you more another time. We don't stand on ceremony. Down with Serenissime!

Felix Mendelssohn Bartholdy

P.S., R.S.V.P.

Ist ne komische Idee.
Was soll der Tand,
Das rothe Band
Du junger Fant?[1]

To Karl Friedrich Zelter

Doberan, July 9, 1824

I would long ago have written you all about our trip, Herr Professor, if anything at all interesting had happened. We are living from one day to the next; bathing, eating, and sleeping are our principal occupations, and what pleasure could it have brought you to hear that the sea is calm, rough, or foggy? Thus I haven't written you for quite a while; now, however, since I have visited the church, the organ, and the tower, I have a few things I can report to you.

The church is an extraordinarily beautiful building dating to the twelfth century. It is built entirely of bricks, and lies in the middle of a rather large park, surrounded by trees. It is both simple and grandiose. I particularly love the exterior view of the sanctuary and of the back end of the church. About ten paces away there is a small, ancient but well-preserved building, which looks like a small round tower and is called the charnel house. This is a special favorite of Professor Rösel, who recommended it to me very strongly; I also like it a great deal. The interior of the church is quite

1. Nonsense verse (Paul had apparently enclosed a red ribbon with his letter): Wha' a queer idea./What is this trifle,/The red ribbon/ You young pup?

splendid too; unfortunately, however, the overall effect
is somewhat weakened by several new additions. Thus,
for example, the pulpit, several rows of chairs in the
nave, the gallery, and much of the decoration, etc., are
all new, and as a result the church is definitely disfigured
in several places; but the basic structure of the church
is still preserved, and it is truly impressive. The organ
too is old, but too old! For an organ 226 years is a long
time. Also, in both manuals and in the pedal the sharp
keys are missing in the lowest octave; occasionally the
individual registers sound quite pleasant, though; but
it's a shame that the lower manual is almost unusable,
otherwise the full organ would probably sound strong
enough overall. But so it is! Moreover, a half dozen
keys stick, so the disaster is complete. By now the cantor
is accustomed to sing a few quarter notes *before* everyone
else; so he always starts off with the first note, when the
organist's little interludes have scarcely begun, and
several times I almost called out: Hey! *iam satis!* Then
after the songs came a sermon; the local pastor is sick,
and had to send in a substitute to speak for him; the
latter read through the sermon, and paused several
times in the middle of every phrase to read from his
text. But when he spoke of, say, Paradise, he practically
roared, stamped his feet, and beat his hands against the
pulpit. In contrast, when he informed the sinners of
their eternal torment, he spoke with a very soft, gentle
voice, etc., etc.

When I noticed such things I began to walk up a
staircase, which I soon realized led up to the tower; at
the top there was a tricky passage with ladders, through
which the watchman's little son guided me, and above
there was a very pretty view out to the sea. But the
tower itself is awful. The old one was struck by lightning,

and so a new wooden one was slapped on top—which is as like the old church as chalk to cheese.

I could tell you a bit about the young sexton here, who is building himself a positive organ, but instead I think I shall save something for next time.

Farewell! Yours faithfully,

Felix Mendelssohn Bartholdy

To Lea Mendelssohn Bartholdy

Weimar, March 13, 1825

So I have just taken my midday meal at the Erbprinz, and am waiting for Felix, who insisted on grabbing me around the neck, forcing me to drive him off; he had to play for the young Goethe this morning. The old gentleman had passed the word that he should save something for this afternoon, and I suggested to him that he not start out immediately with octaves in the bass; they had all once again very kindly asked me to come to eat, and wanted to send a coach, and Ulrike passed word to me that she wanted spend the whole meal talking to me to make up for the fact that none of you are here, but I resisted and said that I needed to rest and recuperate today and possibly tomorrow as well. Ulrike's condition is supposed to be quite peculiar, although since I have not seen her I can hardly tell what is going on from what little I hear, and supposedly one can't talk to her about it; it is said that in the presence of company she appears very cheerful and composed, but that in more intimate circles she acts very sad and depressed; supposedly the doctor has given his assurance that he can cure her, from which it was then assumed that she must be quite ill, and in short I can make neither head nor tail of it. There may also be some spoiling and pampering involved.

Hummel has left already; by now he should be in Frankfurt. Felix is going to visit his wife today.

I find it unpleasant not to have heard anything from home for so long, and that you have only written to me in Paris, where I will of course be arriving much later than planned, since long summer day journeys are out of the question in this kind of weather; all winter long it never looked like it does today, and I shudder to think of the thirty miles to Frankfurt; my head is so full of ghosts from reading Fouqué that I think I have been bewitched, and believe that the Rhine master has sent this weather for me.

Felix had made plans to be in Frankfurt on the 15th, and to congratulate you from there. Today he was most distressed when he found we would probably be on the road on the 15th, and didn't know how he would be able to, and I made the great suggestion that he ought to do so *prenumerando* from here, which hadn't occurred to him—he really is quite awkward about many things, but otherwise most tolerable.

[Abraham Mendelssohn Bartholdy]

On my father's word, I can assure you that I was never in the slightest doubt about how to send my congratulations on your birthday, dearest Mother. I know that you are aware of my devoted love, and that you don't care whether I wish you well from Weimar or Buttlar. Whatever good things I may think or conceive, may God grant them to you, and for the longest time to come.

Now I have just returned from dinner at Goethe's, where things were not at all so stiff and formal. The frightful "Sie" with which he received me yesterday was transformed back to the previous "du"; and when Goethe offers you champagne, and fills your glass, can you really refuse it? And at dessert he produced a piece of paper from his pocket, tied up with a pink ribbon, and told me, as he handed it across the table, that he wanted to give me a small trifle. I found a little red box with the inscription: To Herr Felix Mendelssohn, 1825; and inside a handsome portrait of Goethe on a silver medallion by Bovy. Now that I call a gift!

Szymanowska is so highly regarded here that they rank her above Hummel these days: I was amazed and kept quiet as a mouse. It seems to me that they have confused her pretty face with her not so pretty playing.

I can dutifully report to Fanny that I have not written a single note of my opera so far, and have no inclination to do so at all; laziness is a divine thing; moreover I can report that I improvised poorly yesterday, but well today; and that Frau von Goethe, Ulrike, Adele send their love to you, and with that, *basta*. To Herr Heyse I can report that I ate with Riemer this noon, and that I am also feeling very Greek at the moment. Dictionary writing suits him well. He is wide, fat, and radiant, like a prelate or a full moon. I would send Beckchen a terrific joke, but I can't remember how it starts, so for today—nothing.

To Paul I recommend in a whisper that he behave himself properly, otherwise things may go ill for him! And he should say hello to Rietz for me. Has he still been playing? In accordance with Mother's instructions to always report precisely about Father's health, I can assure you that Father *had* only a bad cold, and is now recovering with God's help, porridge, and a warm stove, so that there is no further cause for concern whatsoever.

Say hello to Professor Zelter, Frank, Klingemann; and Paul should tell Rietz that in Goethe's drawing room there is a very faithful portrait of—Rauch (the sculptor, of course), and with that I bid you all farewell. Yours,

Felix

I grant my royal pardon to the young guard, and promise them the royal order of the *trois rois au d'or* if they behave themselves, which the old guard was unable to earn.

My most fond regards to the children and Herr Heyse, I'll let you know the date of my departure from here, and I embrace you most lovingly.

[Abraham Mendelssohn Bartholdy]

To Lea Mendelssohn Bartholdy

Paris, March 23, 1825

How can I begin to write you a proper, well-organized, and sensible letter on my first morning in Paris? I am much too amazed for that, too curious and too over-whelmed.—But since I promised to send a diary back to Berlin, I will plunge right in, and report that we arrived yesterday, the 22nd of March, at eight o'clock in the evening. After passing the Barrière de Pantin, we drove for a good quarter of an hour with our spirited horses at a brisk trot, through a *new* section of Paris, which Father had never even seen before. This was the Faubourg St. Lazare. Although it does look fairly des-olate and chaotic in some areas, for the most part there are already houses there. We then soon came to the old city, and at long last to the Boulevard. What a hustle

and bustle, scurrying, screaming, and merriment among
the crowd; all of the stores are fully illuminated with
gas, and the streets are so brightly lit that one can read
comfortably. It is perhaps as loud and bright there as
during a great celebration in Berlin. Having arrived at
the Hôtel des Princes, we found only two Entre Sols
ready for us, although Herr Zimmer had made reservations for us, and were immediately given a note from
Uncle Meyer which had come via Nantes. We quickly
changed clothes, and went to visit Aunt Jette and Herr
Meyer, but found neither of them at home.

March 25

Yesterday was certainly an active day. It seems as if it
were a week, and I can write you about only a little, or
I'll be writing until midnight, and after all it's only eight
o'clock in the morning. Before even starting I can report
that I have just taken a bath, in accordance with Mother's
express instructions, and have washed, scrubbed, and
scoured myself more thoroughly than one could imagine. So Mother will feel reassured as far as that goes.—
Now, as for yesterday. Leo and Meyer came to visit us
very early, and seemed completely amazed that I would
no longer sit on their laps, did not overturn any chairs,
did not scream, etc. We then visited Aunt Jette, and
found her on the street already on the way to see us.
Her mild, serious, lively, and completely gracious nature
did not fail to make an impression. And how cleverly
she speaks. How much I am looking forward to bringing
her back to you!—We then returned to her place at
half past eleven, after having seen Rode at Leo's. Rode
has grown old, but he still spits fire. Father told him
about Rietz, and I had to play for him with cold fingers,
and he promised to come visit us today at ten, etc. So

then we arrived at Aunt Jette's, who at once gave me a
plate of pastries to eat (the art is highly developed in
France). I ate! and then the three of us went to see
Ritter Neukomm, at whose home a Stabat Mater for
three voices of his own composition was being give a
run-through. The singers were two boys (both outstanding voices, the soprano was especially beautiful and soft)
and a tenor with a beautiful voice, who sang terribly off
pitch, however. All three gave amazingly polished performances, although they were sight-singing, and put
the proper amount of expression into it, which was only
rarely disfigured by affectation. Neukomm (he appears
to be a very good teacher) accompanied them on the
orgue expressif, a newly invented instrument featuring
one gamba stop, which one can cause to swell and recede
by using the bellows. After each movement of the rather
dry, but melodious, composition, he played the cantus
firmus, and each time wanted to work new harmonies
into it. That just didn't work! It became more and more
monotonous, and the more involved, the thinner it
sounded. At the end there was a fugue. Brrr!

That was the theme and the deepest and most artistic
part of the whole thing was the following,

etc., ad infinitum. He ought to be called *Altkomm* instead
of Neukomm.[1] Afterward he improvised a bit for us.
Then I went to Erard's and found him in the front

1. Name punning; roughly, "late-comer rather than newcomer."

room. I delivered my letter, he was very friendly, told me that he was in the midst of a rehearsal for a private concert, to which he invited us at his house this afternoon, obliged me to come inside, the people were very friendly and courteous to me, and I saw Heinrich Romberg, Halévy, Grasset, and my dear Hummel, who called out, "Hey, look, there's Felix," as soon as he saw me, and after he had kissed me at once said, "But what happened to your pigtails," etc. They played a chorus by Hummel, the Graduale. My suspicion that he is a devout Catholic, which was kindled by a large crucifix in his room in Weimar, was reinforced by the beginning of this piece; for it is very orthodox and serious. But it didn't last all the way through. When a duet from Olympia began to make me want to sneeze, I stole away.—I found Louis Saling at home, and we went to visit Fould, Mme. Valentin, and Baillot, but didn't find them at home; we did see the Eichtals, though, and also Gustav's brothers and sisters, who look exactly like he does and were happy to hear several anecdotes we told them about him. Tomorrow we will eat with them, then onward. This morning the young Eichtal wants to come to pick me up to take a walk. Farewell!

I'll conclude abruptly, contrary to my usual habit. Farewell. Your own

Felix

To Lea Mendelssohn Bartholdy

Paris, April 6, 1825

Yes, yes, Paris is a big city. When you go walking on the Boulevard des Italiens in the evening, and see this crowd and bustle, you begin to acquire some respect

for it. I just returned from the Pantheon; what a divine
building! What an enormous, well-proportioned mass!
Here everyone, everyone, can find what he seeks and
requires! That the state of music here is not quite to
my liking is partly its own fault, since it really isn't too
good, and partly because you, Mother, told me altogether too much about it. I had hoped to find in this
city the hometown of music itself, of musicians and
musical taste, but in truth it isn't so. The salons (although
I hadn't expected too much from them) are *ennuyant*,
and care for nothing besides frivolous music and coquetteries, nothing serious and solid. The orchestras (I
have been to the Italian Opera and the Académie
Royale) are quite good, but in no way outstanding, and
finally, some of the musicians themselves have withered
somewhat, while others complain constantly about Paris
and Parisians, cursing up a storm. Let me enumerate
and prove my ninety-five theses with specific examples.

1. The salons. I shall cite and describe just one of
the many, the Comtesse de Rumford's evening salon.
We arrived at quarter to eleven, and found a rather
large group of people gathered in a room. I was
introduced to the famous Rossini. He has a puzzling
face. A mixture of roguishness, superficiality, and ennui,
with long sideburns, wide as a church door, elegantly
dressed, surrounded by all the ladies, answering their
attempts to entertain him only rarely with a little smile,
and there you have the great Maestro Windbag! He sat
down at the piano and accompanied Mozart's *Ave Verum*,
which as chance would have it is still fashionable. But
he, as a learned composer, wanted to make suspensions
before all of the dissonances, and thus prepared the
thirds, fifths, and octaves for the benefit and enlight-
enment of all his listeners, or rather nonlisteners, for

when music is being played the ladies tell each other
fairy tales, or jump from one chair to the next as if they
were playing musical chairs. Right in the middle, it
occurs to an old man in a corner to call out: *charmant*,
and his two somewhat pretty daughters repeated: *charmant*, whereupon all the young men in the salon called
out: *délicieux!*, and thus the joys of music are savored.
When it's over, they all clap for joy that they have a few
minutes' relief again, and so on and on until one o'clock,
or even later! But more about the soirée! A Mme. Orfila
and a Mme. Merlin sang everything imaginable by
Rossini, and they really did sing quite well, with fire
and as much expression as such music permits. Moreover Mme. Merlin is an exceedingly beautiful woman,
and so has a large audience when she sings, and thus
we were all in seventh heaven. So I had to play along
and improvise. They liked that quite a lot, for with four
trifles, six coquetteries, and several runs you can play
the silliest stuff through, without even thinking. Oh how
pleased you will be when I paint for you a Parisian
fantasy of life in Berlin.—But as long as there are many
places in it where one can respond with an emotional
"Hm," then you play with expression; where there are
none, you play coldly, no matter how much fire the
music contains. As far as I am concerned, I howl along
with the pack, and am sweet as sugar candy; and the
people are courteous to me too. But to return to the
soirée. After Rossini had complimented me many times,
the ladies started singing his music again, and this
combined with the heat became so unbearable to Father
and me that we slipped away, leaving our tea—which
was served precisely at midnight—stranded.—Now am
I unjustified in finding the soirées awful? And they do
it every day! The day before yesterday there was a

terrible social at Valentin's, and then something funny happened which I have to tell you about. A lady who was seated not too far from me wanted to make the heat more bearable while I was playing my F minor quartet, and fanned herself against the beat with a fan which was adorned with steel or tinsel, so that everyone had to listen to the unpleasant sound. I stared at her for several minutes while playing (using Frank's method), and immediately all the ladies turned to look at her and her fan, she turned red, cast her eyes downward, and stopped fanning herself.

2. The orchestras. I heard the Italian Opera Orchestra play *Otello*. You can all well imagine how eagerly I was looking forward to hearing the orchestra and Pasta. I was awaiting a sensation. Hardly! The violins are superb and play well together, but on the other hand the winds, especially the brass instruments, were mediocre at best, and the basses were out-and-out bad. I would hardly call it an outstanding orchestra. And Pasta, though she is considered an outstanding singer, did not delight me either. She has an uncommon amount of expression, fire, and life, a wealth of embellishments, sings nicely, and looks pretty, but—her voice is raw and unclear, and her intonation is not clean, and so far I haven't been able to overlook these two faults. I recently heard the orchestra of the Grand Opera play a "nouvelle Sinfonie de Beethoven." Which one was it? The Second.[1] The performance was nothing special at all. The tempi were altogether too fast, and Habeneck, who conducted from the violin, and would have liked to hold them back, made himself quite miserable, stamping his feet,

1. Beethoven's Second Symphony was first performed in 1803; by 1825 his Ninth Symphony had already been premiered.

hitting the stand with his bow so hard that it wobbled, and moving his whole body, but none of it was of any avail, they simply wouldn't slow down, rushing and rushing until at the end they were almost tumbling over one another. Why isn't it better when someone calmly gives the beat with a baton? In short, I have heard nothing extraordinary so far. Where is the good music in Paris hiding? It's gone! Neukomm claims it's getting worse every day!

Now finally to the musicians themselves, to the extent that I am familiar with them thus far. First of all Cherubini, whom I have seen several times. He is dried up and wizened. The other day I heard one of his masses at the royal chapel, and it was as droll as he is peevish, i.e., beyond all measure. Halévy assures us that there are days when you can't get anything out of him at all. He asked a young musician who had played for him whether he perhaps was a good painter; he told another one, "Vous ne ferez jamais rien"; when he himself shows something to him, and Cherubini doesn't say anything or grimace, then he knows it must have been altogether outstanding. He only played for him once, and of course after Halévy had played his opera for him he said: "C'est bien.—Mais c'est trop long, il faut couper." Everyone who knows him is amazed that after he heard my F minor quartet, performed most miserably, he came up to me smiling and nodded to me. Then he told the others: "Ce garçon est riche, il fera bien; il fait même déjà bien; mais il dépense trop de son argent, il met trop d'étoffe dans son habit." Everyone declared that this was unheard of, especially since he then added: "Je lui parlerai alors il fera bien!" Then they said he had never spoken with young musicians. Halévy too couldn't believe that Cherubini had told me that. In short, I would claim that Cherubini is the one single person who fits Klingemann's saying about extinct volcanos. He occasionally spews forth, but is covered with ashes and stones. Next Lesueur, whom I visited for the first time yesterday—Boucher was so kind as to take me there—he is an altogether lovely, extremely polite man, and he and his family (a wife and three daughters) received me most cordially; we shall soon dine with them, etc., etc. Also, Lesueur (be happy, Fanny!) is very partial to German music and musicians, and speaks of the German masters with the greatest enthusiasm, saying that only the Germans understand the philosophy of music, and that everything good in France comes from Germany. But his church music is supposed to be even more droll and poised than Cherubini's, and that is certainly pretty bad. He is also, by the way, one of the most beloved of all musicians in France, thanks to his personality.—Ritter Sigismund Neukomm is a good man, quite mild and friendly; he complains bitterly about the decline of contemporary music; he told me that there were no rehearsals being conducted at the Conservatory this year, that last year they were already far worse than usual, and that the orchestra cannot play well since they have one rehearsal every morning but at least two operas to play each evening. In short, he complained but had no remedy. His music is also quite gentle, quite charming, and quite mediocre. No fire, no power.—As far as Reicha goes, he is as feared here as the wild huntsman (he hunts parallel fifths, that is), by the way, and although he has absorbed a fair amount of the dryness, the difference between him and Cherubini is still like night and day. Fanny will remember his etudes well.—On the whole, it might also be noted that they all complain a lot.

Everything here is a plot or an intrigue. Kreutzer lost his post in this manner, and Baillot got his through Habeneck; Cherubini demanded that Sosthène de la Rochefoucauld, who was recently named to preside over all musical activity, be dismissed, because when Cherubini went to visit him, he was kept waiting in the front room for quite a while, and when he mentioned his name Rochefoucauld asked him who that might be, and what it was that he wanted from him. Everything in disarray and bitterness—*c'est tout comme chez nous!*

Yesterday evening I saw the famous *Robin des bois*.[1] What a miserable, vile, infamous, lousy, boring quodlibet, in all my life I have never dreamed of such a scandal. The tempi were all wrong, the Bridesmaids' Chorus was twice too fast, Agathe's aria was cut and changed completely—in short, it was a complete outrage. I shall send Rietz a detailed description.

And now comes a difficult matter. We received your letter of March 28 and your scolding, dearest Mother. But I really must defend myself against several things in the latter. You write that I took the score for my quartet *in spite of your request not to.* But I believe I am certain that I packed the score *with your approval,* and you even told me that I could have the parts copied if I wanted to play it, and I hope that Father, who was present, will bear witness to all of this for me. Then you claim that I don't appreciate how much Fanny does for me. I can only assure you that the opposite is true, I cannot prove it. Just believe my protestations, for I have not yet acquired the habit of lying since coming to Paris. As for the rest of the points you made I

1. *Robin des bois*: French title of *Der Freischütz*, by Carl Maria von Weber.

recognize that you were in the right, and I in the wrong, and beg your pardon. Your

Felix

Coda.

I can only thank you in all haste, dear Fanny, for your lovely little letter, and my greetings to the whole crew; to Klingemann I assign the task of engaging the lady he thinks best for me to accompany me to the Mohrrüben Cotillion; a cold greeting to my good Rietz, the next mail delivery he will get a warm letter, as will Professor Zelter, to whom you must give my warmest regards, and with that a fond farewell!

Herr Heyse, I ask your pardon for not having written you a proper letter yet, but I am running around like crazy, trying to see everything at once, and thus I don't have much time to write. But I can report to you that I have a Latin tutor, the brother of the musician Halévy, who has translated the *Odes* of Horace into French free verse, and seems to be a most reasonable man, for he lets me pronounce the Latin in good German fashion. I just read Tacitus with him, *quod Felix faustum que sit!*

Beckchen and Paul, I shall write you very soon; last of all I can report to Fanny that I have not written a single note of my opera, and now I conclude the coda of the longest letter I have ever produced.

Felix

To Johann Ludwig Casper

Berlin, February 6, 1826

In the time when a student was not yet a Ph.D., a Ph.D. not yet a professor, a professor not yet a professor of medicine, and a professor of medicine still had a sense of humor, i.e., in the year one, this particular student wrote poems, which were collected in a yellow volume with a black border, green edges, and the motto: These poems shall not live longer, etc., etc. If only I could just have the book for a few days. There would be such lovely things to set to music in it. You would make me eternally grateful if you would send it to me via the bearer of this letter. Faithfully,

F. Mendelssohn Bartholdy

To Johann Friedrich Kelz

Berlin, July 7, 1826

My dear Herr Kelz,
I am sending you back the three fugues here, which you were so kind as to lend me quite a while ago, and must first of all ask your pardon for not having returned them sooner. You have given me much pleasure with them. For the more one is beset on all sides by silly trifles to tickle the ear, and long for gentle melodies, the more valuable it is when a man such as yourself—who no doubt could easily make himself beloved in this manner—works against the trend, on more serious and powerful things. Which of the three fugues I liked best of all would be hard to say, each one has its own special quality, and if I am especially attracted to the introduction to the second one, with the hidden folk song, and the same song in the fugue now in F, then in C major, now with and then against the beat, then I am also very fond of the first with its lively theme, and the third with its serious and defiant one. So why should one be given first prize? All three are serious and forceful, and so I

thank you most kindly for the pleasure that they have afforded me. Faithfully,

F. Mendelssohn Bartholdy

To Johann Wolfgang Von Goethe

Berlin, September 30, 1826

Your Excellency,
First I must implore you to pardon the inordinate impertinence with which I am imposing upon you, but in which I was emboldened in part by the assurance of Herr Professor Zelter, and in part by the kind generosity and indulgence you have shown me. To wit, I have taken the liberty of enclosing a recent attempt I made at a translation of a comedy by Terence, which preserves the meter of the original verse. My teacher, to whom I gave it, wanted to make it available to the public, and this happened even though it was in no way my intention while working on it; I had intended it simply as an exercise to test my abilities. Since now Professor Zelter has promised that Your Excellency would not take it amiss if I sent you a copy, I have been so bold as to enclose one, and ask only that if you should happen to favor the little work with a glance, you do not forget that it is just a poor attempt by a poor schoolboy.

With the most boundless respect and admiration I remain Your Excellency's most faithful

Felix Mendelssohn Bartholdy

To Adolf Fredrik Lindblad

Berlin, February 7, 1827

If you are capable of listening to a few serious, calm words calmly and seriously, then I would like to tell you* the following:

I could not have failed to observe that you were irritated, piqued, or as you would probably want to call it, melancholy that I did not jump for joy and cry out in amazement over your folk songs, as others did. You want to finish the songs "sometime in the future," i.e., not at all, and I see your brow furrowing up the way it did last fall—and why is all this necessary? Because I had a headache on Monday.—It sounds strange, doesn't it? But that's the truth.

Assuming the songs really hadn't been at all to my liking, would you be one iota worse off, could my personal opinion add anything to their worth? And you, who scorn Rossini, who regard music as something more valuable than mere trifles to tickle the ears, shouldn't you have your own convictions? You say no, but that cannot be—you are either betraying yourself or misunderstanding yourself. You *must* believe something is right and good, for your "I don't understand it" is a good joke, but only once or twice, not more often. So, what you think is good, that *is what is good*, you will never change your mind about it, and you will learn that when you change your opinions, it can only come from changing your own judgments. So what are you doing standing there watching the expression on my face in order to *see* what I am thinking (for you don't trust what I say), why should you care what *I* think. What *you* think should be the most important thing for you—and thus you will totter back and forth, fluctuating according to everyone else's opinion, until you have a firm faith in yourself.

Now, the songs pleased me inordinately, as it happened, and it was only headaches (as mentioned) that made my face look so sullen. So why are you complaining? Think what foolishness it is. You have made an outstanding decision (*I myself*, the highest court in the Royal Kingdom of Prussia, have said so), have undertaken to finish something once and for all, and show yourself to people, everything has been planned and arranged—and just because I ate too much pudding everything is canceled. Doesn't that sound strange. But that's how it is.

Enough of all this, Lindblad, break yourself of this habit—you'll never amount to anything this way, either in the world or in art. Test yourself always, but after so doing be firm and resolved; allow praise and criticism (I beg you) to have only the value to you that they should have, namely that of an opinion. In any case be assured that what I tell you, I tell you from my heart, and always think of you with love, yours,

Felix

*Should all be *du*.[1]

---

1. Mendelssohn's footnote. The letter switches to the familiar form (*du*) in the third paragraph.

To Georg Poelchau

Berlin, March 28, 1827

Esteemed Sir,

Would you be so kind as to pardon my asking a favor of you?—In your comprehensive musical library you surely must have the *History of Italian Opera* by Algarotti or Arteaga, translated by Forkel; and so I am asking if you would lend it to me until tomorrow, if possible, and send it to me via the bearer of this letter. You may be sure of having the book back by Friday, my honor and good name vouch for it, and (if you don't trust these) this receipt as well.

You would deeply indebt to you your faithful
Felix Mendelssohn B.

In the summer of 1827 Felix and his friends Eduard Magnus (later a painter) and Louis Heydemann (later a lawyer) went on a hike through the Harz mountains and Thuringia, as far as the Rhine.

To Abraham Mendelssohn Bartholdy

Erbich (a dump), August 31, 1827
In the evening, under splendid moonlight

If three of the most upstanding families in Berlin knew that three of their most upstanding sons were roving around the country roads at night with coachmen, peasants, and journeymen, and trading their life stories with them—they would be very disturbed—Don't be! For the sons are happy as larks.

Erbich! Even Father doesn't know of it, in spite of all

his travels. And it isn't on any map, so Paul doesn't
know of it. It hadn't been built during the time of the
Greeks, so Beckchen doesn't know of it, and finally
since it is neither at Leipziger Strasse No. 3 nor in Italy,
Fanny and Mother haven't heard of it. It is a miserable
village with an inn which the three of us find heavenly
just out of spite. We had in fact mistaken four miles for
two on the map, and so ended up hiking for an hour
and a half in the moonlight. Finally we arrived at the
village of Lindenbach, where there was an inn which is
highly spoken of by the drivers. The innkeeper could
not give us a room, and together with three coachmen,
all bundled up in their blue frocks, devouring roast
mutton and smoking pipes, we were supposed to spend
the night camped out on benches. For our pains, we
wouldn't get a guide to go to Rudolstadt tomorrow, nor
anything to eat tonight. At this point Magnus became
furious and decamped. We went out to the village, and
followed a brook edged by willows through a stubble
field which was occasionally interrupted by marshy
spots, as far as Erbich. Three cheers!—For we found a
room where we could sleep on our own benches, and
early tomorrow we're leaving with a drayman, who has
promised to take us at an unheard-of clip all the way
into Franconia. At first no one wanted to put us up
here either, since the room is not heated, but finally we
were led up the narrow staircase to our room, which
has wooden benches against all four of the walls; the
proper guest bed is in the corner, though none of us
want to sleep in it—perhaps out of politeness—and in
the opposite corner there are three enormous kneaded
balls of bread and pastry dough, which the landlady
made us swear by our beards not to touch (we haven't

shaved since leaving Berlin, and Magnus' is surpassing.) By way of additional furnishings there are several paintings, worth about three cents, and a fixture for a chandelier. There is a pigskin flask hanging on the door.—*Summa summarum*, a parlor.

By the way, we also attract an unbelievable amount of attention in all of the little villages, towns, and spots we walk through, holding up our walking sticks; the girls (*auctora Magno*) all come to the windows and the alley boys laugh at us for three streets behind. A testimonial to our popularity and white linens.

We are getting along quite well, just as well as we are enjoying ourselves, and that is saying a lot. We speak alternately of choirmasters, sick people, Homer; everyone has his own favorite topic, and we join together in a student's song with refrains. The countryside is also spectacularly beautiful; we walked through the Thuringian forest near Sondershausen today, where we found the most noble beeches and the most splendid oaks; beneath their dense foliage there are springs here and there, from which Heydemann fills his hiking flask. We also reflected, drew, and composed there. Ample inspiration can be found there for both seriousness and pleasant joking, and thanks to this delightful combination none of us will weary or tire of either.

The worst thing is that we won't get to Bamberg before Monday, and so will have to remain without news for quite a while. I long to see all of you horribly from time to time, and especially when things are so altogether pretty and delightful.—So I'm just a mama's boy after all, and used to my daily bread.

If the benches fail us, then we'll have to make an appeal to the bench; we bench-sitters will just have to take our chances with the supreme bench. A justice of the bench would be a fine thing here; his Arabians would be treated like draft horses.

But it's late and our one tallow candle is failing us, and the moonlight isn't bright enough. Tomorrow at five we'll be off. Good night, good night. Sleep well. Your

Felix
stud. phil.

Extrapostscriptum.

My companions send their regards. Say hello to: Aunts Meyer and Jette, Levy and Recha and Uncle Nathan, Schubring, Boguslawsky, and Marx, Heydemann, et al. Also say hello to the lambs; and tell them they may not be shorn before we return; not at all would be even better. Regards to David. And greetings to Zelter. Regards to . . . ∞.

vide subito

To Abraham Mendelssohn Bartholdy

Horchheim, September 29, 1827

Dear Father,

In your letter of the 23rd you write me of your concern and misgivings about the business with Robert's opera, and I am happy to be able to tell you that you may rest assured that the matter has taken a very fortunate turn, and that we parted better friends than we were when we arrived. Whether I will or can receive a text from him, as indeed I must, is not yet quite clear, but it will be soon after I return to Berlin, and so I am not worried. This whole trip has convinced me all over again that people expect something special from me, and much more than was achieved in *Die Hochzeit des Camacho (The Wedding of Camacho)*. I also know that I do not have to disappoint these expectations; but I doubt very much that everything depends on having to present myself today or tomorrow in such a manner. The *Wedding* has been forgotten for a while in Berlin; later they will dig it up again and decide whether it should live or die. If it holds up, then the other theaters will want it; if it doesn't, then performances on other stages will not help this opera either, but they will hurt me, and that is the reason why I have not pursued the matter with either Guhr or Ganz. I shall not stop looking everywhere for a librettist, and sooner or later I'm bound to find one. The time between now and then is not lost, for it isn't being spent in idleness, and when I work I make progress. I have blazed a path for myself in instrumental music (and those are your own words, dear Father), but in other areas I have yet to. I know that I shall also be able to do so in the genre of opera, but I am also convinced that I have only just begun in the area of instrumental music; therefore I shall continue working until I find the opportunity to bring my ideas about opera to light, into the open, and you may believe my firm assurances that then I shall not be dissuaded, whether the work is well received or not.

But now on to tell all of you about my adventures, though this time it shouldn't be so long—since now I won't receive an answer, and shall have to do without well-earned praise, and a week from tomorrow I'll probably be waltzing around in all of your arms already. (*Vide* Horn *med. et chir. Dr.*)

In Darmstadt I went to visit a Rubens (good morning, dear Marx!) and to see the minister of war for musical

affairs, Gottfried Weber. He was friendly and invited
me to stay with him; but he spoke of Herr Beethoven
like a farmer about a diseased cow. He said he was sorry
for him, that he never got enough rock salt, for he
would have remained a great man (*vide* a famous poem
by Goethe), and that now he was half again as crazy as
he ever was divine. As soon as possible I asked him
about the Archduke Marställen.

In Frankfurt I often went to visit Schelble, and Herz—
and Hauser, Hiller, Ferdinand Ries, Louis Saling, and
Carl Maria von Weber's *Oberon* (I actually saw it); more
when I see you.

The trip through the Rheingau was heavenly beyond
description; it was the most beautiful evening I have
ever seen, with the Rhine calm as glass and our little
rowboat cutting through it swiftly. We were all lying
down, stretched out on our coat bags, devouring the
sky with our eyes and enjoying it silently. One city after
another, one island after the next, and one golden cloud
after the other flew by us—oh, how you all should have
been there. Then Rüdesheim, the Niederwald, and the
Binger Loch! How the Rhine roars!

Apropos! I saw Kapellmeister Ganz in Mainz. Since
I wouldn't want to venture a judgment after just
meeting him, I shall simply say that he is a complete
idiot.—But it seems to run in the family; for his
letters were all very clumsily written, except for
the physical orthography, and I have kept two as a
token.

Ferd. Hiller accompanied us as far as Coblenz, just
for fun.

At Stolzenfels I jumped out of the yacht into a
rowboat, and an unfamiliar black man ferried me across

under the light of the half moon. It was a crisp fall evening.

So now I am in Horchheim, well lodged, content, and in short quite comfortable. Everyone is friendly and pleasant, and I am extraordinarily fond of the new honorary member of the Mendelssohn household. Everyone sends their most heartfelt greetings, and Aunt Hinni told me to tell you, dear Father: *Justifiably* angry, and also hello.

Now it is time to return, for I am horribly homesick again. Say hello to everyone for me. Dear Paul, you mustn't work too much, otherwise you will be too scornful of your brother. Oh dear Beckchen, in your red dress, you great General Angereau, why didn't you cross our paths the way you wanted to? Enclosed please find a kiss. Oh Fanny! Oh Fanny! Oh Fanny! General Field Marshal!!

I am getting sentimental, so I'll stop. Farewell, dear parents, and this was the last letter. Your

Felix MB

To Eduard Devrient

Berlin, January 2, 1828

Surely you haven't forgotten, dear Herr Devrient, that we were going to work up some *Bach* on Saturday, and that *you* and *your gracious wife* have promised to grace us with your presence, and must keep your promise? You know quite well how indispensable you are to us, and there are twelve blank pieces of paper in front of me here which need to be filled with invitations to singers. So if you cancel, then I too must cancel, but please don't do it.

If you don't answer then your silence shall be construed as a yes. Yours,

Felix Mendelssohn Bartholdy

P.S. Since I don't know where Herr Bauer lives, but am really counting on him, I ask you just to request provisionally that he not cancel on Saturday, and then I shall invite him in person at Zelter's on Friday, or if you think it better, then please send me his address and I shall write him.

To Karl Friedrich Zelter

Berlin, January 8, 1829

Dear Herr Professor,

Please find enclosed the completed instrumental score of the *Acis*. But the instrumentation is the only thing finished thus far, and it seems to me that many alterations will be necessary, for example in the selection and arrangement of the very frequent and often overly long arias, as well as in the German translation of the English text. I have confined myself to writing the instrumentation for all of the pieces exactly in the order of the original score, and have omitted only the F major aria in $\frac{3}{8}$ time which comes just before the final chorus in part one, because it is not very appealing, and because several long arias precede it anyway.

I have not yet been able to start work on the *Te Deum*, because there are large gaps six to eight measures long in the copy which you were so kind as to send me, and thus I cannot do without the English score. If it would be possible for you obtain one for me I could get started on the work right away. Your faithful

Felix Mendelssohn B.

To Friedrich Schneider

Berlin, March 7, 1829

Most Honored Herr Kapellmeister,
I am taking the liberty of writing to you directly in the hope that you will eventually recall that I had the honor of meeting you several years ago, something which you probably have since forgotten. In the meantime I shall have to remind you of it, since I would like to ask a personal favor of you.

You may perhaps know from the papers that I intend to perform the *Passion* by Seb. Bach, a very beautiful and worthy piece of church music from the last century, and that the performance will take place on Wednesday, March 11, in the concert hall of the Sing-Akademie. The favor I request is to ask if it would be possible for you to suffer the inconvenience of undertaking a long trip, thereby granting us the pleasure of your company that evening—though robbing you of several days of your valuable time—in order to honor an old master, and dignify our musical celebration by your presence?

I ask that you take my request to heart, and hoping most fervently that you will grant it I remain respectfully your most faithful

Felix Mendelssohn Bartholdy

THE FIRST TRIP TO ENGLAND, 1829

*In addition to the triumphant success of his performance of Bach's St. Matthew
Passion, three other decisive events in Mendelssohn's life occurred in 1829:
his first voyage to London, alone, with an excursion to the Hebrides and
Scotland, still an extremely popular destination for European travelers in
the wake of the sensation over Ossian. Not only the Berlin architect Schinkel,
but also the publisher Westermann visited the Scottish islands during these
years. Mendelssohn was accompanied by his father and sister Rebecka as far
as Hamburg, and in England by his friend Karl Klingemann. The two had
known each other a long time; both were friends of the piano virtuoso Ignaz
Moscheles, who had taught Felix in Berlin in 1824. Klingemann's home in
London, where he was an attaché to the Hanover consulate, became Mendelssohn's customary lodgings during almost all of his ten later visits to
London. Klingemann and Mendelssohn also combined their correspondence,
sending joint letters to Berlin. But often Klingemann alone would write,
since Felix could not write "on account of his bandaged hand" (these letters
are not included).*

*The injuries suffered during a coach accident also spoiled Mendelssohn's
plans to return to Berlin in time for the wedding of his sister Fanny and the
painter Wilhelm Hensel. Having to miss this great event was a severe blow
to the young man of the world. He had conquered London as a composer,
virtuoso, and person—and now a trifling accident prevented him from being
able to attend his favorite sister's wedding.*

*But he did arrive punctually for his parents' silver anniversary celebration
(December 26), carrying a composition written specially for the occasion. His
friend Klingemann had written the text for the work, appropriately titled*
"Die Heimkehr aus der Fremde," (Returning Home from Foreign
Lands).

*At this point he had returned home from abroad to his friends and family
as an independent and self-supporting man—for even English publishers
had purchased his works. The entire Mendelssohn family had gathered for
the silver wedding celebration. Within several months, though, Felix would
leave the apartment at Leipziger Strasse 3 and undertake an even longer
voyage than the trip to England—and in fact he never really returned home
again.*

To Lea Mendelssohn Bartholdy

Hamburg, April 13, 1829

Early this morning we received your[1] letter, but after returning from a two-hour walking tour there is hardly time to answer it, for the table d'hôte is waiting for us again; I have no idea whether it is from the Hamburg air or the cooking, but I am constantly hungry. A pretty town, where you can stumble over oyster shells, and where they carry milk to market in red pails; but unfortunately it doesn't seem very German to me, rather more like a cross between London and Jerusalem. The diner at Salomon Heine's was a most *gentlemanly* affair; I sat between Hermann Heine and old Benedick's youngest daughter (Adolph's sister), whose speech resembles her brother's, though her face is similar to Jettchen Benedick's. Beckchen is living like God in France; Salomon Heine is flirting terribly with her, calling her *du*, kissing her at every opportunity, and helping her put on her coat. After dinner we went to the theater and saw several acts of Portici's *Die Stummen von Portici*,[2] of which there is quite a good performance here—then I went to visit the Lindenaus, who received us most cordially. Leopold has changed much for the better; he looks more manly and healthier, everyone praises his playing, he is popular as a teacher, and if his sister were a little less blond she would be quite pretty. She visited Beckchen beforehand, by the way,

1. *Euer* (plural).
2. *Die Stummen von Portici: La muette de Portici*, opera by D. F. E. Auber.

and invited us to visit her Wednesday evening for some music making; tonight we shall see them at the Gesangverein [Choral Society], which is being conducted by Wilhelm Grund—tomorrow night I'm off to the Hesses', and tomorrow morning I will probably tickle the organ at St. Michael's with some Seb. Bach pieces—in short, God is in his heaven and all is well with the world. Methfessel is a cross between Schwachhofer and Dreidenstein, he is full of respect for Saphir and Mozart, and is tolerant of Bach and Beethoven. The young Schwencke is doing a collection of chorales, for which I too have to write him a four-voice one; the merchants of Hamburg prefer Beethoven's symphonies to Mozart's, and that will have to suffice for today.

The 14th

Today I received a letter from Klingemann with the necessary corrections and with the invitation to bring along the double concerto and the octet for voices; when Father returns, I shall ask you, dear Fanny, to give them to him to pack up. The Singverein was quite good last night; Spohr's last works were sung. (I'll write more to Zelter from London about the performance and about the organ at St. Michael's, which I played today.) But the composition was simply disgraceful, people here mistake boredom and dullness for edification, and find the music sacred; in fact it is profane, and a sinful play of trifles. They hang Jews for poisoning fountains; but music is just as valuable as a fountain, I hope, and therefore Spohr will have to die. The soup is being served now, Lindenau is eating with us today, and after supper we are going for a walk to enjoy the clear weather—so I must close.

Just a few more messages and instructions: you[1] must make Devrient swear to sing C-double-sharp, not C-sharp (not #, but ×), on the word "mich" in "er ist da, der mich verrieth" [he is here who shall betray me]. Rietz will know more about it. Thank you for sending the *Flegeljahre*,[2] but I still haven't received it, and when I remembered suddenly at Wilhelmsplatz that I had forgotten it I was too embarrassed to make them stop (just this moment the mailman has brought it). Please tell Rietz that Maurer from Hanover sends his fond regards; he also asked me to convey them to all of you. My first evening here I went to a concert and heard him play a new piece, since then we have visited each other twice, and he is returning home immediately to give a concert of *Der Tod Jesu (The Death of Jesus)*;[3] but if in Hanover on Good Friday his soul is still in hell, and the daughters of Zion are wailing in Berlin, then I shall go aboard, since one has to board the steamer on Friday night in order to be able to leave early Saturday, and God knows what shape my soul will be in then; I am very afraid of seasickness.—One more thing, Rietz would like to keep the C clarinet instrumentation of the first chorale, *O Lamb of God*, and to try to have all four clarinets play in the upper octave—also he should free my score of ink spots, glue, and red pencil marks, i.e., *de ore leonis*. I can't write you much about theater and music, since neither plays, operas, nor concerts are allowed here during Holy Week, and the organist at St. Michael's even asked me to play quietly, for otherwise

1. *Ihr* (plural).
2. Novel by Jean Paul, published 1803–1804, influential in musical as well as literary circles.
3. *Der Tod Jesu*: oratorio by C. H. Graun.

those outside would hear it and the organ playing would annoy them during the week of quiet. For all that, if only they wouldn't promenade their new clothes on the Wall on Good Friday!—that would suit me just fine, and now I can visit the Lindenaus, flirt with Caecilia a bit, don't have to put on my official face or fulfill any musical obligations, can stroll along the Jungfernstieg[4] and gulp in the fresh air, converse with Beckchen and the oysters, and in brief amuse myself as much as I like. Greetings to Marx and the Heydemanns and Droysen, et al. Please pardon this disgracefully poor letter; I'm just not in the mood for writing now, but in London things will be better, and you'll get a more coherent one from here too. Beckchen had just finished the enclosed letter to Caroline and wanted to start one to all of you, but then Herr Keferstein drove up in the most elegant basket carriage and dragged her and Father away by force.

F.

To Abraham Mendelssohn Bartholdy

London, Tuesday, April 21, 1829

Dearest Father and dearest Beckchen,
Having just arrived safely in London, I want to send you word of my arrival before doing anything else. Our passage was not pleasant, and was very long, for we did not land at the customs house until today (Tuesday) at twelve; from Saturday night until Monday noon the wind was dead against us, and there was such a bad storm that everyone on board got seasick; we had to

4. A fashionable waterfront promenade in downtown Hamburg.

stop for a while, once on account of a thick fog and
once to make repairs on the engine; even last night
they had to anchor at the mouth of the Thames in
order to avoid colliding with other ships; also picture
me dragging myself around from one fainting fit to the
next, from early Sunday to Monday night, disgusted
with myself and everything else, cursing the steamer,
England, and especially my own *Meeresstille, (Calm Sea)*,
and scolding the steward as hard as I could, then finally
asking him Monday whether one could at last make out
London, whereupon he replied indifferently that that
was out of the question until midday on Tuesday; but
then, on the bright side, there was the moonlight on
the sea last night, with hundreds and hundreds of ships
gliding past us, and the journey up the Thames this
morning, with green meadows on both sides, towns
veiled in smoke, racing along with twenty steamers
swiftly overtaking all of the skiffs, and then finally the
frightfully massive vista of the city! My thoughts are
still as disorganized as the preceding sentence, and I
am writing this letter only to assure you of my safe
passage; so please don't expect anything more of it. I
also want to write to Berlin at once, since the mail will
arrive there via Rotterdam in four days, and I must go
to my lodgings (for I am still sitting here in Klingemann's
room—he'd send you his regards himself, but has some
business to attend to), must then find Moscheles, who
is expecting me, must *eat dinner*, which I have not done
for three days (oh how miserable am I!), must get a
shave, and in short must reassume human form. Good-
bye.

Felix

To Abraham Mendelssohn Bartholdy

London, May 1, 1829

If only one could get anywhere here! But the noise and bustle continue all day long, and in the evening one is tired. Thus my second epoch-making letter will have to be a very short one, because I was prevented from getting started by having to receive visitors, all of whom I sat down in armchairs in front of the fireplace, and because Cramer's morning concert, which begins in an hour, compels me to finish up. I actually don't have all that much to write about, for I am just now in the process of trying to plan out my future life in London, and if last time I was able to talk about my first impressions of the city, the people, and the music, then by now I have already mailed off my letters, made many new acquaintances, received many visitors, gulped down a few dinners, and planned several more; and not until after I have managed to reflect a bit on all of this society, which I now regard more from the point of view of an outsider, will I again have something new and interesting to write about, and be able to view it more calmly and contemplatively. For in the last few days I have truly lived like the curious traveler and sated myself with remarkable sights, so that you could all find out about my activities just by reading any old *travel guide*.[1] Also, you would not be all that fascinated to learn where I was yesterday (at Count Münster's), or

1. Mendelssohn frequently included English words in his letters, often humorously, writing them in a Latin script which contrasted markedly with his German script; here they are italicized.

where I will be on Tuesday (at Count Bülow's), or on Sunday (at Goldsmith's, where Mühlenfels is to introduce me). Do thank old Reden for me for his introductions, I have such a terrible time with high nobility; for is it Count Münster's fault that his wife was born a princess and he is so proud and boring that he himself has to yawn at every other word he utters? Reden did everything he could, for he invited me most civilly to visit him, and will continue to do so. But the worst thing is that I was asked to go to the Duke of Devonshire's ball tonight, and cannot go on account of some complications too long to explain to you; I had very much looked forward to such a ball, and now I can't go today! But Bülow assured me that he would invite me again, and then what a letter you will all get! Except for four letters I have now delivered all of my introductions. Bülow has been extraordinarily friendly and courteous to me; his wife is very quiet, but one can't really tell whether she's lost in thought or just bored. The Duke of Devonshire received my visit—picture me in an easy chair shouting in French with a deaf duke, and telling him stories about Berlin court life! Thanks to Gans' letter to Dr. König I have free access to the musical manuscripts in the British Museum, which I very much want to peruse, for I have heard that none of the musicians here have taken the trouble to even take a look at them. Monday noon I ate at Doxat's, and then went to the Philharmonic concert with them—they treat me with great kindness and generosity. Sillem also received me quite cordially. I haven't met the Duke of Montrose, nor the Viscount of Sandown, who is out in the country. Later today I shall visit Bute, Lansdowne, and Johnston, and then I'll be through. I know this is all merely a bare outline, but that's just the reason that

I can't do more than scrawl down a few names.—I'm feeling very well, by the way, life here suits me wonderfully. I find the city and its streets altogether beautiful, and once again I was struck with awe yesterday while driving in an open cabriolet into the *city* along a different route, through entirely unfamiliar streets, and found the same liveliness everywhere, all of the houses with green, yellow, and red bills posted all over them from top to bottom, or painted with letters as tall as a man—everywhere people yelling, and the mist (which at first made me feel very uncomfortable and indisposed), everywhere the ends of the streets shrouded in fog, and every few moments a church or a marketplace, or a green square, or a theater, or a view to the Thames, on which the steamers can now travel right through the city underneath all of the bridges, because a mechanism has been invented to lower all the huge smokestack funnels like masts. With the masts from the West India docks looking across, and a harbor as large as Hamburg's treated as if it were a pond, with sluices, and the ships arranged not singly but always in huge clusters, drawn up like a regiment—all of it makes one happy at the great wide world.—The other day I went to see Dr. Spurzheim's phrenological cabinet, shown by a young doctor. A group of murderers exhibited alongside a group of musicians interested me greatly, and my belief in physiognomy (cf. E. Devrient) received strong confirmation; also, the difference between Gluck's brow and that of a parricide is most striking, and probably beyond all doubt. But when people go into so much detail, trying to show me the place where Gluck's musical gift is seated, or his inventiveness, or where you can see Socrates' philosophy on his skull—that is certainly a bit precarious and (it seems to me) unscientific, but can lead to some very interesting results, namely the following: A pretty young Englishwoman who was there with me wanted to know whether she had an inclination to theft or other crime, and it ended up with everyone in the party having themselves phrenologically examined. Whereupon one man was diagnosed as cheerful, another as a lover of children, this lady courageous, that one avaricious, and when the aforementioned Englishwoman had to let down her long blond hair in order to enable the doctor to feel for the sites, and she looked very pretty in so doing, and then put it back up again in front of the mirror—then I gave three cheers for phrenology, and praised everything exceedingly. Naturally it turned out that I must have a good ear for music; the doctor later concluded that I was rather greedy, loved order and small children, and liked to flirt—but music was supposedly the predominant characteristic. And on Tuesday I am to have a plaster cast made of my entire head, complete with skull, face, and appurtenances, and then I plan to determine just how good Hensel's likenesses are!—Monday night was the Philharmonic concert. The orchestra is outstanding, full of fire and strength, and the basses and violins in particular play quite splendidly. More details in a letter to Zelter, which I shall write soon. The overture to the *Magic Flute* and the finale of a Haydn symphony were encored, that is, called forth *da capo*. The public's attention is concentrated exclusively on the instrumental pieces for the whole orchestra, so here would be the best, or rather the only good, opportunity of having my *Midsummer Night's Dream* performed; Moscheles thought so too, having wanted to perform the overture first in his own concert, but has now given up on the idea for the same reason; now I shall probably appear in the Philharmonic with any old composition or other, and then accept the offers for private concerts which will no doubt ensue; and I also shall not play in public (I am thinking) until the Philharmonic has performed something by me. Moscheles—whose advice I sought out on this matter, as in all others, even the most trifling affairs, and who has shown himself thoroughly friendly toward me—thinks that this would be best too, but we are still waiting for the *official* invitation from the director of the Philharmonic concerts, which Moscheles assures me I shall soon receive, however.—I also saw Westminster Abbey two days after the fire, an exhibition of paintings, and the library; and yesterday heard an introductory lecture by a professor at the new university, while tomorrow I am going to see St. Paul's Church and hear the *Messiah* (Sontag is singing, her *first appearance*). Today I have to go to the French Theater, tomorrow to the Italian, and in short I am keeping my ears (as you like to say, dear Father) as wide open as possible. Cramer's concert is calling. Farewell.

F.

Postscripts.

I. I just hope that you received my letter from yesterday in time, and sent me the extra string parts for *A Calm Sea, Midsummer Night's Dream,* and the Symphony in C Minor right away, for I need them all too urgently here. II. Thank Albert Bauer for his letter to Mühlenfels; he's been very pleasant and friendly to me, although I hear he is usually supposed to be rather reserved; he is going to write to Bauer soon. III.

Greetings to Rietz, and tell him that F. Cramer plays a
pretty good fiddle, but—! IV. Greetings to . . .

Felix Mendelssohn Bartholdy
103 Great Portland Street

So far I have received only the one letter from Hamburg;
and this is my fifth from London! Is that fair?—Fanny
and Beckchen must write! and lots of stupid stuff! Even if
Father and Mother don't always have time, I still need
some news and signs of life. Send them often!

To Adolf Bernhardt Marx

London, May 9, 1829

Dear Marx,

Today is the first warm spring day in L.; and the first
spring day in L. is as entirely unimaginable to one who
has not seen it as the glaciers in Switzerland—the smoky
houses have opened up and people are streaming out
from all directions. Even so I want to write you now; I
am so well and gay and lighthearted, but at the same
time very lonely; perhaps your brother will be coming
for your birthday also; if so may he bring you happiness,
good cheer, and lasting strength, and remind you that
even from a great distance my innermost heart is always
with you and all of your family, and that I am enjoying
the great theater around me like a panorama, and that
whenever I think of all of you, even in this great hustle
and bustle, I feel very calm and not at all sad or tired.
Today the weather is heavenly. I was just on a very nice
long street, with alternating tall brown houses (made of
bricks, with signs and colossal letters, sky-high chimneys,
and elegant shops) and noblemen's palaces on one side,

and a graceful ironwork fence on the other, with an arch of triumph in the distance. On the street between the fence and the houses there is the wildest uproar; the dandies gallop by, the old lords ride slowly, the children trot along on fillies; splendid équipages with golden harnesses and velvet-clad servants wait for a coal coach, which blocks the entranceway with its elephantine horses; then there are the dirty rented coaches, all in a long row, with beggars and rabble walking next to the duchesses, who are pretty and look very English and cold, and who are followed by powdered lackeys with satin pants; one fellow with a bell is reading letters aloud; another is singing a new aria while simultaneously holding his hands cupped so as to receive the pennies (an upstanding artist); one man is playing a Scottish bagpipe; most of the men are leading a lady on each arm; many faces are pressed together as they peer out from the coaches. Six mailcoaches with men heaped up on the top race through one after the other, the shops are teeming, that's what the street is like. But through the iron fencework you can see to a broad empty green meadow, on which all sorts of cows are standing and chewing their cuds, and here and there is a tree, while in the distance they become more dense and turn into a woods; on the horizon the white towers of Westminster soar up into the blue sky above the woods; the fog in which up until today all the streets were shrouded has turned to vapor today, which turns everything in the distance sky-blue, and the clouds above stroll across as cheerfully as the people below. In the midst of the smartly dressed gentlemen, who are actually ambitious dandies, there is one who walks deliberately and contentedly, namely myself. On the street corners in thick black letters on the white walls—Piccadilly, which is the name of the street, if anyone asks you; well, I was there a half hour ago and have never seen anything more beautiful in my life. If you can imagine that this morning I was at the St. Catherine's docks and from there cut across L. by water, on the Thames (I'll send the description to Droysen, since he's an Aquarius), and that Piccad. is just one street in the diplomatic area of the West End, a London district, and that the West End is supposed to be dead these days compared with the rest of the city, then you will be quite amazed. I'm giving it my all.—There isn't much in the way of music here; from Klingemann, who sends his warmest regards, and how, you'll get a detailed report on it soon. The musicians are worse than ours, for there is more competition, and unlike the craftsmen this makes them not better, but more mistrustful and intriguing. In general they have everything that can be cultivated by external means, practice, money, formulas, and the like—such as, for example, good arrangement of the orchestra, equality and power in the string instruments, a great number of violins, good precise brass—but everything spiritual is lacking; there is no concertmaster, no tender oboes, clarinets, or bassoons, everything is rough and clumsy; no liveliness, but just speed, no respect for the work of art, in short no conductor. Sir George, whom Fanny can describe for you, is really the best and fieriest of them, no matter how much he powders himself; they worship Beethoven and edit him, they worship Mozart and are bored with it, they worship Haydn and rush him to death. Music is a thing of fashion

The 10th

and is pursued as such, changes like one, and is likewise a subject of conversation.—If only you could see things here today, I am sitting at an open window, the fire is still burning in the fireplace, and fragrant air is streaming in; I am waiting for my friends to arrive, then I shall go on a walk across the meadows with them, today is Sunday and the church bells across from me are ringing loud and clear. Use all your imagination and try your best to picture spring's splendors being any prettier! It's not possible! May God send you today as much warmth and good cheer as I am enjoying here. The flower vendors are yelling dreadfully down below; my innkeepers have put bunches of wallflowers in my room. But now I must go drink my breakfast tea. Write soon, farewell.

To Abraham Mendelssohn Bartholdy

London, June 19, 1829

I received your[1] lovely letter of the 9th on Tuesday, along with the three letters from Zelter, Devrient, and Milder. Next Tuesday my replies will depart with the embassy mail, to Z.—in the meantime please thank him for me for his most welcome and lovely letter—and to Devrient and Heydemann; I am really quite at a loss in Milder's case, as she sent me a dictatorial six-line ukase, which concludes, "If Herr Mendelssohn does not send it right away, Mme. Milder will be seriously angry," and I would very much like to oblige her. But I have been experiencing so many new and unexpected things recently, which upset one's internal peace of mind, that I have neither the leisure, the ideas, nor the dedication to compose, for otherwise something would certainly

1. *Euer* (plural).

come into my head. But I strongly doubt that it would be concert arias, and fear it may be some odd thing, but I still will try to see if I can torture something out of myself by next week, and then send it to her at once; I don't lack good intentions, for I have often sat down at the piano in an attempt to work up some enthusiasm by playing, and then possibly fish out the aria and missing songs I promised, but whenever I get to a piano here I slip into incessant practicing of virtuoso passages and similar stuff, and come away without profit or new ideas. May God grant some improvement, and if He does not, then may Scotland and the lakes.—What you wrote about the theater, dear Father, was probably very much to the point, and seems to me to have been written from the heart, but the theater you speak of has died out here; there is no reflection of national character onstage, except in crude farces which would be indigestible to any other than an English stomach; Shakespeare's plays are so corrupted and spoiled by the insertion of ridiculously bad arias and songs, by omission of their more powerful elements, exaggeration of their pathos, and by complete misunderstanding of the characters, for example the female ones, that they are hardly recognizable or enjoyable, and the new things which are being played are weak attempts to scrape by with imitations of what has already been successful on French and German stages. It can't continue like this, and I think this may be our best hope; since what you say really is true, and since everything up on the stage now is exactly the opposite of it, then things will simply have to turn around in some other direction. For no truth can be lost forever; time and circumstances might obscure it for a while, perhaps, but it always comes to light again in some new form. So I hope.

So, you dear bunch of rascals! I'm supposed to write you a letter? And how shall I address it? To our friend time itself, or to the people, or to two human beings par excellence, and what shall I write in it? Two whole pages of nothing but *bon appétit?* Written words themselves are cold, vultures; speaking is better, even if it has to be just English. I'd like to see Beckchen as an English *lady*, shaking hands with one of these English lambs, for which by the way you should substitute camel or rhinoceros, for lambs are too cute, or Fanny in white *marabous* at a musical soirée conversing over ice cream in the evening, hearing them mumble "charming"; England isn't for you, you rascals. But I am writing a little diary for all of you and shall send it on Tuesday, and we also must start to develop a plan for the celebration in December, for the time is fast approaching, and before any of you know it someone whom you all know will show his face again. I already have some special plans, and ideas about all of this; I'll send them all to you in the diary. But, dearest Mother, when is the wedding? Couldn't the trousseau finally be finished? I'm more interested in this than in the empress' arrival, and many other news items; it's hard to ask people all the way across the ocean, but do make haste! After all it's better and necessary for so many reasons, and if Hensel should die of impatience beforehand, then how can the marriage proceed? I must find the whole little affair and everything arranged already when I return to Berlin, for I of course want to eat with Fanny the day after arriving, and am counting on my favorite dishes; and if the wedding were not until winter I wouldn't even be half as pleased, for I wouldn't be able to participate in the new life for very long, would have to tear myself away soon, and the separation would be twice as hard—in short, I don't plan to be there. *After* my return would apparently be too late, so it will have to be *before* I come back. And so may it rest! Please! I could almost kneel down before my writing desk and beg you. If there aren't enough lodgings then Hensel can move to the Hôtel de Brandenburg, and if there isn't enough dowry I'll send my share of the linens. *I* can't do any more; but *you* probably can, dear Mother. So do it! Isn't it time enough?

Summer has arrived, and the season is drawing to a close; I hope my last concert will be the one for the Danzigers, for which the date still hasn't been set, and I am starting to think seriously about my departure for Scotland with Klingemann. I'm afraid the trip to the coast will have to be omitted, for several reasons, which I'll have to tell you about in person, for it's too involved to go into in writing. I am thinking at present of leaving London on July 20, and going to Edinburgh and Glasgow with the mailcoach; we'll stop along the way wherever we please, for coaches go through everywhere each day, and you can make it from London to Edinburgh in three days. From there there are constant opportunities to travel to the Highlands, and we won't be taking the steamer on Loch Lomond or the other lakes, since we want to go on foot, and because I am going to draw lots of rocky peaks. Perhaps we will make it to the islands and visit Staffa, which must be so beautiful; between here and there I shouldn't need much in the way of letters of recommendation, and Sir Alexander Johnston, who is related to the Duke of Argyll, will certainly be able to give me the best, so that I am counting on a wonderfully happy visit. On the way back I may perhaps see a bit of Ireland and Wales; I am attracted to Killarney because I saw some absolutely heavenly landscapes there depicted in a huge exhibition, and I have been invited to Wales by an English family, the Taylors, to spend a week there at their estate, and either go fox hunting with their sons or draw landscapes with their daughters. I opted for the latter. Then I am thinking of leaving England and crossing over to Ostend, in order to go from there to Rotterdam, Amsterdam, Ghent, Brussels, Aachen, through Berlin and to Italy, but all of these plans are still very hazy.—(Beckchen, they put people in the stocks here; Einbrod has arrived.) (Fanny, they don't put people in the stocks here; Aunt Bute is still out in the country.) I must close soon, for at two Lord Sandown is taking me on a tour through the Earl of Grosvenor's famous picture gallery. Stackelberg is also coming along; he is here, by the way, O Hensel, and sends his regards, and will soon be coming to Berlin for several days. The world has never seen the likes of the pictures which are to be found here!— The private collectors have just brought together some of their treasures, and so the divine works are exhibited together in three rooms; I can't begin to describe it to you. Rubens painted the *Tribute Money*. Titian his young daughter; the old fellow must have wondered quite a lot while painting it how the blond child could stand there so graceful and poised, and so charming and slightly disheveled, holding an apple in her hand and thinking of nothing at all. There are also two splendid pieces by van Dyck, a number of Rembrandts, Murillos, Ruisdaels, and Claudes, so that the whole thing is a real joy. Titian did a portrait of Ignatius Loyola which makes you feel Catholic just to look at it—he peers ominously out of the painting, black and serious—and Rubens' Jews are like escaped bears and wolves. (Cf. *Felicum post reditum*, Leipziger Strasse No. 3.)—Farewell. Wednesday

I am playing Beethoven's E-flat concerto, to the horror of all the musicians—I've had my fill of tedious notes and must play the Beethoven again. (It just now occurs to me that I already wrote you about this.) I'm forgetting the main thing. The Covent Garden business is rolling right along; they have stipulated the most noble and advantageous conditions for me—that I should choose my own text, take it along and compose the music for it where and when I please, and if I finish the opera by December it's supposed to be performed in February. If I want to and am able, I am supposed to direct it myself, they are promising me the best possible cast; as for the honorarium from the theater, they have offered me the proceeds of one of the first performances, and the music publisher has consulted me about my stipulations for the piano reduction. And it's all being taken care of quickly and pleasantly. Since the publisher has asked me, should I accept it, not to publish any of my other smaller things here, so that he can come out with the opera first, I won't have the songs printed now; for I shall certainly accept the offer, and am curious myself to see what my music will look like; and anyway, where would I write them? Apropos the reason I haven't mentioned Baring—because Sillem's letters probably must have been very bad, for I haven't heard a word from either Baring or Sillem since I delivered the letters. The day before yesterday there was a ball at Doxat's; I arrived at twelve-thirty and left at three. Today there is one at Johnston's. This week things are still pretty awful, but it's the last one. Farewell! Fond regards to Aunt Meier.

Felix

To Abraham Mendelssohn Bartholdy

London, July 10, 1829

Today I truly don't know what to write about, partly
from a lack and partly from an excess of things to write
about. From a lack of things to write about, because I
don't have all your letters, nothing arrived for me on
the boat from Hamburg on Tuesday (but I won't be
upset, on account of our agreement), and from an
excess of things to write about, because if I were to start
to describe my life this week and next in detail I'd never
finish, and it would be a diary instead of a letter.[1] What
has occupied me almost exclusively recently has been
the concert for the Silesians; judging from the choice
of pieces, it will be indisputably the most brilliant of the
year. Everyone who has attracted the slightest attention
this season will take part, most of them free of charge;
many offers from good *performers* have had to be turned
down, since even as things are it will last until the
following day. Klingemann is sending you the intermin-
able program, it really is quite interesting. My overture
to *A Midsummer Night's Dream* will open, by popular
demand, then I'll play the Double Concerto in E with
Moscheles. Yesterday we held our first rehearsal at the
Clementi factory, with Mme. Moscheles and Herr Collard listening, and I had a heavenly time of it, for no
one had any notion of our coquetteries, and how we
were constantly imitating one another, and how cute
we were. Moscheles plays the last movement with tremendous brilliance, tossing the runs right off the cuff.

1. *Tagebuch statt eines Tagebriefs.*

When it was over everyone said it was such a shame that we hadn't played any cadenzas, so I at once dug up a place in the final tutti of the first movement where the orchestra has a fermata, and Moscheles was prevailed upon *nolens volens* to compose a big cadenza; we then tried to figure out, meanwhile making a thousand pranks, whether the last little solo (*vide* Fanny) could be left as was, since people would no doubt applaud.[2] We need a little tutti between the cadenza and the final solo, I said. How long are they supposed to applaud? asked Moscheles. Ten minutes, *I dare say*, said I. Moscheles bargained me down to five. I promised to provide a tutti, and so we took proper measurements, patched, turned, and padded things together, stitched on some sleeves à la Mameluke, and tailored a brilliant concerto. Today there is another rehearsal, it will be quite a musical picnic, for Moscheles is bringing the cadenza along, and I the tutti. The full orchestra rehearsal is set for tomorrow at two, and afterward I am planning some *plaisir*; in fact, I will be spending the afternoon and evening in Stamfordhill, a grassy village full of trees, gardens, and roses, with a Herr Richmond and his many daughters. Rosen and Mühlenfels will be with me—since the three of us are all supposed to go to another friend's house nearby for breakfast on Sunday, we decided yesterday to spend the night at the village inn, then go out walking through the fields early in the morning, and amaze people by our presence at such an early hour—this is our plan, and as proper Londoners we intend to behave ourselves with devilish propriety at said inn. Afterward I have to go to St. Paul's (a little trip) to play the organ for the last time, since it will be

2. I.e., applaud Moscheles' cadenza.

my last Sunday in London; then I have to go to Kilburn
(a big trip) to visit Moscheles, who is having a small
party at his house for the first time since losing his
child. And the concert itself is on Monday. Tuesday
evening there will be a party at Dr. Billing's, a physician
here who put an English bandage on my thumb yesterday, and took the opportunity to swear an oath of
friendship; I had been about to drink a glass of wine
with a lady, and was pulling the glass stopper out with
great force, but was very clumsy, and the bottle shattered
in my hand and I cut myself a bit—but it should be
noted for the record that beforehand I began to nod
off and faint, and only then went to see Dr. Billing.
Wednesday there is a ball. Thursday afternoon and
evening we shall all be together at Eichtal's once again.
Friday there will be a going-away tea with musical
entertainment at my place; my guests will be Klingemann, Rosen, Mühlenfels, Einbrod, Collard, Brunel
(the young architect of the tunnel, whose project fell
flat a while back), and Eichtal. Finally Saturday is the
day everyone departs for all four corners of the earth.
Klingemann and I are taking the northern route, Rosen
is heading toward the Rhine, and Mühlenfels is going—
to Berlin. Yes, yes! He gets to see you all before I do.
Please, show affection with him and be friendly to him.
If I tell you that it was he who principally filled the void
I felt from my first taste of being alone and without
anyone to confide in, and which grew even more
pronounced as a result of all the socials and distrac-
tions—or at least he made the feelings less noticeable—
and that I owe to him above all the cheerful and healthy
feeling which has rarely left me here even amid all the
chaos and confusion, then I am sure that you will all be
happy to welcome him in and will also be kind to him.

He is a strong, capable, and virtuous fellow. He will have many funny stories about our time here to tell you, for we've had quite a wealth of them, and have vowed to enjoy each other's company as much as possible in the few days we still have together. Recently the three of us were on the way back from a most diplomatic dinner at Bülow's, and were feeling sick of fashionable entrées, conversation, and trimmings. So then we happened upon an appetizing-looking butcher's shop, where they were displaying "German sausage" for twopence; we were overcome by patriotism, each of us bought a long sausage, we fled into the less well-frequented Portland Street and devoured our purchases, while laughing so hard that we could hardly sing the three-part songs which Mühlenfels led off in the bass. Both professors had concluded their lectures that same day and so had nothing to worry about; Rosen can become quite wild at times.—Just keep on addressing your letters to Doxat's; I will apprise them of several of my travel destinations where they can send everything that comes for me—but you mustn't be too picky about my not writing for over a week *after* today, for the letter I am writing will be the last one from Portland St., and then it may be two or three weeks before I have a chance to send something to you. But like you, I will still keep writing continually on a sheet of paper, and send it—whether small or large—whenever I can find a decent post office which will expedite things to London quickly, and goodness knows there are quite a few of them in this country; thus you will all be kept in direct contact with deep Loch Lomond and high Ben Lomond. The bagpipes will discover in me a great friend; I came across a marching tune which is very amusing and sounds quite funny in F-sharp major. I intend to use the same; but where I shall find time to write I don't know; there is just so awfully much I have to experience here. Perhaps I'll be able to in Berlin in December.—I have to close now, for I have several visits to pay, p.p.c., which Klingemann explains as *pour prendre concertbillets*. I've already sold twenty and will dispose of still more; I hope it will be quite full, and the Silesians will be handsomely recompensed for all their trouble, in which case they would have Uncle's letter to thank, without which the whole concert would never have taken place. I can't write better or more today because I have a headache and am in a foul mood, which is due entirely to the miserable weather we've been having for the last week here. Downpours and flashes of sunshine, autumn chills, stormy winds, and oppressive heat keep alternating; one's umbrella never dries off. It's boring. I only hope it's better where you are. Farewell.

Felix

To Abraham Mendelssohn Bartholdy

London, July 21, 1829, evening

And herewith I bid you farewell, we're about to be off. Rosen departed early this morning. Mühlenfels is leaving at midnight, and early tomorrow morning Klingemann and I shall take our seats in the *stage* and London will be behind us. I can't write you anything sensible today, for my things aren't all packed yet and Cramer has been here since ten-thirty, drunk as a skunk, has already sung some arias for me, asked me if I was also planning to travel to the Isle of Krim, and just now is sitting at the piano improvising better than I have ever heard him, but I don't let it bother me and keep on

writing. A few days after you receive this letter Mühlenfels will arrive (Cramer just slipped gently into
F-sharp) to give you the news in person and bring my
notices, which for God's sake hang on to for me and
don't burn *anything*, they are meant to amuse me at a
future date. Truly, I haven't a moment's peace to write,
this is just so that a letter will arrive on Wednesday.
Droysen, whom I also wanted to write, won't get anything either, because I am too unsettled; tell him how
much I thank him for Fanny's song, and that he should
stop flirting so much, otherwise I might bear a grudge
against him, and also he ought to keep my return in
mind, for I am making a profit here. (Cramer is now
playing brilliantly in E-flat.) I have taken my leave of
everyone, sent off all my notices; the nasty raw weather
seems to be clearing up, promising us a pleasant journey;
I have an entire bundle of letters of introduction and
recommendations to musicians, manufacturers, and
merchants, Doxat's will have your letters forwarded to
me, I shall write you as regularly as possible, on September 15 I am thinking of passing through here again
and concluding some items of business already set in
motion, and with that God be with you! for I am tired
and Cramer is stopping, now I'll quickly pack my things
together, and lie down in bed for a few hours; tomorrow
I'll take my walking stick in my hand, which was just
given to me by the Johnstons (*enquire* Mühlenfels and
Rosen) for my mountain climbing, and will set off from
Portland St. in the brisk air to Charing Cross, where
Klingemann is to meet me, then from there to York,
then on to Durham, and Sunday or Monday, God
willing, to Edinburgh, and on from there. Cramer is
opening the window, saying he needs some fresh air,
and it seems the moon is just coming up, and the sky

looks friendly. The trip to the Highlands will be a nice one. Good night.

Felix

To Abraham Mendelssohn Bartholdy

Edinburgh, July 28, 1829

It is Sunday as we arrive in Edinburgh. We then proceed across the meadows to two devilishly steep rocks, which are called Arthur's Seat, and scramble on up. Below, the most motley crew of people, women, children, and cows are walking around in the green field, and all around the city spreads out before you, and in the middle of it there is a castle perched like a bird's nest on a cliff, beyond the castle you can see meadows, then hills, then a wide river; across the river you can see more hills, then a more imposing mountain where Stirling's castle appears, and this is already way off in the distance; behind it there is a pale shadow they call Ben Lomond. But all this is only half of the view from Arthur's Seat, to the other side the view is simple enough, namely the wide blue sea, immeasurably large, covered with white sails and black smokestacks, little insectlike rowboats and skiffs, rocky islands, and the like. How could I possibly describe it? You simply must see it for yourselves. When God in heaven takes up panorama painting you can expect something terrific. Few memories from Switzerland could outdo this one. Everything looks so stern and robust here, even if it all is half obscured by steam or smoke or fog. Moreover, tomorrow the Highlanders are having a *bagpipe* competition, and so many people were coming out of church in their suits, leading their smartly dressed ladies vic-

toriously by the arm, looking out at the world ceremoniously and self-importantly; with their long red beards,
colorful coats and feather caps, bare knees, and their
bagpipes in hand, they walked calmly past the crumbling
gray castle on the meadow, where Mary Stuart once
lived in splendor and saw Rizzio murdered. It seems to
me that time passes very quickly when I can see so
much of the past in front of me, alongside the present.
In the evening a cool breeze wafts across from the sea,
making all objects look extremely sharp and clear,
standing out clearly against the gray sky, while the lights
in the windows are shining very brightly, and it was the
same way yesterday when I went walking up and down
the streets with Mr. Ferguson, an Edinburgh *friend of
mine* to whom I was recommended by Mr. Droop, a
London *friend of mine*, and picked up your letter of the
13th from the post office. I then read it through with
particular satisfaction on Princes Street in Edinburgh.
In Edinburgh! a letter all the way from under the yew-
tree! I was just as pleased when I went for a swim in
the sea today, paddling about alone in the open water
for a few minutes, and it occurred to me how well we
all know each other; and yet I was well submerged in
the Scottish sea, which tastes very salty—Doberan is
lemonade by comparison. You are all amazed that I
haven't received your letters? It's only natural, the
steamer doesn't arrive until Saturday these days, this
time on Friday evening. But I don't understand how
my itinerary and the plans for getting mail back and
forth could not have reached you; enclosed here is a
duplicate; Doxat's has all my addresses for Scotland and
Wales and will forward everything promptly. And also
I plan to write as often as possible; but I'm afraid I can
predict that it is likely that next Wednesday, after this

letter has arrived, one will probably be skipped, since it will be impossible to send anything from out of the Highlands, although we shall certainly write—everything will arrive later. There are two more things in yesterday's letter I have to answer. First the matter of money; I simply don't understand why Doxat's hasn't written Father yet about this; I need thirty pounds per month, and they gave me a letter of credit for five hundred pounds for this trip, for five cities, but refused to take a receipt from me, saying that they would settle everything directly and report to you, dear Father. Please let me know if I should do anything with respect to this, and what, when I return to London, for it seems that you have assumed that I planned to be in Ireland for quite a long visit. But I was thinking of going over for only about eight days to see a few vistas there which are supposed to be among the most beautiful in all England according to descriptions and pictures I have seen, and to visit Dublin for a few days. The boat trip takes four hours, and so the whole thing is just a short excursion, but one which is well worth the trouble. Whether I shall see Sir Walter here is still completely uncertain, although I have a letter of introduction to him from one of his close friends in London, but I am still hopeful, mostly so that I won't have to endure too much scolding from you, dear Mother, for returning without having seen the *lion* himself. Because the steamer is late, I won't be able to get the flower seeds until after the trip; I am properly ashamed of not having sent them, instead of scissors, needles, and the like, but in London one really does forget that there is such a thing as the world of nature, and just as one becomes almost cold and indifferent to other people there, when there is a fire alarm only looking out the window to see where the flames are, then fall calmly back to sleep if they aren't too close it would never occur to anyone that there are such things as flowers out in the world, or that they grow from seeds. You just sniff them, stick them in your buttonhole, and forget them. But I want to make reparations; the carnations are lovely, and will be pretty in the garden.—Now an explanation for this strange-looking letter. Since people are so uncommonly friendly and forthcoming to us here, we are always booked up at mealtime at midday, in the evening, and in the morning, while in between we run around. We thus took the big sheet of paper and started writing at once, each on one side. There was more room on the last one beneath what Klingemann started, since he writes smaller than I do, and my side was filled up sooner; the letters from the Highlands will be in the same format. (Herz's letter I shall mail tomorrow.) The Highlands journey will be as follows: via Stirling, Perth, Dunkeld, and the waterfalls to Blair Atholl; from there on foot over the mountains to Inverary, to Glencoe, the Isle of Staffa and the Isle of Islay; there we shall stay for a few days because Sir Alexander Johnston forwarded yet another gracious letter to me here in Edinburgh, together with a letter of recommendation to Sir Walter Campbell, the lord, owner, the tyrant of the island, whom a mere word from Johnston will tame, turning him into a guide; from there down the Clyde to Glasgow, and from there to Ben Lomond, since it and Loch Lomond are considered the lions of the Highlands, to Loch Earn, Ben Vorlich, Loch Katrine, then on to Cumberland, etc. What else should I tell you about? How by chance I received the letter from Zelter, Devrient, and Rietz at Charing Cross, five minutes before departing, and read through it in the stagecoach?

How we are going to Roslin tomorrow morning to see the ruins, and now are on our way to dine with Mr. Findlay Dun, then to Mr. Wood's for some music making, then tomorrow to the bagpipe contest (where there will also be some Scottish folk dancing) to amuse ourselves? Time and space are running out, and it all keeps coming back to the same refrain: what friendly people, and how generous God is in Edinburgh. Scottish women are also worthy of note, and if Machmud does follow Father's advice and become a Christian, then I shall compensate for him and become a Turk, and take up residence somewhere near here. If only they wouldn't drink so much whisky! and have so little *pie*! Sir George is better about it, the man with whom I ate my last supper in London, and who drank Moselle wine to the health of my homeland and my family, to whom he attributed several of my good qualities. I made a thank-you speech, we swore friendship together and presented each other with princely gifts; he gave me a drinking song in canon form, and I in turn gave him the overture to a *Midsummer Night's Dream*, which the Philharmonic is playing next season. With whom did I make a bet? With my pen pal. Beckchen, you were perhaps put on the earth in order to be made fun of? Here I take W. Horn's position. Mühlenfels will probably grumble. May God be with us.—A London doctor thought your portrait showed much similarity to Sappho's, especially in the chin. A dandy promised to learn German in order to be able to flirt a bit; an old musician said he saw many beautiful traits in your face. Unfortunately the / man was half crazed, so don't put too much stock in it. At all. Farewell. *Time is. Time was. Time is passed.* Suspended in it is

                                                          Felix

To Abraham Mendelssohn Bartholdy

Blair Atholl, August 3, 1829

Evening, August 3, Highland inn at the bridge of Tummel.
A wild affair. The storm is howling, blustering, and
whistling around outside, causing the doors to slam
shut down below and blowing the shutters open, but
one can't tell whether the sounds of water are from the
rain or from the blowing spray, since both are raging.
We're sitting here calmly around the burning hearth,
which I poke a bit from time to time, making it flare
up. Otherwise, the room is large and empty, water is
dripping down along one of the walls; the floor is thin,
and the conversation in the servants' quarters can be
heard echoing up from below; they're singing drunken
songs and laughing—dogs are barking as well. Two
beds with purple curtains, on our feet Scottish wooden
shoes instead of English slippers, tea with honey and
potato cakes, a narrow winding wooden staircase, which
the maid made use of to bring us whisky, a dismal
procession of clouds in the sky, and in spite of all the
wind and water noises, in spite of the servants' conversation and the banging doors it seems quiet! Quiet and
very lonely. I should like to say that the quiet resounds
even through the noise. Just now the door opened by
itself. It's a Highlands ale house. The little boys with
their plaids and bare knees and colorful caps, the waiter
in his tartan, old people with their periwigs, all speaking
a jumble of incomprehensible Gaelic. The countryside
is broad and wide, covered with dense vegetation, from
all sides cascades of water are rushing under the bridges,
there is little corn but much heather with brown and

red flowers, ravines, passes, crossroads; everywhere beautiful green, deep blue water—but everything is stern, dark, and very lonely. How could I describe it? Ask Droysen, who knows it well and can paint a better picture than I, we are always quoting lines from his *Hochlands (Highlands)* to each other. Now I am addressing him: Dear Droysen, how did you come to know Scotland? It is just as you said it would be. A year ago today we went to the Luiseninsel at night—it was all lit up—and howled a bit. And we also went drinking on the Mittelstrasse.[1] Now I'm doing the same at the foot of the Schiehallion, and am reading some of the *Flegeljahre* tonight, for I brought them along and my dear little sisters are giving me strange looks;[2] Hensel has it easy and can see and retain faces. But the weather is discouraging. I have invented my own method of drawing it, and today rubbed in some clouds, and drew gray mountains in pencil; Klingemann is rhyming cheerfully, and I carry out more of the details when it rains. But it had better not rain tomorrow, for if possible we are to see Loch Tay, Kenmore, and Killin tomorrow. Today is almost an autumn day. I'll tell you all about today soon; I don't lack for material to make me an important figure at Leipziger Str. No. 3. I wish you would send me some letters of recommendation for Flanders and the Netherlands; after all, one must provide for the future too. And when I think of how this piece of paper will be carried out to the garden house, and how yesterday at the waterfall the beginning of the letter

1. *Luiseninsel, Mittelstrasse*: leisure spots and street of restaurants in Berlin.
2. According to Sebastian Hensel, Mendelssohn's sisters had sent a copy of Jean Paul's *Flegeljahre* to him in England, in which Hensel had drawn their portraits.

blew out of my sketchbook and went fluttering down
onto the gravel (we scrambled after it and retrieved it,
though), and how just now the innkeeper's wife is
singing her child to sleep with a sweet melody in a
minor key, and how all of this is on its way to you. So
things will still pass back and forth a few times. But
then when the late autumn weather sets in, I'll put on
my coat for the last day of the journey home, and walk
in one evening. It will be merry. But now I am still in
Scotland, and the winds are blustering wildly. Good
night, I'm going to my bed inside the red curtains. Sleep
well.

Felix MB

To Abraham Mendelssohn Bartholdy

On one of the Hebrides, August 7, 1829. In order to make
clear what a strange mood has come over me in in the
Hebrides, the following occurred to me:

Glasgow, August 11. How much has passed in the meantime. The most horrible seasickness, Staffa, scenery

travels, people; Klingemann can describe them, for in the first place he didn't have to make the London mail, as I did today, for which I had to write several letters, and second he hasn't been plagued as I have been by severe headaches all evening, which make it hard for me to even think, let alone write. Then take into account that it's already midnight, and we've already filled a whole day of our Highlands journey with boat travel, galleries, churches, steam, people, and smokestack funnels, and you will excuse me for being so brief. I can't go on today. Also, the best thing I have to report can be found in the above lines of music, and I'll gladly spare you descriptions of my illness, the thoroughly unaccommodating, damp weather, and so on. So please forgive me this time. I am drawing assiduously, and Klingemann's poems are coming along splendidly, and I also think that several of my pictures were more successful than usual. And expenditures have been more moderate than I thought. We've only spent twenty-four pounds so far. Tomorrow we're going to Loch Lomond and Ben Lomond, to Loch Katrine, the Trossachs, Aberfoyle, Stirling, and Lanark; we'll be back here at the end of this week, and you will receive our last joint letter from here; my own half should be better then. Then we'll part ways, Klingemann is going back to London, and in a week I shall be better able to report on my plans for the rest of my trip. I am thinking of spending another three weeks or so in the islands after that, and then returning to the Continent. Send some good letters to the Netherlands, if possible. Pardon this poor, hasty letter, and farewell.

F.

To Abraham Mendelssohn Bartholdy

Llangollen, August 25, 1829

Anything but national music! May ten thousand devils take all folklore. Here I am in Wales, and oh how lovely, a harpist sits in the lobby of every inn of repute playing so-called folk melodies at you—i.e., dreadful, vulgar, fake stuff, and *simultaneously* a hurdy-gurdy is tootling out melodies, it's enough to drive one crazy, it's even given me a toothache. Scottish bagpipes, Swiss cow's horns, Welsh harps—all playing the Huntsmen's Chorus with ghastly variations or improvisations, not to mention the lovely songs in the lobby—it's the only real music they have! It's beyond comprehension! Anyone like myself, who can't abide Beethoven's *Nationallieder*, should come here and hear them howled by shrill nasal voices, accompanied by doltish bumbling fingers, and then try to hold his tongue. The whole time I've been writing these lines the fellow out in the hall has been playing:

and he does variations on this, while the hurdy-gurdy interrupts with a sacred song in A-flat major. I am going mad, and will have to leave off writing until later.—
August 26. And in so doing I did the right thing; last night in despair I went to visit the innkeeper's three daughters, who have a piano, and asked them to play something on it for me; they are quite pretty and did so—the organ grinder and the harpist fell silent (the

latter is also the barber, it turns out, as I discovered this morning)—the daughters then started up on the organ, but I was blissful, the *muette de Portici* and several contredanses did me good. Afterward they asked me to "favor" them, so I favored them from my heart, racing up and down the keyboard and playing away my toothaches; the evening was quite pleasant, and I returned to my room too late to resume writing. And yesterday afternoon I had already climbed to the top of a high mountain, with the ruins of a Roman citadel at the summit, had looked far out into the blue distance, and down to the dark, lonely valleys below—then climbed right back down into one of these quiet valleys, in which the walls and windows of an old abbey are covered and overgrown with lovely green trees—the abbey is right next to a rushing, babbling brook, mountains and rocky cliffs are spread all around, the choir of the church has been converted into a stable, the altar into a kitchen, above the tops of the gables you can see the tops of the beeches towering in the distance, which could be a chapter in themselves, and the sky was serenely gray. I did a little composing instead of drawing in Hensel's Christmas album; it was quite a nice day. Blue sky and sunshine do so much to warm my heart, and are so indispensable for me! But here they don't exist. This actually grieves me seriously, or almost. The summer is gone, and without having sent a single summer day. Yesterday was a *good* day, i.e., I only got soaked three times, kept my cloak over my shoulders the whole day, and saw the sun a few times through the clouds. *Bad* days are beyond imagination; a raging, whistling storm has been blowing for four weeks almost without interruption and in addition the clouds have come cascading down and it would be raining terribly, if the storm

would just let it fall in peace; but it snatches it up, tosses
it around in the air, whipping the spray against your
face—there's nothing to do for it except to sit around
quietly indoors. In place of the usually cheerful travel
talk all you can hear around you are a few stray cross
words: since time immemorial, flooded roads, or missed
mail deliveries or ships, spoiled travel plans. And so
mine too are spoiled, today I had wanted to make one
more try, and if the sky were blue I'd have gone up
into the mountains again, but instead there's a rainstorm, or stormy rain, again and I'm giving up for
today. My trip to Ireland came to naught in Bangor
and on the Isle of Anglesey—in spite of all the dampness
I was still thinking of making an attempt at it for a few
days; but then the steamer came, having taken fifteen
hours instead of six, and when I saw all the seasick
passengers, wet, weak, and cursing as they tottered
around, I signed up for a mainland-bound coach. I
have struggled just as hard as one can with the weather,
have gotten myself soaked to the skin almost daily, have
seen the mountains looking like furniture, chandeliers,
and rugs in some old palace, hidden beneath gray cloth
covers, with only a few glorious corners poking out, but
now I'm through with it. Tomorrow I'm going to visit
my family in the country (see below), and by the middle
of next week I'll be back in London.

—In the meantime we have had two bright, cheerful
days, like sunshine; and how strange that everything
seems so different from how one had pictured it—it
happened that they were the first two which I spent
completely alone, a stranger in foreign lands. The night
I wrote the last letter Klingemann had packed his things
and gotten ready, and I accompanied him through the
night and the howling rainstorm to the post office; he

climbed up on top of the coach, we exchanged a few
German words up and down, then the guard sounded
the trumpet miserably, the stage clattered away, and
London seemed to me so much like home that I might
have been born there; I returned alone through the
rain to my empty room, and lay down to sleep in the
room with two beds; it had all seemed so different just
a quarter of an hour before—in short, picture for
yourselves the worst evening imaginable, and you won't
even come close to the truth. Added to which bad
innkeepers, expensive bills, a drawing which didn't turn
out, and other such details. —The next day I didn't
depart until two, and just to have something to do, I
walked to the railway tracks, which go thirty-five miles
to Manchester, and arrived at the two tunnels, started
to walk around in them, but since I couldn't even see
the end from inside the large one I found the thing a
bit intimidating. I spoke to the watchman and finally
persuaded him by means of pleas and entreaties to
allow me the use of a railcar to go through Liverpool
all the way to the harbor; the heavy railcar came, a
workman climbed up on the back, and off we went, at
a speed of fifteen miles per hour, there was no horse
and no engine there, the car runs on its own, gradually
working itself up to the wildest speed; this was because
it was going just a bit, quite imperceptibly, downhill;
two lamps were burning up front, the daylight disappeared, the wind blew out the lamps, and then it was
pitch dark, for the first time in my life I saw *nothing*,
and all the while the car racing faster and faster, and
clattering louder—it was a bit rough on my stomach.
Halfway along the route we passed a coal fire, there the
workman stopped and lit up a lamp for himself, it was
also bitterly cold in the passage, then the red, warm

daylight came streaming in from afar, and I was standing by the harbor as I stepped off. It was very invigorating, and as I walked toward home past the market-place building, I felt quite contented. This is just a slight framed building, but much larger than the Catholic church, with a low roof. Inside there are about eight rows of stalls running the entire length, piled high with fruits, meat, vegetables, pastries, loading them down, offering you a long walk through alleyways of victuals; crowds of people of all sorts, blacks, Americans, Italians, Welsh-speaking, naval officers, countless pretty cooks. In the middle hangs a huge clock, on the walls maps of Liverpool; I got very jovial and rode to Chester. Along the way I reflected on something I had already had in my head for a long time—namely, whether or not it was wholly right for me to be running around so haphazardly, without any real purpose, just for amusement, as I had been for four weeks already, and spending much time and money. The thought had already troubled me several times in the last few days. But then I told myself that I was seeing something I would never see again, that I was seeing England freely and unencumbered by business considerations; that I would never again enjoy this independence here, for when I returned I would have too much to do to allow me to go driving around so gaily. And since I probably would never again spend a summer here, since Scotland is a place I shall never forget, since I have never been able to regard times when I felt cheerful and invigorated as wasted time (and whenever I was lazy I was never cheerful), especially since some new things were coming together in my head which proved to me that I had survived the cold-bloodedness of London society and people, and that I had to start composing again, which

I had recently half doubted; thus I discarded my ill humor, and practically acquitted myself! (The only question is whether you, dear Father, will also do so?)— So, and then I felt cheerful, and in Chester there was a splendid view; there is a walkway which runs along the city walls, which are broad and wide, and up there I saw a girls' boarding school out for a walk, I following behind with my sketchbook, the girls were quite pretty, the horizon very blue, the towers and houses close by dark brown; in the evening it rained softly, and in the darkness we rushed toward Holywell, my neighbor talked a lot about his son, who had recently died, and invited me to visit his home (I went too, and he still doesn't know my name), dark pockets to either side of us suggested narrow paths, trees, and mountains, and I lay down in bed after instructing the boy to go to the post office tomorrow as early as possible. He awakened me with letters, which inaugurated the most satisfying day; I received a lovely one from Droysen, to whom you must read aloud my thanks and joy, and then the delightful letter from all of you, and from Mühlenfels! The thought that Father might be able to come to London drove me almost mad with joy; dear Father, if only you would come! You would see the city, I would enjoy showing it, and how you would love it! Klinge-mann and I are always saying so to each other. You say you would need inducements; by God, that's one. I don't want to say any more, otherwise I shall forget everything else. But if only it would come to pass!— That in itself, and all of the letters, makes me feel so content and happy and at home in my loneliness. Then I drove out to the Taylors', in order to confirm for the day after tomorrow; they live in a country house which is surrounded by flowers on an expansive cut lawn, there is not the slightest trace of activity, noise, or people, in the distance you can see the mines which the father directs, mountains everywhere, and then I went on foot across the meadows, and found the elegant, proper London family, but as if transformed. Father and brothers were away on a trip, *never mind,* two daughters were planting in the garden, the mother was riding a donkey, hey!—we then shook hands, I was sorry the prettiest daughter wasn't there; but while walking we heard horse cloppings, and immediately she came up, in a blue riding outfit, and a tall cousin behind her; she was out of breath, very pretty, and is named Susanne. I began to hate the cousin. Until it turned out that he would be most pleased to travel to Wales with me; I accepted, we swore eternal friendship (but in English, for he doesn't understand French, German!), and everything was arranged. When I then found a good English piano there, and played myself a few things on it, when the aforementioned lady rider promised me her garden house (she has one in the park made with fir-tree bark) to use for composing when I returned, in return for which I had to promise to draw the aforesaid hut of bark (it's a kind of shepherding of a favorite sort)—all the girls appeared in white dresses at mealtime, something for which I have a decided preference (whether it has to do with clothes or girls is unclear), afterward I played a little again in the twilight at the burning hearth, and then drove back to Holywell that night—naturally I fell asleep in the carriage, but dreamed pleasant things. Those were two sunny days. The following morning there was another rainstorm, but the Englishman and I set off anyway, spending the night by the sea, in Bangor (Wales is a wonderfully beautiful country, but this sheet is so small that I will

have to describe it to you in person); the following day
we went through Caernarvon to Beddgelert and the
Vale Ffestiniog, then to Capel Curig, finally yesterday
to Corwen, from where we then departed to return to
the estate (it is named Coed Du), and I came here. We
got along well, and spent much time in conversation; if
he hadn't at one point—just as I was singing Fanny's
first song, *Hören möcht' ich (I'd Like to Hear)*, in the
stagecoach—grabbed me by the sleeve and showed me
a salmon-fishing spot, where one can catch the fattest
salmon, I would never have snapped or growled at him.
These songs are more beautiful than can be described.
I speak—God is my witness—as a sober judge, and find
them very pretty. But truly there is music which seems
to have distilled the very quintessence of music, as if it
were the soul of music itself—such as these songs. By
Jesus! I know of nothing better. But farewell! In what
direction I shall go today, whether to the east, the west,
or the north, is not yet quite clear, perhaps I'll even
stay where I am, it's raining too hard. But this is still
the last travel letter, I think, the next one will come
from London, that smoky hovel.—When I look at my
deeds of today, I say to myself, along with Father: *Donde
diavolo, p.p.*. Receive it in the spirit I write it, and I
welcome you. It's strange that the day on which you
wrote your letter, when the sun was shining out in the
garden, and you wished me the same, was one of the
few clear days we had. So a fine, happy, cheerful
morning to all of you!

Felix

To Wilhelm Hensel

London, 35 Bury Street, St. James
September 10, 1829

Here is the matter at hand—as a young female, whom we both greatly admire, dear brother, likes to begin her reports, but then nothing follows thereafter; but in this case I need it, with the special distinction that I am her brother and something important follows.—Thus the issue is that a committee must be appointed to arrange the silver anniversary festivities. Earlier I had thought of Fanny as president, but in her first suggestions she was so accommodating to a certain family (e.g., in the evening we'll be *en famille* at Hensel's, we'll eat our midday meal at Hensel's, etc.), that I have found her guilty of partisanship, reject her with horror, depose her, and Beckchen will have to be chairman. You and Fanny and I shall be ordinary members, Droysen an honorary one, and Klingemann our foreign branch. And now to proceed. I ask for the floor, and have a suggestion to make: how would it be if we celebrated the nuptial eve as follows: three *Liederspiele*, each in one act, with costumes, songs, etc., all properly portrayed, and a complete orchestra below (I will defray the costs of the latter myself, for all anniversary festivities, and to that end engage in a little musical speculation here); the titles as follows: No. 1, *Soldatenliebschaft (Soldiers' Loves),* namely my own famous creation by that name, which the parents are still very fond of, performed without altering a single note, and with the exact same cast as originally (except for Casper, whose role will be taken by Devrient), namely Madame, Robert, Fanny

Aumer, and H. Beer. What do you think? Isn't it brilliant? Then a new *Liederspiel* by Fanny, for which Hensel must write the words—nice, airy, and charming in every detail, very tender and beautiful. Then an idyll by me, for which a number of ideas are running around in my head; it will be handsome, and there ought to be a certain married couple who appear in it, which both of you will have to play, as well as a neighbor's daughter, a mad constable, a sailor disguised as a soldier or who knows what, a peasant's parade, and A major over and over (do ask Droysen whether he can send me his poem soon). In between there can be the appropriate ices and pastries and allegory and pro- and epilogues; I think it will entertain our parents far more than a simple instrumental concert, which in my opinion would be better saved for the following weeks. I won't come forth with the rest of my plans yet today, but will first wait for your own suggestions, your applause for mine, and ideas for the wedding day, which you must send me in detail at once *cheers*.

I ask that you please tear off the following sheet, and give it closed and unread to Beckchen. It contains some more important items and our great plan is progressing forward. Why have we been placed on this earth? Confound it! To enjoy ourselves! And at this opportunity it will be affirmed, O Hensel, that you are a great man. Your etching is heavenly, and fills me with warmth and joy, whenever it looks at me—for it does—it is so genial and pretty, and yet true to life, and yet odd and so forth. Droysen's portrait is the best likeness I have ever seen in my entire life, he even appears to be saying "perhaps." And how you lead into it; and Caroline with the bearskin gloves! But what is the meaning of the moon with the man in it? Fanny's big portrait is beautiful

as well, but I don't like it. I see how splendidly it is
drawn, how strikingly lifelike it is; but in the pose, dress,
the facial expression, and in its whole sibylline, prophetic
quality, or rapturous enthusiasm, it fails to capture my
cantor! In her the enthusiasm is not so much on the
surface, but rather within, and shows itself not in a
glance toward heaven, or in outstretched arms, or in a
wreath of wildflowers, for all of that is something anyone
can see at first glance! But he shouldn't be able to, but
rather only gradually come to understand, little by little.
Don't take it amiss, my good court painter, but I have
known my sister longer than you have, have carried her
in my arms as a child (exaggeration), and am now a
grumbling, ungrateful, unlicked cub, who cannot even
thank you adequately for the rays of sunshine which
you cast upon me from time to time; if only you could
see me sitting quietly so often before your drawings,
and indeed I am in their company nowhere less than
in London, and that would be just the thanks due to
you—but say!? Phooey to these words. Now I would
like to see little Beer and Gans and myself, and many
other things; but in December I'll get to. So do accept
my joy as thanks, that it is your talent to give form to
such pictures as float before all of our eyes, though only
foggily. You can capture it.—Fanny's ideas about Malta
and Naples are nice; I shall probably want to tell all
about the Hebrideans, who are a cold, barren people;
but are you[1] really going to Italy? And not for too long?
A few words on this matter as well.

The 11th. Today I had breakfast at Klingemann's, and
our idyllic *Liederspiel* made great headway, and is beginning to take shape and form; I think it will turn out

1. *du* (sing.).

nicely, and you are worked in splendidly, Hensel; do not be afraid of singing, everything is taken care of for you; the constable is a capital fellow and Devrient ought to be furious wondering—who's supposed to play the young soldier? (For he will.) I am also looking forward greatly to the *Soldiers' Loves*. Please ask Fanny to look around for the vocal parts, I believe they will be found, fairly complete, behind the lower glass doors of my bookcase. Now write at once how you like this idea and what you have in mind for the wedding, and think of me.

F.

P.S. I still have a note how splendid I think it is that the pencil figures in the cockle are wearing blue wreaths. Where the devil do you get such ideas?

To Abraham Mendelssohn Bartholdy

London, September 18, 1829

Dear Father,

I just received your letter from Rotterdam; and hope that this one will still catch up with you in Amsterdam. I would certainly have come, I think; but you will of course be able to see from my childlike scrawl that it isn't quite comfortable for me to write; in fact I am lying stretched out on my bed like a sick lapdog with a bandaged paw, and can only write at all by making special arrangements. What happened is that yesterday a stupid little gig crashed into me and robbed me of a pretty piece of skin with the accompanying flesh, black trouser cloth, etc., and Dr. Kind has pitilessly condemned me to remain quietly in bed for four to five days. Quietly! It will be very hard for me. Meanwhile inflammations are supposed to be avoided, so all I get to eat is soup and rice and fruits, like a Brahman, that's quiet enough in itself. I am very grieved that it had to happen just now, I had much—and many important things—to do, and all my travel plans are ruined. But I still hope to proceed onward soon and recuperate a bit at a professor's country house; so that in two weeks, God willing, I'll return to the Continent. How kindly all of my friends are treating me, like Klingemann who never leaves me, and several have been at pains for over a week. The English are also very friendly, and more people come to visit me than I need. More on all of this in a week, until then farewell; I am just annoyed that today of all days I should have to lie quietly in bed, just when the weather is tolerable for the first time. So, with God's help the weather will continue to stay good and I will be better when I next write.

Your Felix

To Lea Mendelssohn Bartholdy

London, September 25, 1829

So this will be the last letter from me which all of you will receive before the wedding, and for the last time I am addressing Fräulein Fanny M. B., and I certainly would have quite a lot to say, but things still aren't going just right. To be sure, since yesterday I sit up a bit each day, and can thus write better and smaller, but my head is still so completely muddled from lying in bed so much and from the long period of not thinking, and the more I try to collect my thoughts at this moment the faster everything slips away from me, refusing to be captured. Since to me it is all the same whether I say things well, or badly, or keep quiet, you all know full well; but to me it seems as if I had lost the reins to what I always knew how to control quite well, and my thoughts about everything, which now keep shifting and changing, but might have coalesced into a coherent whole as I started writing you, are now nothing but vaguely fleeting, one by one, through my head, half wildly, and it is impossible to organize them. But that is how things are, and when daily you see how all sorts of details that you had imagined for yourself are deformed by reality, enlarged or destroyed, then you are witnessing a truly important event in life, with proper awe and respect, but can hardly make it out. "With awe," by which I mean freshly and cheerfully and with confidence. Live and prosper, marry and be happy, build your own lives, so that I will find it beautiful and comfortable when I return to you (and that will happen very soon), and remain as always, then let it rage outside however it may; also I know both of you very well anyway, and so be it. Whether my sister is to be addressed as Fräulein or Madame means little. The name alone means nothing.

Certainly I have learned that one must regard even the smallest of plans with due awe, and must rejoice even at the smallest success, for even this depends on fortunate coincidence. From Llangollen I wrote you about how my first few days without Klingemann— which I had dreaded from the beginning of the trip— turned into happy ones; people, landscapes, and hours to which I had long looked forward, and which were carefully planned down to the last detail, turned out to be dreary, dull, and often unpleasant; the most trifling pleasures either came to naught or grew into large ones, completely by chance—and everything turned out different from what I had expected, hoped for, or feared.

So it has been in my case, and so it will remain. But instead of making me timid or anxious, it makes me bold and fortunate—and far from worrying in advance over small plans, I instead approach great ones with confidence. And with that a winter good-bye.

No doubt I should have written far better things, but I just can't; say what you will, the soul is just too closely tied to the body. I recently saw this, to my great annoyance, when they bled me, and all the free, fresh thoughts I had just had dripped into the dish with my blood, and I grew pale and bored. Klingemann's epigram also shows how it's spirited away what little poetry I have, and this letter shows it too, and I would bet that in every phrase you can tell that I can't bend my leg. But as soon as I am well again I intend to fly away from here, for I have had enough of this smoky hovel, and want to get on my way, to the Mediterranean and then to the West; I can hardly even picture anymore how the dinner table at home looks at midday mealtime, or on Sunday evening surrounded by all those dear faces. Now, the days are growing cold and short; they put the coals on the weekly bill again, the way they did when I first arrived, everything points ahead to the coming season, which in the spring was reckoned a matter of months, now is a matter of weeks, and soon will be a matter of days; soon I'll be free again, soon we'll see each other again.—But don't anyone hold it against me that I am somewhat sentimental now; when one is sitting in a heap of nothing but ruined plans, as I am, one has a right to be. Father's first letter, holding out the promise of our meeting in Rotterdam, which came to naught as a result of my doings here; his second, in which he invited me to meet him in Amsterdam and then travel further with him, which I received the day after the accident, in bed; two letters from home which have since arrived, all full of expectations of my being with Father, perhaps even back in Berlin already for the wedding; Fanny's instructions about the organ piece; English business faces all around me, among which I must retain my composure in order to take care of a few items of business, since I have "become quite obtuse" all the way down to the canceled invitations sitting next to the mirror—they make for altogether dismal surroundings. May it be granted to me to look ahead to the immediate future with all the more cheer—and may whatever joy and good fortune the blue heaven above can bestow on people be yours, and may time bless you, and make it unforgettable!

I had thought of a splendid idea for the organ piece; but now I won't be able to present it until I arrive. Likewise with the quartet, for which a few things remain to be smoothed out and sanded down. But do write me immediately to tell me whether you ever received a letter from Klingemann, with a song of his own composition in G major, titled *In den Wäldern (In the Woods)*, and whether Marx ever received a letter shortly after the concert for the Silesians regarding it among other things; you never mentioned either of them, and I fear they may have been lost. That you abhorred my *Kloben Lied der Tragödin* I cannot comprehend;[1] to me, having known it for a long time, it doesn't seem so bad at all, and Goldschmidt worships it. If I hadn't had Klingemann, I believe I should have croaked from vexation and boredom. But instead I have gotten over it, and shall soon feel fresh again. I owe much to him.

Your F.

---

1. *Kloben Lied der Tragödin*: composition for the singer Anna Milder-Hauptmann (see letter of June 19, 1829).

To Eduard Devrient

London, October 29, 1829

I am writing this letter out of generosity and wrath; for I only owe you one answer, and after all you promised to write without an answer; now of course you could also write a letter just as a matter of generosity, but that won't be necessary, I hope, for God willing I'll greet you myself soon after this letter arrives, and shall stand before you "bent over my cane"—and you will find I have grown thin, grown whiskers, and a few other things, but in certain respects remain unchanged. It's the same old story of inside versus outside all over again.—I have nothing at all to write you about, dear Eduard, for I don't want to write about the immediate past, since it is sad and gloomy and boring, and describing my delightful, serene spring and the remarkable Hebrides is something that would be better done when I am sitting with you around the coffee table, with your wife listening, and then one story will lead into the next—and when I have congratulated you on your latest child. To be sure, I had intended not to mention that in the letter at all, and would rather have said it better, with a handshake, but it is important, after all, and can't be kept quiet, and I simply can't mention your wife's name without adding the same tired old congratulations, which one can take as one likes. You both must be very happy!—Now, I shall soon be there to see it all too, and we shall have to chat a great, great deal, for I have tremendous plans whirling through my head, for beautiful music, old and new, which should be performed and for which you might also perhaps sing along, that

is if you want to. But if you don't want to, I shall kill
you. Therefore you want to. And for other reasons too.
It just occurred to me that I have something to write
you about after all; in fact I'll probably be bringing a
Liederspiel along with me, which I am composing here
for my parents' silver wedding anniversary, and which
Klingemann and I had already sketched out on the trip
through Scotland; it won't be anything but a small idyll,
takes place in summer, out in the country, and the
major role in it is of course for you; this is a wandering
tradesman, who plays the braggart, lusts after girls,
honor, and money, and among other things must dis-
guise himself as a night watchman and is obliged to do
a serenade with his horn underneath a window, which
I plan to write just to fit your throat (you know that I
can), and which you will perform splendidly. If you
want to, of course. But I'll kill you, etc., etc., *ride supra*.
Seriously though, we want to perform this bit of amusement along with other trifles on the evening before, or
whenever, in a proper (miniature) theater, with a proper
(miniature) orchestra, and thus I ask you all the way
from here to take the matter in hand a bit, decide on
the costumes, be the director, show my eldest sister how
to act the part of the village mayor's wife, and so on.
You know of course what I mean; and the first chance
we have to finish off a rice pudding all by ourselves I'll
lay out everything at greater length. Apropos, I laughed
about Dr. Spontini while lying in my bed, the fellow
will certainly drive himself mad. By the way, the musical
situation in Germany looks execrable. Here they pursue
music like a business, calculating, paying, bargaining,
and truly a great deal is lacking; but if you compare an
English musical festival with these shabby Germans,
there is unfortunately a big difference. The people here

may be just as calculating and avaricious, but they still remain *gentlemen*, otherwise they would be expelled from polite society, an area in which our own dear Royal Chamber Musicians are all too lacking (they're princes of whining, full of vanity, ignorance, crudeness, and emptiness). When I think of the musicians in Berlin, Devrient, I feel bitter as gall. They don't even have that quality which I expect of my cobbler, they aren't even honest, and at the same time all are such sensitive souls who supposedly live only for art! I don't mean to be praising English musicians here, by the way, they are also miserable dross, but when they eat an apple pie, at least they don't speak of the concept of *pie* itself and about how it consists of crust and apples, instead they just cheerfully gobble it up. In short, may the devil take a lot of things! You can see my wrath all the way from Berlin, and are very calm, and are laughing at me, and can speak calmly, but soon things will be reversed and you'll be furious, and I calm and reasonable. Therefore it is very fitting, and to me, amid this weed field of musicians, we seem like people who are calmly sitting in a warm room, listening to the wind blowing outside and keeping happy and warm by the fireside. The simile forces itself upon me because it's cold and windy outside, but here a brisk fire is burning in the hearth, and I'm warming myself. In Ballachulish I wrote a song for you in the rain, but it's not worth much. Whenever I write home nowadays, toward the end I start rushing so much and have such an aversion to writing that it seems as if I need to hurry there and talk. And so I must.—Until then, yours,

Felix MB

To Abraham Mendelssohn Bartholdy

London, November 6, 1829

I have just come from going out for my first drive, on
which I went with Klingemann; air and sunshine are
lovely things indeed. They made me tired and pale, yet
I can feel how refreshed I am, and am in a healthier
mood than ever. Even as I was walking slowly down the
stairs, and once again opened the front door in front
of me, and the people in the inn came out of their
rooms and congratulated me, and the driver offered
me his arm to climb into the carriage, I suddenly felt
relaxed and well; but when it turned the corner and
the sun shone on me so warmly and the sky did me the
favor of being deep blue, then I *felt* what health is for
the first time in my life, for I had never before done
without it for so long. We drove to Waterloo Place,
down all the way through Regent Street and Portland
Place, then via the New Road to Gloucester Place,
Portman Square in Hyde Park, and through Piccadilly
back home. London was indescribably beautiful, with
the red and brown chimneys standing out sharply
against the deep blue sky and all of the colors shining
so brightly (often I was blinded here by people's red or
yellow clothing, which really hurt my eyes), with the
gay shops gleaming, and heavy blue air pouring out of
every cross street toward me, obscuring everything in
the background, and in place of the green, fluttering
leaves on the bushes, which I had been seeing from my
gig before, there were now red sticks, and only the
lawns were still green, and how beautiful the sun shone
on the hill in Piccadilly, and how lively everything

seemed to me—it made a strange but very comforting impression, and I felt the strength of returning health. Arriving home I found a friendly, lovely letter from old Horsley, who made me the present of several of his compositions, so that perhaps I might, as he put it, be diverted for an hour on the sofa. I shall take along many dear memories of the city, and when I drive away on the *stage* (or rather in it, for I am a wounded child), I shall probably sometimes look back and think of the joy I have felt here. For it does one altogether too much good when people are friendly and stand by you, and it gives me the deepest pleasure to be able to say honestly that they do so here; thus my sojourn has not been in vain, and these times will always be dear to me whenever I look back on them.—I am all the more sorry that I had to lose two months out of such a year, for soon it will have been that long, it's now approaching the eighth week, and I spent five of them lying constantly on my back in bed, and although all serious troubles have been gone for three weeks and I have been making visible progress this last week, so that I can almost walk without my crutch, can sit properly in a chair, can dress practically all by myself, and occasionally something musical makes its way into my head, things are still proceeding very gradually, step by step (in every sense), my knee is still weak and stiff, the wound still hasn't closed, and I fear that another two weeks will pass before I am able to depart. But I hope not more, either; this letter should be the second to last one, I think. And I won't need to rent a coach, but can travel as far as Cologne with the express mail, which leaves every day, and rest up in Brussels, Aachen, or wherever I like while waiting for the next express mail (for they leave daily), and thus travel to Cologne in comfort. How I shall arrange things from there on I don't know yet, but there won't be any difficulty at all, and my child: I could certainly travel through as many nights as I wanted to be there, and Lawrence: I could make the whole journey on foot. In the letter of October 27, which I just received via Hamburg today, Fanny scolds me for being impatient; this again misses the mark, for since the third week I have fallen into a lazy apathy which knows no bounds: I could sit on the sofa the whole day long, and do nothing, I rarely get up before one-thirty, recently I sat alone for a half hour in the twilight, looking into the fire and thinking of nothing at all (an undertaking which otherwise could be counted on to put me to sleep, but here I remain awake and content); I am reading everything from the end of the eighteenth century: Kotzebue, Iffland, Meissner, Engel, etc., in short, if I were just to smoke a long pipe, and had on a nightcap, with my crutches in the background, one might take me for a stout old uncle with gout. That I was fuming in my letters home was prompted by such a variety of reasons that I need not enumerate any of them; but to name only the first, always writing by myself became very disagreeable to me.—(Lady Mollar has just sent fresh Dutch herring, with *Mr. Mendelssohn's best thanks and compliments.*) Rosen had wanted to write Father, but I asked him to address the letter to everyone instead; to judge by the address, though, he doesn't seem to have done so. Rosen was most pleased with the Edinburgh hospitality of Hogarth, who wrote a long letter to Klingemann in order to find out exactly how I was doing, and in order to praise all of you in detail, according to John Thompson's reports, and he will probably also have told you about it; it is very nice and generous on the part of these dear people. The professors are here almost every evening, Rosen usually for breakfast as well; he is altogether wild and riotous. For example, he noticed that we always recognized his knock and thus always expected him when he comes, so since then he has knocked once like a servant, once like the milk girl, and this morning like the postman, and recently he had himself announced as Count Reden. But when he claimed seriously that the currants I was eating in my pudding were dried *Johannisbeeren*, I naturally made a bet with him, and won a dinner, which in the next few days I shall be able to claim at his place.—You see what insignificant things I have to write you about, but there's nothing for it, so do pardon me if on Tuesday I only write a little or not at all. I'm not experiencing enough to fill two letters a week, and that I've finished copying the Handel manuscript will be of little interest to you. Nothing more is yet set regarding the concert in which I am supposed to appear like the lame postman,[1] or with regard to my songs, and now the mail for the 6th has come to an end. A cheerful, happy evening to all of you.

F.

To Abraham Mendelssohn Bartholdy

Hôtel Quillacq à Calais
November 29, 1829

So England lies behind me and is a thing of the past. It is a beautiful, lovely country, and as the white coast disappeared and the black French coast rose up, I felt

1. An allusion to the saying *Der hinkende Bote kommt nach,* roughly, "The lame post brings the surest news."

as if I had taken leave of a friend, and all of the dear friendly people were waving a last friendly wave to me. That was quite a picture. But now it's past history. And I am hurrying to join all of you and shall even take this letter along with me as far as Lille, perhaps even to Brussels, if I stand the trip as well as I have so far. I just arrived here safely after a three-hour trip, am staying here until this evening, when I shall depart for Lille with the diligence. I haven't written you for a long time, the last days in London were so rushed, the haste so great, and there were so many important things to do that I lacked the leisure, composure, and patience to describe everything to you, instead of experiencing and taking care of new things. I can call my last two weeks in London the happiest and richest I ever spent there. Horn, to whom I could show everything, and who shared my delight and amazement at everything, thanks to whom I was able to reexperience the city's tremendous impression as for the first time, who soon felt at ease and comfortable with my friends, was responsible for much of it. And a circle of people gathered at my place late every evening, making for a rare assemblage: Rosen, Mühlenfels, Klingemann, Kind, and Horn—now that was beautiful to hear, the lively and cheerful conversation, with nothing dull or false permitted, but at times turning into something of a jury in deliberation, and all present were spewing sparks and flames when they were excited, and all so different and various and yet still in agreement on certain points, without ever having had to come to an understanding; truly, when I would return home at night, knowing that everyone would be sitting around my hearth (for we usually didn't assemble until eleven), it gave me the oddest, happiest feeling. Beforehand I hadn't been at parties, as before during the wild season, but rather among closer, more intimate circles of my English acquaintances, and one remarkable, interesting, glorious moment followed the next. Every once in a while you realize that you are experiencing something unforgettable, and such a feeling goes right to your very bones. This often happened to me in these days, but no more of this, instead I'll tell you everything in person, God willing. I was just tired, and wrote too much recently, and without searching through all my notes I would have had a hard time writing all this in detail, for on the whole I lack all patience for writing at present. But for now just one more thing, which is that tomorrow I'll add a few words to this letter from Lille, from where I am thinking of sending it. Perhaps this will be the last one.—Goldschmidt, who was so kind as to accompany me as far as Dover, and of whom I thus took my leave this morning, sends his best regards to all of you. He was often present at our evening soirées, and when we pressed him a bit from time to time, he was very pleasant and better than I have ever seen him. There is a great well of virtue and geniality in him, and I enjoy being with him very much. Oh what all I have to tell you about! How will I manage with just a single mouth? You'll manage, says Reden; apropos of Reden, he has met with much honor. But everything in person, I hope.

Brussels, December 1. So here is Brussels, and I feel so healthy that I shall take the letter along with me again tomorrow, and hope to send it from Cologne—for it is to there that I hope to go with the express coach tomorrow. And so this letter will thus be the last for this trip, God willing.

Maastricht, December 2. Here in the most comfortable

room, in front of a hot stove, with the first German-speaking people, enough empty music paper in front of me, after a nice trip, in beautiful moonlight, hoping to depart tomorrow for Cologne, the day after for Berlin—here I write the epilogue to this letter. A mailcoach is passing through here tonight, I think, and should pick it up. I'll be following right behind, God willing, and with that farewell, be happy and cheerful when I see you again. In five days, God willing!

FMB

THE GREAT TRIP OF 1830–32

"The great trip" was what Mendelssohn himself called the journey which began in May 1830 and then developed, carefully planned, into the longest Bildungsreise *undertaken by any musician in modern times. Mendelssohn's reputation as a letter writer was based on the reports sent from this trip. They were clearly intended only for his family, who in turn saw to it that—as in previous years—the rest of the relatives, from Paris to Vienna, would all be kept well informed by means of hand copies.*

There is a way in which the "great trip" was a self-contained chapter in Mendelssohn's life. The months spent in England and Scotland in 1829 were a sort of rehearsal, and it is no coincidence that the most debonair portrait of him stems from this time; the watercolor by James Warren Childe of London depicted him with top hat in hand. The by now full-fledged cavalier traveled through all the centers of central Europe. In Leipzig he still had to go knocking at the doors of the publishers, with success, but in Vienna the publishers came to him. In Munich Mendelssohn cast about for the composition of an opera, which of course came to nothing on account of the libretto; here he "rasped horribly" with the beautiful Delphine von Schauroth, played four-hand piano with her much too long, and then reported even this to Fanny. He had become a man of the world, who no doubt would have liked to walk in Goethe's footsteps in Italy, but then suddenly saw more, because he was looking in other directions, and above all heard more.

His love for the Swiss Alps, instilled in him by his parents, was deepened, but new for him was his sudden recognition of how German he felt himself to be, regarding the trip from Munich to Stuttgart, Heidelberg, Frankfurt,

*and Bonn as the "high point" of the trip (in the letter to Zelter dated February
15, 1832). Paris, with which he had gained familiarity as a child, disappointed him completely, and subsequent to this visit in the spring of 1832 he
never returned there.*

*In the familiar city of London, close to Klingemann and other friends,
Mendelssohn felt at home once again. It was here that he found himself in
the proper frame of mind for the letter to his father (dated June 15, 1832)
in which he—ever the well-brought-up son—summarized the many months
spent traveling, and aired his self-assured plans for the future. But the future
shaped up differently for him than he foresaw in London.*

To Abraham Mendelssohn Bartholdy

Leipzig, May 18, 1830

Such is the way of the world.—Once again it's time to
write and describe, once again time to be off for distant
lands, and once again I feel so strange and calm the
moment I think of all of you. Moreover it's late in the
evening, tomorrow I want to continue on, and spring
is not a bad invention at all; and Father, who poked his
head into the room here the day before yesterday, is
now sitting peacefully by your side, God willing, and
you are probably also thinking of me. And if it seems
to you as if I returned from England only just yesterday,
and today have already traveled onward, and if you
remember how often I wanted to leave and was always
held up by cold weather, birthdays, measles, Reformation symphonies, and probably other things as well, and
how now I have finally gotten away, then it's nothing
new and probably nothing special either—just the way
of the world, as I stated already. So let us proceed.—
Good evening then, now I've just returned home, tired
from having taken in so much, and have quite a lot I
want to write about, but I don't know where to begin.

For such a variety of things have happened in the past few days, the basis for many a joke I could tell in person, but which now will have to be salted away for several years; it's good that Father knows all about Dessau, and will have reported everything, and I need only a few words to tell you how infinitely small the city is, and how beautiful the countryside is—green, bushy, and full of meadows and woods—and how happy and content Schubring feels. That Madame Müller is altogether adorable you know already without my having to tell you; she remembered the tiniest details of our house, declined to praise your punctuality in correspondence, O Fanny, had the most beautiful, serious, and friendly eyes, and a sister who sang your songs very nicely (I behaved impishly and found fault with a few things— "The author intended a ritard. here, and there a diminuendo"—Beckchen will be jealous again), and who also embroidered the Madonna della Sedia on a reading desk (oh what a muttonhead I am! says Father). A pretty cousin in a blue dress with a bright border was also present, I had to play my three Welsh pieces, and praised Susan inordinately, then we hurried to visit Mlle. Olivier, who didn't sing anything for me, and I found her most agreeable—there was a morning of musical entertainment there. The program; Trio in D Major by Beethoven, with the prebendary, the court musician, and the traveler; trio by Haydn, with the same; *Fantasie ou Improvisation sur les thèmes du célèbre Beethoven*, by the latter; and additionally, chocolates and childhood reminiscences of Vienna. Herr Rust is a small, anxious man, who has a lucrative organist's position in Vienna; he got the urge to move to Dessau, went there twice and came back, and couldn't make up his mind; then Beethoven died, that was the last straw for this customer, as they say in Dessau—he gave up his position, went to Dessau, visits his old aunt there daily (he himself must be almost sixty), gives lessons for six groschen, plays from memory on Sebastian Bach's organ, and is happy with his life. Schneider arrived ahead of me, as did a tradesman on Saturday, who had sold much during the week and now wanted to enjoy a drink; I found him annoying. But it's only Dessau, I wished that I were already here in Leipzig, and still must tell about how wildly they sight-read *A Calm Sea* at the rehearsal, how the duchess praised me highly, as did her cousin from Rüdolstadt, how I described our schedule conflict with the Redens' soirée with Sontag and imitated her own cadenzas for her, a counterpart to the galloping Katzenberger,[1] how Her Excellency gave me messages in her own hand to deliver in Italy, which I am now carrying like a *billet doux* in my May-beetle purse, how in the evening at the homes of Rath and Erdmannsdorf (*est! est!*) there was tea and music, how I drove with Schubring under cheerful calm skies to visit his cheerful calm sister in the country, where we sat under a pear tree with May bugs looking at drawings from the military campaign in Champagne, drawn by his brother-in-law, how I slowly returned to Leipzig that night—thank God I was here then! and how I met Father here, and Dorn visited me, how we went to the Rosenthal and the Birnbaum and to Auerbach's Keller—

The 19th, evening. I am still here, and can't depart until tomorrow morning, but prolonging my stay here has been useful, and now this letter will have to become a business letter. I am as tired as a saddle horse at the station; the music dealers have broken me in, or I

---

1. Katzenberger: *Dr. Katzenbergers Badereise*, novel by Jean Paul.

them—I have made music, heard it, collected it, and now want to make a leisurely trip to Weimar tomorrow, having just recovered my breath and senses an hour ago. M. Levy will bring along to you, Father, ten louis d'or and a draft due in the fall for the same amount, which I gave him; this is the honorarium for my two violin quartets, which I sold this morning. I had played my A minor quartet for Marschner, and he asked me whether I perhaps wanted to publish it; since I said yes, he came to see me at St. Thomas' School and brought me the offer from Breitkopf and Härtel, to whom he had already introduced me on account of their old manuscripts; I was pleased with it, and went there this morning, and though I didn't even have my quartet with me they paid me the ten louis immediately, and gave me a hand copy of a cantata and an organ piece by Seb. Bach, neither of which had been known to me. From there I went to see Hofmeister in order to pay him a long-promised visit; he then bought my other quartet (in E-flat), gave me the draft, which I ask you, dear Father, to redeem when it comes due, and offered to publish all of the piano pieces I might give him. When I began to speak of the Symphony in C Minor, however, he told me to my great astonishment that it was already being pirated from the English edition in Leipzig, and when I pressed him for the man's name I learned that it was Probst. So I made contact with him as well, and he too wanted to buy pieces from me, but I didn't much like him, so I turned it down; he boasts hideously, continually calls himself an artist, rails at all of the other publishers, and in short he's not my man. But I had to let him keep the four-hand reduction; there was nothing I could do about it. Now I ask you, dear Fanny, to write to Klingemann right away with the next mail, and ask him if he would ask the Taylors if they would permit me to publish the three small pieces—that is, whether it would please them—and then have Attwood let me know how much I should ask for them from Cramer. In addition I've enclosed an announcement of some copies of works by Bach which are to be auctioned off here over the course of the next several weeks. Their authenticity is beyond all doubt, and so I ask you, dear Father, if you would be so good as to give the notice to Zelter and Rietz and ask them to mark down what of it they already have; and perhaps you might want to purchase those pieces which they don't have, here at the auction? If you should care to, I would ask you to send the sum you want to bid for them, which Zelter can probably suggest to you, along with your bid, to Herr Weisse here; he promised me to take care of everything then. It would be lovely if you should care to, for among them are the most splendid pieces.—The Passion according to St. Luke is and remains the work of Telemann, though; here they put Bach's manuscript of it down in front of me, intending to strike me dumb with awe; luckily, it is written in such a beautiful and graceful hand that one can clearly see that it is just a copy.—*Later.* This letter is wooden, but that comes from Leipzig and all of these business transactions; I just looked through the cantatas once again, they are absolutely gorgeous, and I wish we could acquire them. But the lamps have burned down—tomorrow morning the conclusion and farewell. Good night then.

The 20th, morning. Now I am setting off, the horses have been sent for, and everything is ready. Still, a thousand thanks for your lovely first letter to Leipzig, I still can't get used to writing at all, wanting to take wing with my quill pen in order to babble on, and in so doing forgetting everything; therefore pardon me for today and the next time things will go better. Rellstab must have received two boy's albums, but unfortunately I can't send him one of my two girl's albums, because I gave it away already. Please ask Father to pardon me that the first time I let myself be heard from is to ask for a present; but the thing is just too important to me.—M. Levy's crown thalers have just arrived, along with the bill from Friedlein, the coachmaster—farewell. On the outside perseverance and on the inside good cheer. And think of me and keep happy.

FMB

Copyright Agreement for Friedrich Hofmeister

Leipzig, May 19, 1830

The undersigned hereby confers to Herr Friedrich Hofmeister in Leipzig the sole and exclusive rights of ownership of a quartet in E-Flat major for 2 violins, viola, and bass, designated as opus 12, applicable to all countries in which music is published. He acknowledges receipt of the proper honorarium.

Felix Mendelssohn Bartholdy

To Lea Mendelssohn Bartholdy

Munich, June 14, 1830

Dear Mother,
I promised to write twice a week, and so I intend to keep to it, although today I can only send a few lines. To wit, I want to start conducting myself like a curious

traveler today, and if last week I mailed my letters in
the morning, made my visits, and ascertained that on
my first trip to Munich I was very unsatisfied with the
weather but quite edified by the city—then this week I
want to make for the three galleries (the Royal, the
Leuchtenberg, and the one in Schleissheim), see the
library, Glyptothek, Pinakothek, and all the other theks
(cf. Hr. Märcker), visit painters, try out organs, etc., etc.
Then I can write all of you in proper detail about how
and what I have done. Of the past few days there is
nothing to tell, except that Thursday they held the
beautiful Corpus Christi Day procession, of which I
shall soon send Beckchen a description. After the
procession there was a dinner at the home of Montgelas,
where I attempted my London Harrowby face in front
of many noblemen, and where Prof. Walter, without
knowing me, said many good things about Benni, called
him a very erudite man, explained to me that he had
just traveled with his brother to London, where he saw
him, then I got into an English quarrel with him, and
when it came time for the theater and we left at the
same time, he even took me there in his coach, and we
went in together, although he little suspected what a
bourgeois he had in front of him, and although I kept
trying in vain to introduce myself to him. In the theater
King Ludwig was received with jubilation and *God save*
(I'll send all the details soon in a diary), after the theater
there was a big reception at Kerstorff's, where all of our
acquaintances asked about all of you with great interest;
even the upstanding Herr Boisserée, His Excellency,
and Herr Bertram, who to judge from a brief acquaintance appears to belong to the natural species *Schautus
maximus, Lin.*—they too remembered you. On Friday I
moved out here to Burggasse No. 167, the home of

Herr Lindpaintner (brother of the musician). Friday at
noon there was an informal *dîner* at Arasburger's, with
Greek performances and pictures by Heidegger, in the
evening I wrote letters, Sunday morning I was introduced to various clubs, the Art Association, and the
museum, and made my other visits. In the evening
there was the so-called *Liederkranz* (the Munich *Lieder-
tafel*), where King Ludwig once more was received with
jubilation and *God save* (it must bore him, since he can
hear it elsewhere), but it was so hot there, and not to
even have a chair (since for every man there were
perhaps thirty ladies), that I disappeared after the first
part, and went to visit an elderly musician, a friend of
Weber, who lives in a nice house with his daughters,
and there we played Weberiana on their fine piano until
late into the evening. Yesterday morning I finished the
E minor piece completely, gave the manuscript to
Schauroth very gingerly, and am having it copied for
publication; I ate at Bärmann's at noon, was invited to
a musical coffee hour in the afternoon, and saw *Tell*[1] in
the theater that evening. It was the first time I had seen
it, and it put me in such a wonderful mood, it looks so
lively and lifelike, that it moved me more than anything
has for a long time, and when the old red lamplight
shone on the Grütli I would have liked to cry, if that
were appropriate for a musician to do at a play. We
shall soon see what today has to bring us; but may it be
a happy and cheerful one for all of you!

F.

P.S. Because of the symphony and the dedication I still
can't make definite plans, unfortunately. I myself don't

---

1. *Wilhelm Tell*, drama by Friedrich Schiller.

even know yet whether it will be published, and I am almost beginning to doubt it. As soon as I hear for certain about it I'll let you know.—Benda I declare to be completely mad, and not even amusing; whenever he isn't in the mood to praise Bach, he always rails at Napoleon. Give my best regards to *Corno Inglese*, that is, Horn. I shall write him soon, and tell him a bit about the ladies of Munich, and then also about art and life as an afterthought; tell him he should speak freely and report on Berlin—farewell.

To Fanny Hensel

Munich, June 23, 1830

Oh my little sister,
I know everything! I just received a letter from the 16th, which contains much about young Sebastian, and they are congratulating me on being an uncle, and are merry, making a lot of noise, and my head is buzzing. If only tomorrow's letter were here already, and you past all discomfort, *quite charming*. But what? You want to congratulate *me*? With that I wish you much happiness, but a happiness more lovely and serene than anything I can think of; and "you" now means not just you, but includes another as well, besides the rest of us, who are also included; nothing but happiness and cheerful existence, and may the lovely creature bring you the most intimate happiness and peace, and may you often think of the *waiting* uncle, and so on. And what do they mean by new distinctions, and uncle? We've all been promoted! I wish you happiness at the new honor, dear parents, or rather grandparents; you, Father, now Grandfather, and you, Grandmother, now

Mother (or the other way around, anything's possible)—
and Beckchen is an aunt, and Paul an uncle, *ach!* And
perhaps I ought to congratulate you, Fanny, and Hensel?—I wanted to fling my arms around Kerstorff's little
bookkeeper, who delivered it to me, and I babbled on
a bit in his presence; then I wanted to compose a song
for you like the last one, but it turned out poorly, just
as stirred milk turns into cheese, then I wanted to do
several more things, and finally here is a letter. I would
very much like to see the full name—Sebastian is not
bad, however. But I ask you merely to send me everything relating to all this: cards, cut-out newspaper
articles, if possible even his baby rattle. I wish you would
also give him the name Felix; the name does have
something pretty about it, after all, and I think later I
might really love the little rascal if he carried my name—
otherwise not. Also don't forget to have some lout
present at the baptism to represent me, as if I were
there; just use someone who likes me, and I him, for
that purpose. Let the man drink a lot of hot chocolate;
I would certainly have done so. And above all imagine
that I was there with you the whole day—for I am.—
May God bring you gently through the difficult times
which you still have to endure, and stay healthy and
happy.

F.

I am doing well and gloriously beyond all expectations,
people are spoiling and pampering me with piles of
sugar.

To Lea Mendelssohn Bartholdy

Linz, August 11, 1830

Dear Mother,
"How the traveling musician bore his great day of bad luck in Salzburg."

Fragment of an unwritten diary by Count F. M. B.***
(Continued)

Just after I had sealed the letter to you the most unbelievable day of bad luck began to wash over me. I took my pencil in hand and ruined two of my favorite drawings from the Bavarian mountains so badly that I had to tear them out and throw them from the window. This annoyed me, and to relax a bit, I climbed up the Capuzinerberg. That I lost my way can of course be assumed; the moment I arrived at the summit it began to rain frightfully, and I had to run back down quickly, underneath my umbrella. Then I wanted to at least have a look at the cloisters below, and rang the bell— then it dawned on me that I didn't have enough money for the monk who appeared; they take great offense at such things, and I made hastily away without even answering the doorkeeper. Then I sealed up my packet for Leipzig and took it to the post office; first it would have to be inspected at the customs house, I was told. I went to the customs house; they kept me waiting for an hour before producing a three-line certificate, and conducted themselves so insolently that I had to quarrel with them all over again. *Hang* Salzburg! I thought, and ordered horses to go Ischl, where I hoped to recover from all the bad luck in that dump. "You can't have any horses without permission from the police."—So to the police. 'You can't have permission until your passport from the gate is here." Am I rambling too much? After walking back and forth for things countless times, the long-awaited mail coach came, I ate, had my things packed, and was now thinking it was all behind me; bills and tips had been taken care of. Just as I walked up to the door, two elegant traveling carriages drove up in step, and the people in the inn all ran up to the gentlemen, who were walking toward them. I took no notice, however, and sat down in my carriage—at which point I saw that one of the coaches which had just arrived was pulling up right alongside mine, with a lady sitting inside. But what a lady! Just so that you won't all think at once that I fell in love and that that was the crowning event of my bad luck, I shall begin with the fact that she was elderly; but she looked very charming, and friendly, and wore a black dress with a heavy gold chain, and handed the postilion his tip, smiling most dearly. God knows why I continued to arrange my luggage and held the coach from leaving, I just kept looking over, and as unfamiliar as she seemed to me, she still made a strong impression on me, as if I really had to speak to her straight away; it may have been a product of my imagination, but I won't let myself be talked out of the fact that she was also looking across at me, gazing at the boorish traveler in his student's cap. But when she even climbed down on my side, hanging on to the door of my coach with an almost intimate air, then stopped for a while, resting her hand calmly on the coach door, I had to have recourse to my well-practiced traveler's manners in order not to jump out and say: My dear lady, what is your name? But manners triumphed, and I called out politely: Onward, postilion! At this the lady quickly withdrew her hand and I went on. I was vexed by all this, reflected on it a bit, and fell asleep. A coach with two men which rolled past us awakened me. The following conversation then ensued between the postilion and myself. *I*: They're on their way from Ischl, I won't be able to obtain any horses there. *He*: Oh, the two coaches which were stopped in Salzburg were also from there, so you'll get your horses after all. *I*: So they were also from Ischl? *He*: T' be sure, they come here every year, and were here last year as well. I drove them—she is a baroness from Vienna. (Dear Lord! I thought.) And she's frightfully rich, and has such beautiful daughters—I took both of them down to see the mines in Berchtesgaden; what a pretty sight they were in their miner's garb, and the upstanding gentleman from Berlin, who was always with them (could that be my Oppenfield, I thought?)— he was also a handsome gentleman; people said he was a Hebrew, but I shan't believe it as long as I live, he was a nice man, just like other people. They have fortunes too (oh no, I groaned), but are very base with the likes of us.—Hold your tongue, I cry. What are their names? Couldn't say.—Pereira?—Don't think so. Drive back, I said, firmly resolved.—Then you won't be able to make it to Ischl tonight, and we're just over the worst mountain; you can find out at the station.—I hesitated again; I drove on—at the station they didn't know the name, nor at the next one. Finally after seven unbelievably trying hours I arrived, and asked before getting out of the coach: Who left for Salzburg this morning in two open coaches?, and received the calm answer: The Baroness Pereira, tomorrow morning she's going on to Gastein, but will be back in four to five days. Now I knew for certain, so I spoke with her coachman as well—no one from her family had stayed behind. The two gentlemen in the second coach were the two sons (the very two whom I didn't know), and to top it off I remembered a miserable portrait which was shown once at Aunt Hinni's, and the lady in the black dress was cousin Pereira, God knows when I shall ever have the chance to see her again. I don't believe that she could possibly have made a more agreeable impression on me, and I shall certainly not soon forget her charming manner and such kind countenance; but premonitions are dangerous things: You have them easily, but can only tell in retrospect that that's what they were.—I would have turned around on the spot and driven back through the night, but when I remembered that at best I might catch her just as she was leaving Salzburg, perhaps not even at all, that it would spoil all my travel plans and my trip to Vienna if I were to go on to Gastein with them (for I thought of that too), and finally that Salzburg had been nothing but a den of bad luck for me, then I bade farewell once more and went to bed moping. The next morning I had her empty house pointed out to me and drew it for you, dear Mother (*vide tabula A* in the appendix). My bad luck was still thundering in the distance—I couldn't find a good vantage point, at the inn they demanded more than a ducat from me for a single night, and so on. I cursed in English and German, drove on, put Ischl, Salzburg, the Pereiras, and the Traunsee behind me, and now I am here, where I have declared today a day of rest. Tomorrow I am thinking of pressing onward with the first coach, and so God willing will be happily ensconced in Vienna the day after tomorrow. More

from there. Thus ended my Great Day of Bad Luck,
but it was all true, not Klingemannesque storytelling;
not even the part about her resting her hand against
my carriage was added—everything was a true-to-life
portrait. The most incomprehensible thing about it to
me was that I didn't ever see Flora, who was also along;
for the elderly lady in the Scottish coat who was going
into the inn was Frau von Weinroth, and the old
gentleman with the green glasses who followed her
could hardly have been Flora either. In short, when
things start going amiss there's no end to it.

I shall not write anything more than this today; it
still annoys me too much. The next time I'll tell you all
about the Salzkammergut, and how pretty my trip
yesterday was, and how right Devrient was to recommend this route to me. The Ebensee, the Traunstein,
and the falls at Traun are absolutely gorgeous—what
an altogether charming place the world is. It's good that
you are all in it, that I shall find letters in it the day
after tomorrow, and many other such things. Dear
Fanny, I plan now to compose my *Non nobis* and my A
minor symphony. Dear Beckchen, if you could hear me
singing *Im warmem Tal (In the Warm Valley)* in my falsetto
voice you would find it practically pitiful; when Marx
and I suddenly wagged our heads, singing *Man geht und
kommt (One Comes and Goes)* it was not too pleasant either.
You do it better. Oh Paul! do you now know how to
get around with gold florins, heavy florins, light florins,
Viennese florins, standard florins, and the devil and his
grandmother's florins? I don't. Thus I wish you were
with me, perhaps for other reasons, however. But dear
Hensel, the corner measurements of your red box are
not quite right (it's here in front of me); the frame from

Ischl shows it. Beckchen's picture will be more precise, I think, and that's all for today. Farewell from me, a cartload of personal letters is coming soon.

F.

To Rebecka Mendelssohn Bartholdy

Vienna, August 22, 1830

My dear precious sister,
Good morning. Here is Vienna and there is Berlin; and since they are not together I have to write you a personal letter once again. It is Sunday morning, I have just composed the beginning of a very serious bit of church music on the chorale *O Haupt voll Blut und Wunden*; this sort of thing already interests you, I know, so I shall send you the gloomy thing and you can have it sung wherever you like. But it is very morose—have an art dealer on Unter den Linden show you the engraving of a Spanish picture by Zurbaran; there are several hanging there, showing Saint John, who accompanied Mary home from the site of the Crucifixion; I saw the original in Munich, and I think it one of the most profound pictures I have ever come across. Moreover, I also have a small piece of Latin music which I intend to send to the Sing-Akademie; I hope to finish both pieces before leaving here. For a stranger in Vienna to be serious is something quite new, I think, and also I swear to you that I don't feel serious the moment I go outside, and until now that's what I've been doing all day. But I think there will be little time left over in Italy for resting and reflecting, so I would like to have spent a few serious hours here. The people give you little chance, to be sure, I have already been interrupted

three times while writing these lines. First came Levy, the Waldhorn player, who ordered a serenade for voice and horn which he wants to bugle beneath the windows of some beautiful young lady, then came Merk, who tossed off some violin variations so that the windowpanes were clattering and applauding, then I was invited for a quartet on Thursday—with Mayseder, etc.—then Herr Rau invited me to eat with him tomorrow. Madame Cibbini and Thalberg will be present—it doesn't all quite fit chorales. In the evening I usually go to the Burgtheater, where they present only plays, and quite outstandingly; if Mlle. Müller were still there things could get a bit nasty. Meanwhile Mlle. Pistor isn't doing too badly either, bites her lips, has a sweet speaking tone as well, and the way everything works together and meshes together into a whole—which we miss so much—makes it quite lively and satisfying to me. In short, I am living like a Viennese, doing nothing at all, and spend all day occupied with so-called diversions, which in the long run are actually very boring. And finally, in all Vienna not a single reasonable young lady can be drummed up, and how can a man of my caliber survive three weeks without a lamb? In Venice things will be better, says Rau, but what shall I live on until then? Can't you recommend someone to me for that purpose? (It's now the 23rd already, by the way.)—I certainly can't flirt with Hauser; he is much too grumpy, rails at everything, quarrels with everyone, finds fault with the world, but if the dear Lord were to give him a free hand I doubt if he would arrange things as well as the dear Lord has. Simon Sechter is no young lady, either, but an old counterpointist; we pelted each other recently with sweet, canonical phrases, if only I could remember some of them. There isn't much more to

Thalberg than a pretty hooked nose and stupendous fingers; Merk smokes a cigar while performing a gloomy Adagio and certainly doesn't let it go out. Czerny is like a tradesman on his day off, and says he is composing a lot now, for it brings in more than giving lessons. Lachner recently asked me, as I was beginning to play a few chords on the organ, whether the Passion was by Bach. Beethoven is no longer here, nor Mozart or Haydn either, and when Stadler shows me the piano on which Haydn composed the *Seasons*, it doesn't help me much either—in short, I'm not pleased with the world. If in the meantime our dear Lord would give me a free hand, I would . . . , etc., *ut retro.*—For I'd never come by anything as pretty as my trip on the Danube; I just can't do it. But you should know that I waited in Linz only just long enough to enable me to travel to Vienna by boat; the swift current and the stories about the Danube eddies and the mountains on either side greatly attracted my attention, and I was tired of the hired coachmen and their swindling. But the mail boat didn't come, and so I finally rented a quite small new skiff with a gondolier's deck for me, sent my things to Vienna by mail in case we should capsize, the old skipper (his name is Johann Leindle) promised to take me down in a day and a half, and so we flew away from Linz like an arrow at noon. At first it was scorchingly hot, and the banks flat, but as the sun sank down the banks climbed higher and higher, toward evening we came to the eddies, which rush and whirl, and when one is past the narrows the river continues softly on between two dark, high mountains. The evening pressed on, and on both banks steeples and cloister windows were peering forth out of the bushes; and you could hear the following tones:

in infinit. Then right away came another bright bell (for we were moving fast),

D.C. in. infinit., and then right away,

etc. I wrote down this bell sequence in my little book from Anna Fränkel, and then fell fast asleep in the skiff, and the ceaseless soft bubbling sounds from the tiny wake and eddies whispered very softly in my ears, since I was lying on the deck of the boat; one could easily fall asleep to it. But now I wish I could describe to you, dear sister, what it was like when I awoke; but all words pale. Night had arrived, the whole starry heavens had opened up, the rowing sounds resounded sharply, for everything was completely quiet, and all around me nature was full of mysterious movement. For in the sky shooting stars were falling constantly in every direction, darting back and forth, on the water the little eddies were mumbling high notes and low ones from all sides, and the current pushed on terribly fast, rushing onward, and even on the banks there would be a light from time to time, bobbing up and down—and in addition everything so serenely calm and peaceful;

it seemed to me almost as if I were eavesdropping on the music of the spheres, as I rode down the smooth water so quickly, seeing and feeling nothing around me but the distant starry heavens.—Later, toward midnight, the lights on the bank increased in number, a flute piped out a bad dance tune, the skipper said that it was the place where we would stop for the night and that things were still merry in the inn, so we put ashore and went into the village. I shall not forget the trip; the feeling of my independence as I traveled around in a foreign country, alone and unrecognized, suddenly struck me and I thought about all of you very much, and it was sweet. The place where we are staying is called Mölk and can be found on the map, everything is true (I have to keep adding that now). The next morning we set off before sunrise, it was beautiful again, but the right moment didn't come again; a couple of Hungarian officers called from the shore to ask if they could ride along, and I rode on to Vienna with them. At Stein there were more pretty reflections in the water, and the bells sounded low in B-flat minor. I drew them in my book, and am glad from my heart that you are drawing, my dear pipkin, and are copying my Scottish pictures; now I'll complete all of the detail in my sketches and then send them to you. Then you could follow my path through the Tirol and the Kammergut on the Danube; it is splendid that you are starting to draw, it will certainly bring you much pleasure, and we'll do it together sometime. But you mustn't be too grotesque about using the eraser. It doesn't help. *I don't want it* is what Anna F. says about erasers, but then blushed immediately at her immodesty, and I teased her a lot about it.—But what the devil, I just received the letter of the 18th; Mantius Tamino has gone mad. If Mme. Schulz with that nose of hers doesn't run rings around him, then Mlle. Schätzel can say of him that he is as big as her heart, and if Mme. Milder weren't already retired, it could be claimed that he sings like David and she like Goliath. Why doesn't he appear as one of the three boys instead? But seriously, it annoys me, and all the more so when he is such a huge success—and since my lungs are still healthy, by the way, from now on I shall stop wearing them out by preaching like this. But if the Redens don't invite him anymore on account of it, then—I ask you, dear Mother, not to think me all too inexperienced a traveler; especially when one is traveling a long way, he wouldn't even think of getting out of his carriage again and going into an inn where he has checked out and all the bills have been taken care of in order to ask for the name of the people who were just arriving there. It often happens to you that people arrive just as you're leaving, and to ask for their names and then leave again would be a bit of a bother; as I said, one only recognizes premonitions when they come true, and I am afraid that despite all forebodings I will not turn around in the future and ask whenever I see strangers driving up, for it would get to be quite a habit to have to keep up these meetings and farewells to people one will never see again. For heaven's sake do lend my portrait to the exhibition, and cut out the catalog entry and send it to me—where it will say: No. 25, Portrait of a composer practicing, and No. 26, Pipkin in oil, without hands; for Beckchen, you too must hang in it. If the Beers don't donate Ludwig, then they themselves should be hung, but I doubt whether it would make people as happy as the beautiful picture.

It would be scandalous, and also, Gans is mad. The prudent 4 percent ones are doing badly on the market, by the way. But now this letter is out like a mouse; but first I must confide to Fanny that the chorale melody is in the soprano voice, and is doubled in octaves by the oboes, and played by the flutes, and all of the violins. But if she should ask now who carries the other parts, then I remind her that there are such things as two violas, two cellos, two bassoons, and double basses in the world. I am looking forward to the piece, in which no one will know whether it is in C minor or E-flat major; you know my style, Fanny. Now finally you must know that Tobias Haslinger, to whom I was introduced yesterday, spoke to me as follows: I am very pleased to make your acquaintance, perhaps we can do some business together as well; wouldn't you like to have me publish something? Something can be done for the man, for I am known to be available; so I ask you now, my dear little sister, groats, nephew, or skeleton key, to send my original score for the quintet in A major which begins:

the moment you lay eyes on this variation, endorsed to Arnstein and Eskeles, via the mail coach immediately to me here; I've calculated that it will still arrive in time, since I shall probably wait here to see Pereira, who is arriving on the 5th or 6th. You won't find it in the bookcase—Rietz has it; have him give it to you, and then send it to me, but right away. Thank lanky old Eduard again for his hand copy too, and tell him I would give him a copy of the piano reduction in return as I did Schlesinger. If he then writes me: "My good friend, your stinginess etc.," then it's certainly he who is writing. But I shall certainly write him in the next several days, also Devrient, to whom I am greatly indebted; I'll send him a song for bass voice at once, which you can sing too. But farewell; we've been gabbing, but now I must wait until you answer, but do for once try this format and write a long—or rather wide— letter to me. The letter for Froriep will go off with the next mail; I haven't yet been able to get hold of him. The clown is leaving—I've things to do—adieu Garn— but do keep happy and cheerful and stay serious and draw, be a good Beckchen, you couldn't be anything better in your whole life. But to me you are perfect, and I have a sensitive soul which will always love you.

FMB

To Paul Mendelssohn Bartholdy

Florence, October 30, 1830

My dear Paul,
Even if today I don't plan to wish you any particular luck, since I always do anyway, and am also happy at what good things are happening to you every day—still one gets a little sentimental on such a hallowed, familiar date, when one is used to drinking hot chocolate together in the morning and having company in the evening, when one, instead of enjoying such pleasures, is breakfasting alone in an inn, reading the newspaper, which always looks so dismal and crazy these days, and can only take part in the joyous day in his thoughts. Thus today I would especially like to be close to you, and tell you how I wish you both perseverance on the outside and progress on the inside, and how much it

warms my heart that all of the little discords we may
have had with one another from time to time three
years ago—since that morning when we were quarreling
so awfully and I threw you off the chair, whereupon
you scratched me, whereupon I told on you, whereupon
you couldn't stand me, whereupon I became very angry
(I think you will remember)—have completely disappeared, and probably forever. It seems to me as if since
then we have become much closer, and as if the unpre-
dictability of both of our moods has moderated somewhat. Thus I have taken so much pleasure in the course
of your education and projects, and can certainly hope
that your lively interest and your warm sympathy in
everything was not just temporary and that there will
never again be any sort of unpleasantness between us.
And if I can bring myself to stop snapping at you so
horribly when you turn the page too late, and you can
manage to be "at home" from time to time when I
desire it and not go out so often, like when you were
lying in bed with the measles, then I am convinced of
it. But these things won't be too hard, so I am convinced.—Even had I not said all that, we still can't write
each other often for a while, and thus it is good for us
to shake hands again, and wish each other something
proper, such as—good morning. Also I am feeling
properly festive, and if instead of being with all of you
and stealing some flirtatious attention away from you,
I will be sitting in a coach heading for Rome this
evening, then I would like to peer over the Alps a bit
and spend the evening with you and take pleasure in
your merriment. For I can just imagine that a crowd of
young people are gathered today, and would be greatly
offended if that were not the case. You would then have
to repeat the party on November 30 for me and set out

a chair and a cup of tea with a huge pound cake in order to soothe my raging spirit, but I do hope for something better. You could all play in the garden today, perhaps, for after yesterday's warm rain the air is so comfortably warm that I am sitting here at the open window and writing. And there's nothing really wrong with the fact that people are wandering around the streets with the prettiest flower baskets, offering fresh violets, roses, and carnations for sale. The day before yesterday I was tired of all of the paintings, statues, vases, and museums, and so decided to go walking from twelve until sundown, bought myself a bouquet of tazettas and heliotropes, and climbed up through the vineyards into the hills. It was one of the most pleasant walks I have ever taken; you can't help feeling refreshed and enlivened when you see all of nature around you, and thousands of gay thoughts were floating around in my head. Then I went to a château named Bellosguardo, from where you can see all of Florence and the wide valley, and where I took great pleasure in the rich city and the thick towers and palaces, but mostly in the countless white farmhouses which covered all of the mountains and hills as far as the eye could see, as if the city were spreading out all the way across the mountains into the distance. And when I took the telescope and looked through the blue haze down into the valley, everything was still covered densely with white farmhouses and bright dots, and I felt at home and comforted in the middle of such an immeasurably broad panorama of dwellings. Then I walked far across the hills to the highest spot that I saw, on which there was a tower, and as I arrived I found everyone in the whole building occupied with making wine, drying grapes, and mending casks. It was Galileo's tower, where he used to conduct all his experiments and make his discoveries. Looking down from above there was another wide panorama, and the girl who led me up to the top of the tower told me a heap of stories, in dialect, which I hardly understood, and then gave me some of her sweet, dry wine grapes afterward, which I gobbled up with great virtuosity, and thus I continued on, to another tower which I had seen, but couldn't quite find my way there, looking all the while at my map, and in so doing walked into someone else, who was also peering constantly at his map. The only difference between us was that he was an elderly Frenchman and wore green eyeglasses, and asked me: "È questo S. Miniato al Monte, Signor?" and so I answered with great solemnity: "Sì, Signor," and it turned out that I was right. Immediately Anna Fränkel came strongly to mind—she had recommended this cloister to me, and it is indeed amazingly beautiful too. Now just think that I went from there to the Boboli Gardens and saw the sun set and that I then enjoyed the most beautiful moonlight that evening—then you will certainly agree that the walk was invigorating. I shall write about the pictures another time, for it has grown late, and I still have to take my leave to the Galleria Pitti and the big Galleria, and have to have one more look at my Venus, which of course we can't speak of in front of the ladies, but which, however, is divinely beautiful. The courier is leaving at five, and God willing I shall be in Rome early in the morning the day after tomorrow. From there I'll fill in the rest. But now allow me to interpolate a small aside to Father:—Dear Father, I have taken the liberty of making you a present; but if you would only just not take it amiss, for unfortunately there is still a catch. The local wine is in fact the most wonderful that

I have yet savored, and since Schadow is sending a case from here he talked me into sending some of it home too, and took care of all the arrangements for me. But then it occurred to me afterward that in the end the wine would cost you more than it did me, and although Martens assured me that it would not be expensive I am still somewhat apprehensive, and therefore ask you not to be angry when the case arrives. Once you have opened it and sampled the wine I won't worry anymore, for you will then sing my praises; it is the noblest wine I know of, and I think that you especially will like it very much and that it will do you good, for it's supposed to fortify the stomach. It is two-thirds Aleatico, and one-third the first pressing of it, the so-called *vino santo*. Hopefully it won't seem too expensive to you, so please don't be angry, and after it has arrived please give some of it, perhaps eight to ten *little* (French) bottles to Zelter, and five little (likewise French) ones to Rietz. I am enclosing a few lines to each of them in the case. And now just a few words to all of you: write me much and often while I'm in Rome, and keep me informed about everything. A fond farewell and keep healthy. And you, dear Paul, be cheerful and think now and then about Italy, as I do about Germany and you, and I wish you nothing but the very best. Your

Felix

To Fanny Hensel and Rebecka Mendelssohn Bartholdy

Rome, November 22, 1830

You two dear rascals,
Enclosed a personal letter. Put it away carefully and don't read it to anyone. First I shall sing your praises

and then afterward you'll both be reprimanded with unbelievable severity. But no. Therefore I shall first put on my cantor's face and then tell you the truth afterward, which other people would call scolding, but you regard as strong praise. So pay attention: Tell me for once, what on earth is this about? Have you turned dumb? Has the devil incarnate gotten loose? You know how much I hate to give advice from two hundred miles and over two weeks away, but for once I want to do so myself, for I am very wise. You are making an error of conduct, and the same one, to be sure, that I also once made. (Perhaps I may err, though.) I have never in my whole life seen Father write in such a bad mood the way he has since I have been here in Rome. To speak seriously now, I don't want to reprimand you for this, since of course I don't know how things stand, but I only wanted to ask you if you could perhaps alleviate things a bit by means of some domestic remedy? I mean by indulging, by giving in, and by your showing Father the side of things which he likes to see more than the other one, and keeping altogether quiet about many things which irritate him, and saying "unpleasant" instead of "scandalous," or instead of "splendid" saying "tolerable." It helps unbelievably once in a while, and, I also would like to ask quietly, perhaps also in this case? For even taking into account the momentous events taking place in the world, it still seems to me that his bad moods come from the same thing that they did when I began to go my own way in my musical undertakings, when Father was continually in the foulest mood, and railed at Beethoven and all of the visionaries, and I was often depressed and often unruly as a result. Then too something new had happened, and it was not quite agreeable to Father and perhaps made him uneasy,

The composer's father, Abraham Mendelssohn Bartholdy.
Drawing by Wilhelm Hensel.

A drawing of the composer by Wilhelm Hensel, 1821.

from you; and if I spoke well then just follow my good advice. Furthermore I am reprimanding you, Fanny, for railing at the Academy so much; Rungenhagen is truly a completely different sort of fellow from Baini, and Hellwig as Astolfi and Grell as Marian the soprano, and Mantius are all better than some old tenor dressed in black priest's garb with a tonsure. Furthermore I am reprimanding you, Beckchen, for nursing your sentimentality; are you on this earth in order to be sentimental? Heavens! Learn to play the trumpet or enjoy your life in some other splendid way. But now I want to tell all of you the truth: you are splendid folk.

The 23rd. Curses! I was just about to work on the *Hebrides* and then Herr Banck—a musician from Magdeburg— arrived and played an entire book of songs and an Ave Maria for me, and asked my opinion of them for his edification. It seemed to me as if I were wise old Nestor, and I delivered a hypocritical speech to him. So you have missed your words of praise, I my B minor, he his advice, and a morning in Rome has gone to waste. The chorale *Mitten wir im Leben sind* has been completed in the meantime; it is probably one of the best church pieces I have written, and either growls angrily or whistles darkly. When the *Hebrides* is finished I am thinking of working on Handel's *Solomon*, for which Santini gave me the score, and preparing it for a future performance with cuts and so forth. But don't speak about it or Hans Taps or some little person will come along and give the thing a coiffure with flutes and spoil the first noisy stage effect—perhaps I shall write about this to Zelter myself—but you rascals provide the foremost example in the world. After this work I am thinking of composing the Christmas music *Vom Himmel hoch* and the A minor symphony, then perhaps a few things for

I think. As long as I praised and eulogized Beethoven the unpleasantness got worse, and if my memory serves me correctly I was once asked to leave the table, and then it finally occurred to me that I might very well speak the truth, just not exactly the one that Father couldn't stand to hear, and from then on things got better and better and finally all was well again. Perhaps you have forgotten a little bit that here and there you must indulge and not provoke, that Father considers himself older and more ill-tempered than he really is, thank God, and that it is up to all of us to give in to him once in a while, even if right is on our side, as he has often done. So praise what he is fond of a little, and don't criticize what is near and dear to his heart, namely nothing old and venerable, and don't praise new things until they have come to pass and are recognized—such as me when I have become Kapellmeister, for example, for until then it will always be a matter of taste, and take Father into your confidence for me and dance around him, in short try to smooth things over again, and remember that I, a well-traveled man of the world, have yet to find a family that—*even with all* its weaknesses and crossness taken into account— was as happy as we have been thus far. I also take into account "failure to recognize happiness," and if we grumble about it, our grumbling as well. But still, it's as I've said. So think it over together, you dear rascals.

I suspect that all of this is a bit wretched, and does not belong here at all, for you are both as smart as I am, but in the meantime I simply have to say it, and so here's out with it—don't answer me right away, for it won't arrive for four weeks and by then things will have changed already. You don't really need to answer at all, for if I was stupid I don't wish to invite a tongue lashing

The composer's mother, Lea Mendelssohn Bartholdy, née Salomon.
Drawing by Wilhelm Hensel, 1829.

A drawing of the composer by Wilhelm Hensel, November 14, 1822.

The composer's sister, Fanny Cäcilia. Drawing by her husband,
Wilhelm Hensel, 1829.

A page from Henriette Granbau's autograph album. The composer's watercolor is of the Gewandhaus in Leipzig, the music is from Luigi Cherubini's opera Ali Baba.

The composer's drawing of a waterfall in Dunkeld, Scotland, 1829.

The composer's drawing of the Spanish Steps in Rome, 1831.

A portrait of the composer by Eduard Magnus, 1845.

A portrait of the composer's wife, Cécile, née Jeanrenaud,
by Eduard Magnus, circa 1845.

A pencil drawing of the composer by Wilhelm Schadow, 1834.

The composer's study in Leipzig, copied by Marie Wach, the composer's granddaughter, after a watercolor by Ferdinand Schiertz, 1847.

A letter from the composer to his friend Heinrich Konrad Schleinitz,
February 19, 1844.

Caricature of the composer, 1829.

The composer's view of Luzern in a watercolor made on July 2, 1847.

"Souvenir of an excursion to Mürren," July 1847. Watercolor by the composer.

Lausanne, August, 2, 1842. Drawing by the composer.

A LIFE IN LETTERS

piano and a concerto, and so on as it comes to me. I am having happy and gay times with Bendemann and Hübner and the young painters—it's a cheerful country. (Dear Lord, now they're all approaching, with Schadow leading, and are insisting that I go along with them to visit Camuccini, and the mail is leaving in a half hour.) Dear rascals, I want to go forth out of the door, I'm already starting to freeze anyway, for the weather is brutish today, and when the sun is behind the clouds it's as if I hadn't turned on the heat in Berlin. Now bearded Hildebrandt is sitting there and just confessed to me, O Beckchen, that he didn't do his little picture for the Kunstverein, as I asked him to, but as a gift for "someone." O world! O misery! This letter may be short, but what does it matter. The next one will be longer. *The 25th.* My heart couldn't bring itself to send you such a thin, short personal letter, thus I kept it for two days more instead and will now finish covering the sheet altogether. A year ago today I had my pointless adventure in Maastricht, found a warm room, people around me were speaking German for the first time again, and I composed a song in G minor with flutes, *So mancher zog ins Weite.* That same day I also drove through Tongres, Löwen, etc. How it must look there now! I doubt if in all Holland anyone is composing a *Liederspiel.* But I am no less fond of mine than you are, and recently played through it—I would like very much to hear all of you do it, or at least to hear someone play something. I miss that very much here; I have no acquaintances with whom I can share new things, who can take a look at a score or know how to play along with the bass or flute, and when a piece is finished I have to put it away in the trunk without anyone's having enjoyed it. I really do miss that very much; I was spoiled in that regard in

London—for a friend such as Klingemann, who is so unusual, and so fresh and strange and at the same time possesses a gentle soul, and furthermore people like Rosen and Mühlenfels and the others, I shall after all probably not find gathered together again. One certainly doesn't find them running around the streets here, at any rate; here you always have to say things only halfway in order to keep quiet about the better half—there you would say things halfway because the other half went without saying, and the other person understood it already. But that's just the way of the world. And admittedly it is wonderful here; the warm sunshine alone is enough to thoroughly invigorate you, and the venerable artworks do their part too. In addition, having your hands so full, and the many friendly, well-wishing people—here too it's not hard to feel content. Recently we young people were in Albano. We drove off one morning in the bright, clear weather, underneath the great aqueduct, which stood out sharply, dark brown against the clear blue sky, followed the road all the way to Frascati, from there to a cloister, *Grottaferrata,* where there are beautiful frescoes by Domenichino, then to Marino, which sits picturesquely atop a hill, over which the road leads, and down below there is a spring where the girls were chattering and washing. There your picture was well remembered, Hensel, and we waltzed down the Galopp to Ahlborn in order to give a lesson there, remembered to honor the Madame with praise, and Oviesieska with awe (in Marino the names and everything sounded funny in the air)—Emil and I waltzed right on through a little forest in Albano, and arrived at Castello Gandolfo by the sea; none of the landscapes are—like my first impression of Italy—at all striking or so astonishing as one had imagined, and not

especially *out of the way* either, but they are so pleasing
and gratifying, all of the lines are so soft and painterly,
and form such a complete whole, complete with staffage
and illumination and so forth. Here I must deliver a
eulogy to my friends the monks; they always complete
a picture right away, lending atmosphere and color to
the whole with their loose-fitting gowns and pious, quiet
gait and dark countenances. From Castello Gandolfo to
Albano there is a beautiful *allée*, lined with periwinkle
oaks, which leads to the sea, and there it's teeming with
monks of every kind, who enliven the landscape and
yet make it seem lonely. Near the city a couple of
mendicant friars were out for a walk, as well as a whole
troop of young Jesuits; while an elegant young clergy-
man was lying in the copse and reading, a couple of
others were standing in the woods with muskets, waiting
in ambush for birds. Then comes a cloister with a
number of small chapels surrounding it; for the first
time it felt completely deserted, but then a stupid dirty
Capuchin monk came out, laden down with thick bou-
quets of flowers, and placed them all around in front
of the pictures of the saints, first kneeling down before
each one and then adorning it. We continued onward
and met two old prelates engaged in a lively conversation, at Cloister Albano the call to Vespers was sounded,
and if you turned your head in the direction of the
highest mountain you could see a Passionist's cloister
on top. They are only allowed to speak for one hour
each day, and occupy themselves exclusively with the
Passion story. One of these coal-black, silent monks
made a very strange impression on us, amid all the girls
carrying vessels on their heads, the vegetable and flower
vendors and all the crowding and yelling—he was
starting his trip homeward up the Monte Cavo. Thus

they have taken possession of the whole wonderful area, lending a strange, melancholy atmosphere to all of the revelry, free-spiritedness, and cheerful people, and to the eternal serenity provided by nature. It is as if people here needed something to offset them. But that sort of thing is certainly not at all for me, and I don't need any contrast to be happy with what I have, etc. Here would follow a long tale if we were sitting together in the yellow room, but then I wouldn't need to wait four weeks, and this sheet would have to be infinite, which as you can see now it isn't; so that's all. Keep happy and so forth, and may heaven grant you the rest. Good cheer!

F.

To Abraham Mendelssohn Bartholdy

Rome, December 7, 1830

Dear ones,

Yesterday your letter of the 23rd arrived and today it is now a year since I was riding homeward at full gallop in a post chaise through the snow, and eating chocolate, since I didn't have time for anything else. I would love it if Christmas, New Year's, and my birthday could all be canceled this year, for I shudder at the thought of it. And I also won't get to the detailed letter that I had wanted to write today either. God knows how fast time flies here. Many thanks for Rösel's letter and fond regards to him; he is often thought of in front of the keyhole at the priory in Malta and by the fountains on the Monte Pincio in front of the Villa Medici. This week I met several very charming (and pretty) English families, who promise me several pleasant winter evenings.

I am often with Bunsen. I also intend to thoroughly savor Baini, who is the craftiest priest one could imagine, and at the same time the most popular confessor in all of Rome; he creates an artificial halo around himself, and I think he takes me for a *brutissimo tedesco,* so that I can get to know him quite splendidly. Of course his compositions are nothing much, as is the case with all of the music here. It may not lack for sensuality, but it lacks the necessary means altogether: The orchestras are beneath contempt, with neither pianists nor pianos; Mlle. Carl is engaged for the entire season as *prima donna assoluta* at the two principal halls, and has already arrived and is beginning to make *la pluie et le beau temps.* Even the papal singers are growing old, are almost completely unmusical, and don't even get the traditional pieces right; the entire choir consists of thirty-two singers, who, however, are never all together. Concerts are given at the so-called Philharmonic Society, but only with piano accompaniment, no orchestra—and when recently they wanted to attempt Haydn's *Creation* the instrumentalists thought it was impossible to play it; no one in Germany could even imagine what the wind instruments sounded like. Now, since the pope has died and the conclave begins on the 14th, the burial ceremonies and those connected with the election of the new pope will take up a large part of the winter, so that it will be lost to all music and large social functions, I almost doubt that I shall manage any sort of proper public undertaking. But I am hardly troubled by this, for I am profoundly enjoying such a great number and variety of things here that it would probably hardly be a shame if I were to carry it all around with me for a while and digest everything. The performance of Graun's *Passion* in Naples and especially the version by Sebastian

Bach show only how what is right *must* prevail; they won't capture and inflame people's taste for something fiery, but in this case things are no worse than with tastes in all of the other arts. For when one sees a portion of Raphael's loggia scratched away with unspeakable vulgarity and incomprehensible barbarity to make room for pencil inscriptions, when the whole base of the climbing arabesques is completely destroyed because Italians have carved in their miserable names with knives, and God knows how, and when one sees "Christ!" scrawled beneath the Apollo of Belvedere with great emphasis and even bigger letters, when right in the middle of Michelangelo's *Last Judgment* an altar has been erected which is so large that it obscures the very center of the picture and thus ruins the whole, when cattle are driven through the wonderful rooms of the Villa Madama, where Giulio Romano painted frescoes, and hay is stored there, simply because the people are indifferent, then one can probably say that this is even worse than bad orchestras, and it must grieve painters even more than awful music does me. The people's spirits have probably been besieged and destroyed inside; they have a religion but don't believe in it, they have a pope and government but make fun of them, they have a splendidly bright past history but pay no attention to it. So it is no wonder that they take no pleasure in art, since they are indifferent even to all that is more serious. The indifference shown at the pope's death and the inappropriate merriment during the ceremonies are really horrible; I saw the corpse lying in state, and the priests were standing around it whispering constantly among themselves and then laughing out loud, and now, while masses are being said for his soul, they are constantly hammering away at the scaffolding of the catafalque, so that everything is drowned out by the echoes of the axes chopping and the noise made by the workmen, and the service cannot be heard at all. As soon as the cardinals are in conclave satires come out against them, where they parody the litany for example, and instead of naming a sin in order to ask that it may end, they name particular qualities of the well-known cardinals or have an entire opera of cardinals performed, where one is a *primo amoroso,* another a *tiranno assoluto,* a third a lamplighter, and so on. It just can't be this way if the people are supposed to be rejuvenated by art. And it was no better before, but they believed in it, and that makes all the difference. But nature and the warm December air and the lines of the Albanian mountains down into the sea—these have all remained the same, and there they can't carve any names or compose any inscriptions—*that* is something anyone can enjoy afresh and in solitude, and to that I remain faithful. I miss having a person here with whom I could share everything openly, who could look at my music while it is in the process of being formed, making it seem twice as charming to me, with whom I could rest and relax completely and from whom I could honestly learn (he wouldn't have to be a very wise man for that purpose). But since trees don't grow all the way up to heaven, as they say, so too a man will probably not find himself here, and here in particular I miss a pleasure that I have always had everywhere in rich measure. So I'll have to hum to myself here, and even so things will be well enough. Next Saturday is your birthday, dear Father; this time I'll not be able to bring you a gift, and just as my congratulations go to you daily, you understand, on that day of course they do so even more especially, since up until now I had always brought them in person. But things are such that trees don't grow all the way up to heaven.

F.

P.S. The mail leaves at noon, which is why the letter is so brief and hasty. Farewell to all of you from me. I plan to go walking a bit now; outside there is warm spring air, I hope that we will slip through the winter unnoticed. Soon the shortest day will be here, at five they are sounding the Ave Maria. Have Hensel describe St. Onofrio to you; it's my favorite spot, for all ages are united there—the newest one makes its appearance in a tailcoat. Keep well and happy and think of me!

To Abraham Mendelssohn Bartholdy

Rome, January 9, 1831

There are moments when it seems as if all of one's life is compressed into a single instant, and tries to speed up—such have been these times I have spent in Rome. I write these lines only because you were all recently disquieted at missing a letter from me, and I assure you that I am living happily and in good health. The rest I'll have to spare you, for right now every moment is occupied with something or other remarkable or delightful. By means of a small Fantasie at the Philharmonic concert recently one evening I made a number of the most pleasant acquaintances, and I have only to choose where I would like to spend my evenings; but happily the season for balls has now arrived, and so one meets people several times during the week, and dances, and I assure all of you that Thorwaldsen, and Horace Vernet—with whom I share my lady in the *extratours*—make quite a handsome sight. Vernet told me yesterday in his garden: "Si vous n'avez pas vu mon portrait du pape vous n'avez pas vu le plus affreux barbouillage qui existe"—brr! whereupon he took hold of his musket and shot a cat dead, and said, "J'ai assassiné le pauvre chat." He waltzes very well, though, and to see him paint is a joy. Now I must be off to the underground crypt at St. Peter's, thus my haste; but now just a couple of words on the receipt of your last letters. As it happened I had played in the Philharmonic concert, it was almost midnight, people made a terrible racket afterward, many strangers came up to me and introduced themselves, a very charming Italian family (Giustinani's) had taken me there and then driven me back home, and I returned to my room as if in a dream in which the whole strange world was buzzing before my ears. There I found the two letters lying on the table, and even just the sight of them brought me calmly to myself again and back to you. Then I wanted to open them just to see if you were all in good health, and there Fanny's A major song greeted me, which of course sounds quite different from all of the trifles I had to listen to and play. Now that was a moment of celebration! And then Father's letter, with reference to which, however, I still want to defend myself as to the lack of illusions, for I am a creature of illusions. And Beckchen's descriptions of Christmas! Well, you did provide me with a lovely, unforgettable moment, for which I thank you all.

Pardon me for closing; after all, your letters too are short from time to time, when the occasion demands. I always want to begin writing a few days earlier, but then it just doesn't work again, and that my life is pleasant and that I am happy with thoughts of you is evident from these lines—more isn't really necessary. Keep healthy and happy.

F.

To Abraham Mendelssohn Bartholdy

Rome, February 15, 1831

Now it seems everything has changed completely, to be sure. The carnival has been interrupted, people arrested, patrols in the streets—it all bears little resemblance to the carnival and its jesting. Hopefully you will not have become anxious over the news from Bologna and its surroundings; here all is calm and people have gotten over their fears. But how quickly the scene can change, and how time flies. I draw a lesson from it for myself, to hold fast and enjoy that which I have as fully as possible, and then carnival in Rome becomes one more dear memory that I can add to my storehouse of experiences. There is something very moving about this sudden switch from the wildest merriment to the most bitter gravity, and when I think of the crowded, colorful streets of last week and then the empty workaday atmosphere today I want to begin this dialogue with current events, which you, Father, did not want to go into at all the evening of the silver anniversary, but with reference to which I am again collecting arguments in order to take it up with you again some day. The measures taken by the government (*vide infra*) seem to me to have been very good ones, by the way, and thus the general peace is disturbed only by an element of fear on the part of the people of Rome, but by nothing further, and here the whole thing is probably over; how things will shape up elsewhere we shall have to wait and see. First I want to respond to everyone's letter of the 25th, and then tell you in detail what has happened since then. You write me, dear Father, of a confusion concerning a payment from Arnstein and Eskeles to me; this can only refer to a sum which I withdrew in Venice, where I found myself greatly embarrassed. It happened that Arnstein and Eskeles had forgotten, incomprehensibly, to send an *avviso* pertaining to my letter of credit in advance, and it appears that in this country this is so essential that the bankers in Venice not only refused to give me any money, but appeared to regard my letter as forged. I spent several days waiting for Pereira; Herr von Sternfeld, who had been recommended to me by Fränkel, ran around with me to several other brokers, who were uniformly even more impolite, and it was a matter of only 100 florins, which I wanted to draw on the letter from Vienna for 2,000 florins and on the one from Doxat for 500 pounds. In short, Herr von Sternfeld gave me the 100 florins himself and I had to write to Eskeles to have him send them to him. I thought it unforgivable that they should cause someone such embarrassment, for if Sternfeld had not given me the money I wouldn't have been able to do anything; an honest face got you nowhere in Venice. Otherwise everything went properly, in Florence I took 200 florins from Borri, and here in Rome 50 scudi each month, which is unfortunately what I need on a monthly basis, since the necessary social expenditures, such as coach, linens, etc., are exceedingly expensive here. In addition I withdrew 50 scudi for the Duchess of Dessau's concert at Valentini's. Since Bunsen, to whom she referred me for the transportation and the payment, would hear nothing of it, and since it is unpleasant to receive a negative answer in such matters,

I preferred to take the money myself, have myself given the exact sum required by Valentini in Augsburg (104 florins, 12 xaviers), and will write you to have this sum returned to you, and have the music shipped by freight or whatever works best from here.—Thus for my stay from November 1 to April 1 I have withdrawn 250 scudi, and in addition the 50 for the Duchess of Dessau. Of them 150 were withdrawn at Torlonia's, and the other 150 from Valentini's, where from now on I shall take my traveling funds exclusively, since now Lent has started and the ball season is over; Valentini still hasn't sent in anything to Augsburg yet, since he is keeping a record, as he says, until he has a larger sum together. As far as a diary goes, since England I have arranged things so that I always carry around smaller books with me, in which I note down in a few words what I have done or am going to do each day, some things written down in advance in order not to forget to do them, and some written down afterward in order not to forget them later on. Thus I know precisely where I have been each day, what I have taken in, and if something needs to be described in more detail then I do it in letters to you, or in drawings or music. Thus I don't need to write down too much each day, but still don't lose track of things. You, dear Mother, desire to know something of W. Benedict; those who saw him in Naples told me he was not at all seriously ill and that there isn't much to be said about him. Julius Benedict is not here, nor Platen, whom I can't stand even at a distance. You regret that I look so shabby, but it doesn't help, one puts on some weight in exchange for some pleasure, and I am feeling quite healthy, and hopefully am only disheveled on the outside, while black inside. But many thanks to you, Beckchen, for the idea about the suspenders, they really have long since become quite crippled, and I had to wear other ones, so send me something again, and think of me leaning out of the window, reading Hebel's Alemannic poems, and shouting for the fun of it across the Spanish plaza, my favorite is yours: the "Porridge," and then especially "Transcience" and the "Conversation on the Oxcart." I thank you, Fanny, for your praise of my arrangement of Handel for winds—I have certainly not made any changes in it, and that is the best thing in this case. But my favorites are the flutes and clarinets with the G major chorus (the number of the twelve apostles). And now to the story. Thursday (*giovedì grasso*) things were still splendidly mad—confetti, bonbons, flowers, bills, all in crowds across the Corso. In fact I jumped up from behind at Vernet's and bombarded from there until I'd exhausted all my ammunition and they emptied out their bags over my head. The horses ran well, in the evening the masques moved out across the Spanish plaza, and an elegant lady could be seen sitting in the coffee house smoking her cigar. Friday was a day of rest, and on Saturday morning we went on an excursion on horseback around Rome's city walls, which kept us occupied until three. We return through the Porta del Popolo, amazed to still not see any coaches. I hastily change clothes, buy myself pocketfuls of confetti, with people laughing secretly at me for what reason I don't know; and so I arrive in splendid spirits at the Corso. But it turns out to be filled with dour-faced men, no masques, no ladies, no coaches, and made a strange and most disagreeable impression, and finally I found an edict posted at the corner, whose brevity and certitude made for a striking contrast to all of the buffoonery. It began: "La sopra occorenza di gravi circonstanze impone che

cessi il Carnevale nei tre giorni che da oggi ne riman-
gono.—Niuno pertanto si permetterà di andare in mas-
chera, le corse dei cavalli ed i festini non si eseguiranno
e taceranno altresì le rappresentazioni teatrali." Anyone
violating this would be severely punished, and that was
the end of it. The news of the unrest in Bologna,
Ancona, etc., had arrived, and even in Rome agitators
had been discovered, and the militia, instead of keeping
watch over the masques, was standing with loaded rifles
on the various plazas. In the evening ten to twelve
young people really did attack the soldiers at the Piazza
Colonna, but were immediately arrested, and since then
no further trouble has occurred. Even so, edicts are
constantly appearing, with increasing severity and firm-
ness. Saturday evening all foreigners were ordered to
report to their embassies, innkeepers to turn in their
names, and the embassies to vouch for their country-
men; most refused to do the latter, and probably rightly
so too. Sunday all were called upon to pray for the
preservation of the peace, and to this end two miracu-
lous pictures of the Virgin Mary and the chains of Saint
Peter were publicly displayed in *Pietro in vincoli*. Yesterday evening an edict appeared calling on all citizens to
arm themselves and report to their own sections the
moment the cannons were fired and the bells were
sounded. The Vatican is closed and the Swiss guards
are not even letting anyone into the colonnades of St.
Peter's. Everything is watchful and calm, and since the
lower classes of society are the pope's strongest *support-
ers*, and have proved it with deputations, *vivati*, and so
on, it seems to me that everything is already settled.
The middle classes appear to be terribly afraid, though;
all of the houses are bolted shut at night, one has to
ask three times before they open the door, the stores

are closed, with not a soul on the street. Again there is no lack of humorous touches, but the best of all is that the German painters are cutting off their mustaches out of fear. It seems that they think the mob's rage will vent itself on the closest target (which they probably regard themselves as being) or rather actually against foreigners, and since a mustache is the hallmark of a German painter, which he displays as prominently as he can, they trim it back in, and in times of war look very tame. I have a very particular aversion to this brood. They affect disgust. And through all this the sun is shining so bright and clear, and the weather is so warm, that it is a real joy. One goes walking, drinks in the air, and it smells altogether beautiful, *verte*. After this faithful depiction you will all not worry, I hope, even if the French newspapers start talking about battles in the streets, barricades, and so on, which they no doubt will not fail to do. We know nothing of such things here, but should anything new happen I'll write again the next mail day. If not though, so things will rest until a week from today. And that is to be hoped. Farewell.

F.

To Abraham Mendelssohn Bartholdy

Naples, April 20, 1831

One must become accustomed to the fact that everything always turns out differently from what one had expected and counted on, so you will not be surprised if instead of the promised diary letter only a short one arrives, reporting only that I am well and not much besides. As far as the scenery goes, I can't describe it, and if you have no impression of it from all of the people who have talked and written about it, then I shall hardly be able to provide one, for the reason that it is indescribably beautiful is indeed that it cannot be described. What I otherwise might be able to report on is my life here, but that would be so simple that I'd be done in two sentences. I haven't wanted to make new acquaintances, since I shall only be here for a few weeks at the most before taking tours through the surrounding region and because the only thing I want to get to know properly in the region is nature. Thus I went to bed at nine in the evening and arose at five in the morning in order to take in a refreshing view from my balcony of Vesuvius, the sea, and the coast of Sorrento in the morning light. Then I went for several long and solitary walks, sought out a few of my own favorite spots, and was pleased to find that the most beautiful spot I found was practically unknown to the Neapolitans themselves. On these walks I would seek out some house on the heights to scramble up toward, or follow my fancies, and then let myself be surprised by the night and moonlight, and become acquainted with the *vignaruoli* in order to find my way back, so that I would finally arrive, very tired, back home through the Villa Reale around nine. What a beautiful sight the sea and enchanting Isle of Capri made in the moonlight from the villa, with the blooming acacias giving off an almost tranquilizing scent, how strange the fruit trees stood out, all covered over with pink blossoms, like pink-leaved trees—this too was indescribable. And since thus I have spent most of my time out in and with nature, I cannot write as much as usual. Perhaps we can come back to it in person sometime—then the little pictures above the pink sofa would provide the material and inspiration for stories. But just one more thing, which is that I agree with you, dear Fanny, in what you once said many years ago, that your favorite was the Isle of Nisida (perhaps you have already forgotten it, but I haven't). It looms out in front of you as if it had been created just to be a pleasure spot: one is almost shocked coming out of the Bagnolo Wood, because it lies so close at hand and emerges, so large and green, out of the sea, while the other islands, Procida, Ischia, and Capri, are looming indistinctly farther off in the distance, veiled in blue shadows. Brutus went into hiding on the island immediately after Caesar's murder, and Cicero visited him there; then as now the sea lay in between, and the cliffs jutted so steeply out over the sea, all covered with vegetation on top, just as now: these are the antiquities I like, and which give me something to think about. Something more than a few bits and pieces of stonework. By the way, you, dear Beckchen, would make a really grotesque sight against the backdrop of Vesuvius; at least all Neapolitans do. I would never have imagined such an intense degree of superstitiousness and deceitfulness as that found among the people here. It has often spoiled my pleasure in nature here, for the Swiss, who annoyed Father, are really innocent, natural men by comparison. My innkeeper regularly shortchanges me for a piaster, then I tell him so, and he casually produces the remainder. I met with Benedict here, and we see each other rather often. And I also often meet with both Benedicts. They seem to be doing quite well, and will be leaving Naples in a few days and commencing their journey homeward, on which they hope also to stop in Berlin. The only acquaintances I shall make here are to be musical ones, in order to leave nothing unfinished—thus, for example, Fodor, who does not sing in public, Donizetti, Coccia, and so forth.

Now a few words addressed to you, dear Father. You wrote me that you would not be pleased to see me go to Sicily, and in accordance I abandoned this plan. As to how I shall arrange my trip from here on out, I am thinking I shall be able to write you in the next several days, as soon as I have a general idea of how much time I still need here. From here I shall turn northward again, and you can well imagine with what anticipation I am awaiting your answer to my question, which is so important for me. That it is a bit difficult to abandon Sicily I cannot deny: for it was really more than just a whim of mine. There is nothing dangerous to be feared, and there is even—just to make my heart heavy—a steamer which leaves on May 4, which is making the whole tour and on which many Germans, and probably the local envoy Lottum as well, will be going along. And I would have liked to see a mountain spitting fire, since naughty Vesuvius isn't even smoking. Your instructions have nonetheless until now always very much accorded with my own wishes, so that I certainly shall not pass up my first opportunity to obey you even against my desires of the moment, and thus I have crossed Sicily off my travel plans. Perhaps we shall be able to see each other all the sooner.

And now farewell; today I still want to go for a walk to Capodimonte. Your

Felix

I forgot to tell you, dear Mother, that I have kept the duchess meticulously informed, and that I hope that she will reimburse just as meticulously. Also you asked me about Hofmeister's honorarium. I sent his voucher to Father from Leipzig, and Father has promised to take care of cashing it for me. The things from the Fränkels have been taken care of, as you already know. Farewell.

To Lea and Abraham Mendelssohn Bartholdy

Rome, June 18, 1831

Dear parents,

This is, God willing, the last letter I shall write you from Rome this time. Accept my thanks for all of the splendors I have seen and enjoyed here. Tomorrow morning at four I'll be going by *vettura* via Terni and Perugia to Florence, where I am thinking of arriving on Friday. From there I will provide more news, and hope to find letters from you in Genoa, whither Mirabaud and Reichmann will forward them. Now the actual traveling begins again, and I am happy that I am moving closer to you once again. Pardon me if I write only a few sentences today, but you know the commotion and the hundred little things to be taken care of when leaving a place where one has already settled in. To you, dear Father, I still have to report on the money that I have used during the first year. I thought that it would be less than the sum set aside for me, but it turns out that I have had to spend exactly this sum (for a visitor's life in Naples is a more expensive one than I had thought), and even 7 florins more. As it happened, I didn't have with me your letter in which you wrote to ask how much I had withdrawn since departing from Vienna (incl.), and thus didn't know quite exactly. Since Vienna up to the first anniversary of my departure from Berlin (which I celebrated in Naples on the sea), I have spent exactly

800 Prussian florins, that is 400 scudi (which as you write in the same letter are equal to 1½ Prussian florins) and 300 guilders, thus 800 florins altogether; since previously, according to your letter, I had used 707 florins, I have thus exceeded the 1,500 florins set aside for me by 7 florins. Meanwhile I shall probably make up for it during the coming year, I think, and since you also wrote me at the time that this was a guideline for me to keep to I hope that you will not take the transgression too much amiss. I constantly try, at least, to keep in mind what you told me—namely not to spend money on anything needlessly, but not to deny myself anything which is essential or important, as far as possible. You think that in Naples something or other happened to me that I am keeping from you, but this is truly not the case. The reasons for my displeasure there are precisely those which I gave you in the last letter from Rome, and none other, and since my return here I have heard from many people that exactly the same thing happened to them, I can see quite well that what happened to me was no exception. It is fiercely hot here right now; during the midday hours one can hardly do anything. If you walk out of the house it gusts at you as if from out of an overheated oven, the slightest bit of activity in your room causes you to perspire, on the Spanish Steps one can see the hot air flickering, and then after sundown it becomes so bitingly cold that you need to put on a coat to go for a stroll. In spite of all this I so much prefer to be here rather than in Naples, where there are none of these inconveniences, that I can hardly begin to tell you. Meanwhile I am happy, though, that I don't need to stay here any longer, where one has to live in a constant state of battle with the climate, keep cool when it is hot and keep

warm when it is cool, and where one is obliged to be worried about every draft and protect oneself against it as best one can, like the old ladies back home.—I hope Hensel's toothaches and nervous episodes are over with by now; the man strains himself too much, I have always said so. And if I could take his pulse I would certainly prescribe that he should stop drawing all the time in the evening. You, dear Fanny, wished to have a personal letter, and one ought to arrive within the next few days; I had planned to work on it in the mountains, whither I went last week, and where I amused myself divinely for six days; now I must send off a little travelogue with *raisonnement* to all of you, about the cliffs, the chestnut forests, and church windows, and the costumes I saw in this colorful country. But for today farewell. The time of departure draws near, and I still haven't paid my farewell visits to anyone. By the time you read the letter I will hopefully be a bit closer to you, and with that think of me and keep well and happy. Probably not again very soon from Rome,

F.

To Fanny Hensel

Vevey, August 18, 1831

Dear little sister,
Just a few short words in haste, and about business matters at that. For I am en route again and still have to keep all my senses opened wide to make for a good finish, and I shan't be in the mountains again soon— and a proper letter from Interlaken should follow, so forgive the haste and dull business today. You remember in fact the last business letter I wrote you, what it

was concerned with, and what pleasure you all gave me in consequence. I have not yet thanked all of you for it and do so now wholeheartedly. For next year too you have all promised me a similar favor (in case I am not in Berlin and cannot do it myself), and here is where my business for today comes in. I wrote you in fact for the coming year (now in progress) as well, to make one hundred thalers available for you to use, and perhaps even more, which I have been saving from my travel funds. It will be quite easy too, but now I have received a letter from Father in Geneva in which he also repeats to me—among many other serious matters—that he has suffered very significant losses, more significant than he had thought, and Mother tells me as much in almost every letter, and in the last one even underscored quite prominently a section dealing with this matter. Now I almost have to fear that when all is said and done a great change has taken place during my absence, or at least there is something there about which I am not clear, and since naturally I don't want to turn to our parents with such a question I ask you to write me very honestly and precisely what the thing is, whether anything has changed in the household or otherwise, and what you know of the whole matter, for that is roughly the same as what I would know myself if I were at home. Write me whether life at Leipziger Strasse is still the same, or whether there is perhaps just a little bit less in the big iron chest, or whether you have had to curtail anything in your life—for you see that if so it would be my bound duty not to just put aside for myself and my friends, but as a family obligation. I fear this because I imagine to myself that our parents perhaps don't want to let me know anything on account of the lovely trip I am having. But you are candid when I ask you frankly, so please tell me everything that you know.

My dearly beloved Frau Sister, what blissful joy you give me by your letters, in which you speak of domestic happiness, and whose words convey happiness to everyone—that is simply beyond all expression. I shall probably share it with you sometime, God willing, and then perhaps be able to express it too, but thanks, a thousand thanks, for being so kind as you are. And thanks too to you, lovely couple, that you are so splendidly cheerful, and not happy alone, but also feel and share and thus hate and feel things twice as strongly—there is no end. You cannot imagine how happy the letters make me, talking of Moor's head pastries with bread and butter, or of the Jewish heads, or of birthday celebrations, or even of music making—unless you think of the pleasure that experiencing them yourselves has afforded you. Although I only have the story many days later, it is still enough to warm a person to the cockles of his heart. And with that my thanks.

And send me your music, my dear Fenchel.

Stand united!—That doesn't fit in at all here, for here it is Switzerland, to be sure, but you do so anyway without my exhortations. Beckchen doesn't make a bad third place-setting either, and as a fourth perhaps

F.

The elder Mendelssohn's "significant losses" came about as a result of the collapse of a Hamburg banking house in which the Bank of Mendelssohn and Company had interests.

To Karl Friedrich Zelter

Munich, September 22, 1831

Dear Herr Professor,

Permit me to introduce to you herewith Herr Adolf Henselt from Munich. He is thinking of going to Berlin in six months' time to hear the music there, make the acquaintance of musicians, and make himself known to them, and thus I did not want to omit to give him a letter to bring to you, so that he will find his way to the source right from the start. He will be able to give you news of many of your acquaintances, since his teachers are friends of yours; until now he has had composition lessons with Herr von Poissl, and is now going to study with Hummel in Weimar in order to perfect his piano playing. Good music interests him and thus you shall not want for the most varied opportunities to provide him the greatest pleasure. I told him about a few things and in so doing made his mouth water, as I am now making my own as well. Thus I would be greatly indebted to you if, for example, you would grant him access to the Friday concerts, so that he could hear a few things by Sebastian Bach. Pardon me for the many requests, dear Herr Professor, but the great generosity with which you have always received my recommendations in the past makes me so bold as to call upon it once more, and although I could not become further acquainted with Herr Henselt I know from everything that I hear that he is certainly worthy of your hospitality, a very talented and unassuming young man.

Now I am going to the organ at St. Peter's to practice the footwork in a few Bach fugues. The bearer of this

will be able to tell you all about it.—A thousand greetings to Doris and Rosamund and all of your family, and happiness and good cheer in these times! Your faithful
Felix Mendelssohn Bartholdy

To Fanny Hensel

Frankfurt, November 14, 1831

Oh my dear little sister and musician,
Today is your birthday and I wanted to congratulate you and wish you good cheer, and then came your letters about Aunt Jette and now any real joy is certainly over with. Yesterday the engagement announcement came, today this one—things are strangely back and forth. I want to give you one of the new unbelievably moving Seb. Bach organ pieces which I just got to know here—they are fitting for today in their pure gentle solemnity, it is as if one were listening to the angels in heaven singing.
The 17th. I wanted to write out the piece when I was starting the letter, then set aside the paper, and in the morning when I arose it had already been finished—Schelble had arisen earlier, having heard me speak of it, and got there before I did. From this small tidbit you can fill in the rest of the details of my life with him for yourself; every moment he puts me to shame with some new item of generosity. And I learn something from his clear judgments. Would that you could be here once to see and share my life with me, for it is made even more dear by Philipp Veit, who is one of the most splendid people I have ever known, possessed with such charm, gentleness, and yet lively-spirited, so that it is a joy, and at the same time a great paint—you should just

see his latest picture. We are usually together, in the evening there is music making *in corpore*, and recently at the Caecilienverein Schelble performed some Handel, a chorus by Mozart, the *Es ist der alte Bund* by Bach, which sounded heavenly, the Credo from the great B Minor Mass, and a chorus by me. This evening he is having *Ihr werdet weinen und heulen*, a piece of church music from my Roman, etc., sung in a special concert. Tomorrow, though, I am departing, and expect yet today to receive Bendemann's reply about whether I should go north or west; then on to France. Now play this chorale with Beckchen, as long as you are together, and think of me while so doing. At the end when the chorale melody begins to flutter and dies out way up in the air and everything dissolves into sound—there it is surely heavenly. There are many others as well, just as powerful, but they are more remorseful. This one fits today exactly, and so I am sending it, and my regards and kisses to you and Hensel, and I wish that you will remain mine, as I am yours.

F.

N.B. The chorale is with double pedal, eight feet, Schelble arranged it thus, not a note is missing.

To Karl Friedrich Zelter

Paris, February 15, 1832

Dear Herr Professor,
I have surely wanted for a long time to write you and beg your forgiveness for my silence, but now that I begin my letter and remember that the last one was from Rome and spoke of Holy Week I feel my wrong-

doing twice as keenly. But do not be angry with me over it, and realize that I have been racing around rather a great deal in the meantime, with many new and wondrous things that need to be seen in order to be able to have something to write about from Paris, and that I also wanted to have something significant to tell you about, and that I had to become acquainted with Paris all over again in order to be able to say something about it. But of course all of that doesn't excuse me, as I am well aware, and if you want to be furious with me all of the various excuses won't be of much help anyway, but the best thing would be if you would never let me get around to the excuses when I have committed some wrong or other, but instead would always show me by your friendship that you well knew how I meant things. And you still tender me this friendship, I trust? Allow me to hope so.

But even if I had wanted to write you just about the high points of my trip, then I really ought to have done so from Germany. For this time when I arrived back in Germany—after all of the beauties I had savored in Italy and Switzerland, after all of the wonderful things that I experienced—and in particular while en route through Stuttgart, Heidelberg, Frankfurt, and down the Rhine to Düsseldorf: That was really the high point of my trip—for there I noticed that I was a German and wanted to live in Germany, as long as I could do so. It is true, I cannot enjoy as much beauty there, experience no splendors, but I am at home there. In not a single one of the spots—even those which especially captivated me—would I particularly want to live; it's the whole country, it's the people whose character and language and customs I don't need to learn and follow or imitate, among whom I feel comfortable without having to be surprised at it, and so I hope that in Berlin I shall be able to find my own livelihood and that which is necessary to it, and that I shall not feel less at home there, where I have you and my parents and siblings and friends, than in all of the rest of the other German locales. If someday people in Germany no longer want to have me anywhere, then I can always go to foreign lands, where life is easier for a foreigner, but I hope that I shall not need to. And so I can't even tell you how sincerely I am looking forward to seeing you again.

It has occurred to me quite strongly that in Germany music and appreciation of art is widespread and keeps propagating more and more, whereas in other places (e.g., here) it is being concentrated. From that it follows, perhaps, that with us it is not raised to great heights, nor taken to such great extremes—and in consequence we are able to send musicians to other countries while still remaining sufficiently endowed ourselves. I have thought all this out for myself while being obliged so often to listen to and occasionally even talk about politics, and when people, but in particular Germans, rail at Germany or complain about it, that there is no focal point, no supreme figure, and no concentration—and when they claim that such things will certainly all soon come to pass. No doubt it will not come to pass, and I think it may almost be a good thing. But what will and must come is the end of our all-too-great modesty, with which we regard everything that others bring us as right, and even fail to appreciate what is ours until others have done so. I hope Germans will soon cease to rail at the Germans for not being united, thus making themselves the most disunited ones, and that some day they will imitate the solidarity of the others, which is the best thing that they have. And if indeed they do not do so soon, I will not give up on them even so, and will continue composing as long as new ideas occur to me. But I am always sorry when we ourselves will have nothing to do with those things in which we are superior.

I came to Stuttgart and once again enjoyed the outstanding orchestra, which plays together so completely beautifully and precisely, in a way that one could only dream of. Lindpaintner is at present, I think, the best orchestral conductor in Germany, it is almost as if he were playing all of the music himself with his little baton; moreover he is assiduous, holds rehearsals with his orchestra almost daily, and with his quartet once a week. Molique plays in it—he has such a swift, cool perfection and can make such breathtaking leaps that he would be famous if he lived anywhere else; but he is such a fat *Weinbürger* and doesn't want to be disturbed in his comfort. They were about to give their first subscription concert, in which they play the great symphonies every year; I was supposed to play something in it and offer a few compositions, but was in a hurry and could not wait so long. But upon my return I promised Count Leitrum to stay a little while, and I don't have any idea whether I shall return. The count spoke of you a great deal, by the way, and of the friendly reception you gave him, telling me everything in great detail—how he found you dining, how you compelled him to join you at the table, etc. Lindpaintner is on very good terms with him and all of his subordinates praise him. In the summer the people don't have much to do, and so when there are no rehearsals for a few days the Kapellmeister goes hiking through the countryside with his wife, taking along linens and a tobacco pipe, and arrives back home again from the vineyards several days later. The main thing is, finally, that they all complain all the time but wouldn't want to leave for anything—thus I have become acquainted with musical life in a small German city quite close by. In Frankfurt everything is more upstanding, businesslike, and more metropolitan, but much less fun; may the devil take the republics, they're simply not suited for music. They are altogether stingy, asking first what it costs, and don't have the least bit of flair. But on the other hand the Caecilienverein is there, which alone is enough to make one glad to be in Frankfurt; these people sing with so much fire and are so in unison that it is a joy to behold. It meets once a week and has about two hundred members. But in addition Schelble gathers a smaller group of about thirty voices at his house on Friday evenings, where he has them sing at the piano and little by little works up his favorite pieces, which he doesn't dare present to the large association right away. There I heard a bunch of small Sunday pieces by Sebastian Bach, his *Magnificat*, the great *Mass*, and many other beautiful things as well. The women are also there—as at your Academy they are the most enthusiastic ones, whereas the men are a bit wanting, for their heads are full of business. I even think that it must be the same everywhere; when all is said and done our women have more of a community spirit than our men. At least certainly at the Caecilienverein, for there the sopranos are altogether wonderful, the altos and basses are very good, but the tenors are a bit lacking, and Schelble complains, as you do, that the men are too frivolous. At the full Verein concert I heard the motet *Gottes Zeit ist die allerbeste Zeit*, which we used to sing at your place on Fridays from time to time; the piece *Es ist der alte Bund* was quite divine with the big chorus and the beautiful, soft sopranos. One can scarcely believe what

an effect a single person who wants to accomplish
something can have on all the others; Schelble is not
alone in this, of course, and a taste for serious music is
certainly not primarily restricted to Frankfurt, and yet
it is remarkable with what joy and how well the amateurs
there play the *Well-Tempered Clavier*, the Inventions, and
all of Beethoven, how they know everything by heart,
fix every wrong note, how really musically trained they
are. He has built up a very important circle of influence
and brought people farther along in the truest sense.
At the same time Philipp Veit is there calmly painting
his pictures, which are so beautiful and pious in their
simplicity, in a sense with which I am familiar only
among the old masters, there are no airs or affectation
in them, as may be found with the Germanophiles in
Rome—instead a sincere artist's soul. And then one
comes to Düsseldorf, where Schadow is once again with
his pupils, and works as hard as he can to produce
something, where Lessing creates and executes his
drawings from time to time when people order them,
and then again they have their little orchestra and their
Beethoven symphonies. . . . I don't know why I am
writing you all this, for you are more familiar with it
than I, but I just got absorbed in it while thinking of
all the people who seem so distracted in every city, and
of whom this country consists.

But here it is France, and thus one cannot compare
any German city with Paris, because here everything
flows together, which is what distinguishes France,
whereas in Germany everything spreads out. Germany
is composed of so, so many cities, but as far as music—
and I believe art in general—is concerned, Paris is
France. Thus they have all their conservatories here,
where people are trained, schools are formed, whither

all talent from the provinces must be sent if they wish to become at all accomplished—for outside of Paris there is scarcely a tolerable orchestra in all of France, and there are no outstanding musicians. And while here there are 1,800 piano teachers, and there is still a shortage of teachers, there is as good as no music at all in the other cities. How thousandfold are the ways in which this forms the focal point, what a convivial hustle and bustle it is when you can behold a whole country before you in a single city, and have the elite of all the people around you; I cannot describe it, and you know it. Therefore it also happens that here everything is divided by subject, for everyone seeks and finds his own place. I stand by what you and my dearly loving parents taught me and thus am immediately classified among the *école allemande*. As far as fashionable music goes, I shall not write you anything about it, for it is just the same as I found it seven years ago; the most significant and important thing, which I had not heard before, is the Conservatoire orchestra. It is only natural that it should be the most accomplished one which can be heard in France, for it is the Paris Conservatoire which is giving the concerts, but they are also the most accomplished performances to be heard anywhere. They have all joined together, the best in Paris, have taken some young violinists from the school, given the directorship to a spirited and skillful musician, and then rehearsed for two years before venturing a performance, until they have become completely attuned to each other—until there could be no question of a wrong note any longer. Every orchestra really ought to be like this, wrong notes and rhythms should be eliminated once and for all, but since this is unfortunately never the case, this one is the best that I have ever heard. The school of Baillot, Rode, and Kreutzer furnishes them with violinists, and it is a joy to behold the young people coming to the orchestra en masse with their instruments, and then commencing, all with the same bowing, in the same style, with the same serenity and fire. Last Sunday there were fourteen on each side, with Habeneck leading them, giving the beats with his violin bow; Tulou is the principal flutist, Vogt the principal oboist, Gallay the principal French hornist (the horns are particularly outstanding, the best wind instruments in the orchestra), the principal cellist is Norbert, and so on with the principals. The worst drawbacks are the double basses, which having only three strings can only go as far as G; they are lacking in power and tone, so that wherever there is a forte the real support pillars are lacking. Moreover the first clarinet is shrill and has a stiff and unpleasant delivery and tone. Also the trumpets are unsure in the high notes and modify the difficult passages, and lastly the tympani have a hollow, muffled kettle sound, somewhat like drums. The latter and the basses do the most damage to the overall effect. On the other hand, there is never the slightest question of hesitation or wrong notes, nor of even the slightest disunity; it is the most precise ensemble that can be heard in the world today, and at the same time they manage to play quite comfortably and calmly. One hears how each member completely fulfills his role, is in full mastery of his instrument, how each has his own part and knows everything which is demanded of him by rote, in short how the entire orchestra is made up not of individual musicians, but of an ensemble. The external arrangements are also purposefully and reasonably managed; the concerts are infrequent (every two weeks), and on Sundays at two o'clock, so that it is a holiday in every sense and people don't have to do anything afterward except return home for mealtime and retain their impressions, since there is almost never an opera in the evening. Moreover the hall is small, so that in the first place the music is twice as loud and one hears all of the details twice as precisely, and in the second place the audience is just a select few, and never a large crowd. The musicians themselves really enjoy the great Beethoven symphonies now, and have become quite familiar with them, and it gives them great pleasure to have mastered such things; several, such as Habeneck himself for example, are also certainly sincere in their love for Beethoven. But I don't believe a word the others say, the great squawkers and enthusiasts, for they disparage the other masters on his account, speak of Haydn as if he were a powdered wig, of Mozart as if he were a simpleton—and such narrow-minded enthusiasm cannot be genuine. For if they felt what Beethoven intended they would also know what Haydn was and would be compelled to behave more humbly; but they don't, but instead launch right into their critiques. The audience too loves Beethoven uncommonly, because they think one must be a connoisseur in order to love him; very few of them experience any actual joy in it, and I simply cannot stand the denigration of Haydn and Mozart, it drives me mad. Beethoven's symphonies are like exotic plants to them, they don't really have a look at them, but they're a curiosity, and should someone happen to count the filaments and discover that they belong to a well-known family of flowers he leaves it at that and doesn't think anything further of it. Thus already they are even complaining about people's coldness during this and the previous year, and several Beethoven string quartets will be performed in an arrangement for full string orchestra with twenty-eight violins, contrabasses, etc., without wind instruments, in order to have something new by him. I was even supposed to arrange them, and transcribe the *Pathétique* Sonata for the Conservatoire orchestra, but I delivered such a pretty lecture to them that they have no doubt given up on the idea, and the performance will be without the wind instruments. Now it seems they want something new, and that I can grant them, for thus next Sunday they are offering my Overture to *A Midsummer Night's Dream*, and in a subsequent concert my Symphony in D Minor. I am also supposed to play there once, and when all of this is over with, I have some inclination to give a concert in the hall; but this is still a long way off. But I must tell you about the program for the last concert: it began with Beethoven's A major symphony, then came Weber's *Choeur des chasseurs*, which was a verse from the huntsmen's chorus from *Euryanthe*, and then suddenly an anxious, sad piece with horns, then the huntsmen's chorus once more, then the sad music again, which kept getting softer and softer, and finally stopped. It turned out that this sad piece with the horns was by Castil-Blaze, and that they had done *Euryanthe* in the great opera house in his revision, of which this was a sample. It annoys me that they did this in a concert, for without it the concert would have been a model one, but that was once again one of those matters which are not supposed to occur between men of honor. At the end of the first part Kalkbrenner played his *Traum (Dream)*—a new piano concerto that he composed and in which he has gone over to romanticism. He explained beforehand that it begins with hazy dreams, then comes an episode of despair, then a declaration of love, and finally a military march. No sooner had Henri Herz heard this than he too quickly came up with a romantic piano piece, likewise explaining it beforehand: first comes a conversation between a shepherd and shepherdess, then a thunderstorm, then a prayer with evening bells, and finally a military march. You won't believe it, but it's completely true. Kalkbrenner plays his piece wonderfully beautifully, by the way, with an affability, elegance, and perfection which nothing can rival. That was the first part of the concert; the second consisted of *Christ du mont des olives* with the Conservatoire chorus and singers from the Grand Opera house, who all distinguished themselves. The next concert begins with Beethoven's F major symphony, then a duet from *Armide (Esprits de thaine)* and a cello concerto. The second part is the Kyrie and Gloria from the new Beethoven mass, and my overture. Now if that isn't a motley assortment!

Besides all this I should tell you about Baillot's soirées, the Grand Opera, and the newly reopened Opéra Comique, but I'll save it for my next letter, otherwise you will lose all patience with my lengthy letters. But please, my dear Herr Professor, write me a few lines in return, even if it's just a few words, so that I will know whether you would like to have a sequel to my life and doings in Paris and whether you remain faithful and friendly toward me. I have heard nothing from you for so long. I must also write you about my new pieces, for I have been rather diligent lately. How I am looking forward to being able to play them for you and finding out whether you are satisfied with them, and what about them doesn't seem right to you, and what I should improve. For you will have to hear a great number of instrumental and church pieces. But please, send me some word, and tell me that you are well and happy, and thus lift my spirits. My warm regards and best wishes to your entire family. Farewell. Your faithful pupil,

Felix Mendelssohn Bartholdy

To Breitkopf and Härtel

Paris, April 19, 1832

Your Excellencies,

I enclose today, courtesy of the Bossanges, three of the manuscripts we discussed, namely: the parts for the octet, the six songs, and the parts for the *Midsummer Night's Dream* overture. I ask that you have them published as soon as practicable. I shall send you the arrangement of the octet, which I have started but have been prevented by illness from finishing, at the earliest opportunity from England. I request that you have the parts for the overture engraved as soon as possible, but put off the date of publication until I have written to you from England, where it is also appearing. In London I shall play both of the piano pieces we discussed in public, and send you the one which seems to make the greatest impression. I shall then send the authorization and waiver, and ask you to forward the copies and the honorarium not to me but to my father, Herr A. Mendelssohn Bartholdy in Berlin.

Finally I beseech you most earnestly to see that the person who does the engraving for the octet and overture takes note of both of the enclosed slips of paper, so that all of the notes I have made on them, which are of the greatest importance, are followed. Similarly I request that you retain the title exactly as I have given it, or at least notify me if you should prefer to alter it.

In several hours I am departing for London, where your letters may reach me at the address of Messrs. Doxat and Company. With deepest respect, faithfully,

Felix Mendelssohn Bartholdy

In Paris Mendelssohn fell very seriously ill (typhus?) and reported home only occasionally. The letter and package from Karl Immermann, an old friend of the Mendelssohn household—Mother Lea raved about him—had to do with a planned opera, for which Immermann supplied the libretto, although the composition came to naught.

To Abraham Mendelssohn Bartholdy

Literary Union Club
May 11, 1832

Dear ones,

Yesterday I received your first answer to my letter from London; now I am reproaching myself for perhaps not having told you in sufficient detail how well I am, for I had not thought that you would be so horrified after I had put the trip, the sea, and much time between myself and the great danger. God be praised it is past and I behold my life as if given to me anew, and to be enjoyed as if it were too.

For I cannot describe to you how happy these first weeks here have been. If from time to time bad things all pile up, as in the winter in Paris—where I came to miss the loveliest people, never felt at home, and finally became very ill, then for once the opposite comes to pass, and that it is how it is here in this lovely country, where I find my friends again, know myself to be well and among well-meaning people, and where I can enjoy the feeling of returned health in the highest measure. Moreover it is warm, the lilacs are blossoming, and there is music to be made, just imagine my joy. I must describe to you a pleasant morning this last week when things piled up in just this manner. Of all the outward signs of recognition I have had so far, it was the one which pleased and touched me the most, and was perhaps the only one which I shall always think of with renewed pleasure. Saturday morning there was a Philharmonic rehearsal, in which they couldn't do anything by me, however, because my overture was not yet copied out. Rosen and Klingemann came over for breakfast, we are getting on so happily and comfortably with one another, as if it could never have been otherwise; just as we were about to leave, a letter from Immermann arrived, asking me to how he should address a package to me—it seemed my opera was completed and he wanted to send it to me. I stuck the letter in my pocket, set off down bright Regent Street, and met a couple of stunningly beautiful young English girls at the entrance, of whom I am quite fond, and who took me along to their box. Right away Beethoven's *Pastoral* Symphony began, which sounded pleasant too, and made for easy listening alongside the pretty children, and in the meantime I read through Immermann's letter and thought of the present and the future. Then, after the symphony, I wanted to go to the lobby in order to greet a few old friends. But no sooner had I arrived down there when someone called out from the orchestra: *There is Mendelssohn*, whereupon they all began yelling and clapping such that for a while I didn't know what to do, and when it was over, another called out, *Welcome to him*, whereupon they struck up the same racket and

I had to make my way through the hall and to the orchestra in order to take a bow. You see, I shall not forget that, for it was more dear to me than any other distinctions; it showed that the musicians are fond of me and were glad that I had come, and it was a happier moment for me than I can say. At the same time I now also have the pleasure of finding all my acquaintances unchanged, Cramer and Addison are very gracious about paying, and always order more—what more does one need, we are singing happily.

Tomorrow morning Klingemann or Rosen or Stentzler or both or all three are coming; then we will have breakfast and talk politics. We have tea and *tops and bottoms* for breakfast (this is historic). Then to work, my Rondo with Orchestra is more than half finished and will be wild enough. Then there are visits to pay, or curiosities to see; so for example I emerge from the great *meeting in Guildhall*, where they ask the House of Commons to prohibit taxes, and the Lord Mayor appears and says finally and once and for all that he has no trust in other councillors *(cheers)*, they are men of disgraceful principles *(cheers)*, *if it be that they have any principles at all* (huge roar), and Lord Grey would have to stay on (all hats tossed up into the air). Then good old Taylor gave a most delightful speech, after which the emissaries from Birmingham arrived—this too was a world-historical event. So every noon and evening I am out with friends, and we make music and coquetteries and all manner of good things, arrive home rather late, sleep rather a long time, and for breakfast arrives Klingemann or Rosen, etc., *dal segno*.

I have significantly changed and improved the *Hebrides*; it will be rehearsed for the first time at the Philharmonic tomorrow morning, and performed on

Monday. On Friday I am conducting the *Midsummer Night's Dream* in Vaughan's concert; please pronounce his name "Von." On Sunday it's out to the green countryside to visit the lovely Horsleys, etc. Now the letter must be off, and I on up Regent Street, for here I am at my club, of which I am an honorary member, and thus entitled to write, read the paper, and eat here as much as I please, but today I'm not dining here, but with Moscheles, and so now I send you all my regards and ask that you all keep well and happy for me. I am, and think of you.

F. MB.

P.S. The Literary Union's pen is worthless. A personal letter to Hensel will soon follow, using a better one. O Fanny and Beckchen, my salutations to you.

To Abraham Mendelssohn Bartholdy

London, June 15, 1832

So this is, God willing, the last page that will be sent off to you from my great trip. My travel letters take their leave herewith.

For a week from today I will pack myself off on a steamer, and expect to arrive in person on Wednesday in place of a letter; then we shall see each other again. Actually I have aged ten years, and am very serious and composed, though shabby on the outside, but that doesn't matter at all, for I am fond of what I have always been fond of, but even more so, and hate perhaps more strongly what I have never been able to suffer, and am happy with my life. Father's first letter concluded: Enjoy your youth and your happiness. This I have done from the heart, and shall do, and I thank you all for it.

I fear your next letter will scold me for not wanting to accept the position at the Academy, and I am all the more sorry that the last letter I receive might be an ill-humored one. But now we do not need to correspond about it anymore, and the way I feel now I truly would not like to accept any fixed, binding position. People buy up from me what I write, and for the time being I can live from that, and continue writing, which is the main thing. And also I must come back to this country again soon, for I have very remarkable plans pertaining thereto, which I shall not unveil until a week after my return. It is very good to be here, though, and such friendly people and pretty girls are nowhere else to be found. It is very pleasant to be able to feel oneself so much at home when abroad, but when I am truly at home, things ought to feel a bit different indeed. I shall also bring along flowers for you again, and a lovely gift from the Philharmonic, and perhaps some eau de cologne, but the main point is that I am coming home again. Forgive me, dear Father, for not being able to write seriously; when I began, thinking that this would be the last letter, it still seemed serious, but now I am thinking of home and my return via some express coach or post chaise, and that brings other thoughts to mind. How much has changed in the meantime! And how I hope to find you all unchanged!

That's it for writing, nothing more can be brought forth, so I shall come myself—and tell all the rest in person. I hope that is no longer too far off, and so farewell and be happy. In a week it's aboard the ship and homeward; until then good-bye, and put this letter on top of the stack of travel letters. May God grant us, as I hope, cheerful and happy times.

Felix MB

I had a number of things to bring up, but still won't do so—for time is pressing as always and great plans have yet to be carried out. Therefore simply and above all my heartfelt congratulations to the newlywed couple, of whom I know only half, but nevertheless well, and for a long time—and anyway, what more could one wish for in the way of youth and talent than that which they already have? Theirs remains an infinite share indeed.

This is the last travel letter and one would really have to wrangle with it to avoid becoming sentimental—how I am wont to yawn when the likes of an Iffland tries to bring me to tears. Then it will become a bit lonely here.—As for the man himself . . . take it from the man himself—or his notes—or compositions—but not me. He is as healthy as iron, or rather as elastic rubber—few can emulate what he himself puts aside, and yet so much is happening here. I shall need to rest for a whole year to recover just from watching it.

When the man played his Munich concerto at the Philharmonic the triumph was ridiculous; once again I felt as overcome with emotion as a young mother, and the silly gray-haired people swore *to me*, as if I had played or written it, that it was played and composed so divinely and extraordinarily that no one could remain composed, so to speak, much longer. Everything else remains enshadowed and the cause of art has been furthered. Much, indeed much more than all this was true of it—such performances unheard of.—But I cannot go on—I wish I could this autumn. Then I would accept your gracious

invitation and lodgings, my dear Frau City Councillor,
and remain, in person, always yours,

K. Klingemann

INTERMEZZO IN DÜSSELDORF, 1833–35

The decision reached in London, that he "truly did not wish to accept any fixed, binding position during the first years," was soon forgotten in Berlin. Though Mendelssohn's application to succeed Zelter as director of the Berlin Sing-Akademie was unsuccessful, but Düsseldorf opened many doors for the twenty-four-year-old, who with his fiery enthusiasm hoped to turn the musical life of the city upside down, in the churches and theaters as well as in the concert halls. Moreover, Mendelssohn felt extremely comfortable in the proximity of many of his close friends: he lived with the Schadows and spent time in the company of the painters he had befriended in Berlin—Hildebrandt, Hübner, Schirmer, and Bendemann. He could visit his cousin Benjamin Mendelssohn, who taught geography at the University of Bonn, and his uncle Joseph Mendelssohn at his vineyards in Horchheim, near Coblenz. In this respect his family was close at hand. Mendelssohn kept a riding horse, swam, composed, rehearsed, performed himself, and practiced with an intensity which Klingemann had observed in London, writing: "I need a year just to recover from watching it."

The expected recognition did not come, however, and Mendelssohn was very dissatisfied, although Karl Immermann, thanks to whose good efforts he was brought to Düsseldorf in the first place, attempted again and again to use his age and influence to introduce Mendelssohn there. But Mendelssohn could not risk the renown he had gained abroad on bad performances in this Prussian province. The orchestra was simply unsatisfactory, and the organist likewise. Things rapidly came to a precipitous break between Immermann and his theater, Mendelssohn resigned as director of church concerts, and finally gave notice halfway through 1835. It was easy for him to resign, for the city of Leipzig had been courting him for some time. First the publishing house of Breitkopf and Härtel had tried to win him as the editor of their Allgemeine musikalische Zeitung (Musical News), not knowing, of course, that Mendelssohn prohibited himself from writing about music as a matter of principle. Then the directorship of the Leipzig Gewandhaus concerts sought to obtain him—with success. Leipzig thus became the artistic focal point for the young conductor, and remained so, apart from occasional absences caused by travel and another brief Intermezzo provided by a position in Berlin, until his death.

To the Lower Rhine Musical Festival Committee of 1833 in Düsseldorf

Berlin, March 16, 1833

I wish to express my deepest gratitude to the esteemed Lower Rhine Musical Festival Committee for the current year for the honor, the delightful offer, and the confidence you show me in wanting to confer upon me the directorship of this year's music festival. It is every musician's duty and pleasure to be able to participate in such a wonderful undertaking to the best of his abilities, and so it is natural that I am able to accept, with my best, most sincere thanks, the directorship which you entrust to me.

But now I have accepted an engagement in England for this spring which will require my presence in London in late April at the latest, at which time I thought of traveling there by way of Düsseldorf. To remain in Düsseldorf from this time until the music festival, as you asked in your letter, would thus be impossible for me since I would have to miss the Philharmonic concerts altogether, on account of which I am making the trip; I would thus be compelled to return to Düsseldorf for the music festival from London, and I would most gladly do so, provided it is not a necessary condition that the director be there so far in advance of three weeks beforehand. If this is *not* the case, I would commit myself to arrive back in Düsseldorf again on May 16, passing through on the way to London during the first half of April in order to make up the lost time. Since I believe that conductors have arrived only a week in advance for previous festivals, I remain hopeful that this conflict will not deprive me of the pleasure of being able to accept your offer, and ask only that you send word of your decision to me here as soon as possible, so that I may make my travel arrangements accordingly should it be favorable to me, as indeed I hope and wish.

I have inquired about the score and orchestral parts for *Israel in Egypt* at the Sing-Akademie, and have been promised that the same will be loaned to me for the music festival; they only desire to know how long they will be needed there and how soon they can be returned here. Thus if you would be so kind as to send me a brief note addressed to the directorship of the Sing-Akademie, in which you state by when the scores will be returned, I would then be able to forward them on at once, or bring them myself.

Whether it will be possible for me to write an overture for Handel's oratorio I am not yet sure myself; nor have I been able to find a suitable piece of music for the second evening thus far, but will occupy myself with the matter at length while waiting to receive your gracious answer. Additional plans and arrangements could probably also be taken care of when I pass through in April.

Reaffirming my assurances to you of my heartfelt gratitude, I remain, with deepest respect,

the esteemed Committee's most faithful

Felix Mendelssohn Bartholdy

To Abraham Mendelssohn Bartholdy

Düsseldorf, September 27, 1833

Dear Father,

I want to take a few short lines to report my safe arrival to you and otherwise make this just a business letter. The day before yesterday I arrived here, and still have to stay at a hotel, since Wach and his sister are still staying with Schadow in my rooms—but I will be able to move in shortly. I wrote to Beckchen yesterday, but remain altogether without any news from her or from any of you.

As I went to drop off the coach yesterday it occurred to me that I had forgotten to obtain from you the certified invoices for the repaired wheel, from Groschop in Enrenbreitstein, and thus ask you, if you can find them among your papers, as no doubt you can, to send them to me, since the man says he will reconsider them. I borrowed fifty florins from my uncle in Horchheim, so that I would not have to wait here until the first of October, and so ask you to return to him the same sum, with my thanks, as soon as he comes to Berlin (he departs from Horchheim next Monday). And when I have the bills here and can negotiate with the saddle maker, I shall write you about the matter again and we can finally resolve our complicated travel finances.

Here everything bodes quite well, and I am looking forward to the winter and much work; yesterday I received a letter from Rosen, who will be coming to Berlin around the end of October. All the rest in the next letter, in answer to one from all of you, to which I am very much looking forward.—Best regards to all

of you from the Woringens and Schadows, and from
the Hübners and Bendemanns. Your

Felix MB

To Benjamin Mendelssohn

Düsseldorf, November 29, 1833

Dear Benni, says Aloys Fuchs in Vienna:
"This very day (November 6) the mahogany-wood piano
selected for you was sent by Conrad Graf from here to
Bonn. The packing crate is numbered *M.B. No. 2003*
and the freight charges set at fifty francs (courant marks,
payable in Bonn); the shipping time should be thirty-
six to thirty-eight days. Next to the dampers it carries
the words, in my handwriting, 'Chosen for Herr Felix
Mendelssohn Bartholdy by Aloys Fuchs.' With regard
to the quality of the piano I would simply call your
attention to the fact that it is the best instrument out of
more than twenty which Graf had ready in their show-
room, for he places no small stock in your approval and
thus took great pains to satisfy your wishes and stipulations adequately. When I tried it out . . . I could
hardly tear myself away from it, and wished only—that
I could have heard you, my dear friend, play on it.
Herr Graf asks you whether *he* should inquire at the
House of Arnstein and Eskeles *himself* about obtaining
the purchase price, or whether he may expect an *aviso*
from there—this when I made inquiries there several
days ago when no invoice had yet been received. I
therefore appeal to you for further instructions. I hope
too that soon after the instrument arrives you might
also find it convenient to relay your opinion of it,
whether it is satisfactory, etc., etc., etc."

As concerns the last point, I herewith accept absolutely to spend Christmas Eve at your home, that is if you are all spending the evening quietly at home and want to give me apples and gingerbread. Otherwise I'm not coming, will not try out the instrument, and you have not invited me, you nasty neighbors. As far as the other point goes, please write me all the details and tell me whether the port wine, which Alexander claimed in a letter to have left in Bonn, still exists. Confess! Did you take it for ordinary old *Ahrbleichert* and drink it all up? And if not, would you care to send it to me?

So write me whether I should come for Christmas, because I would very much like to, give my regards to Rosa, and farewell. Your

Felix MB

To Benjamin Mendelssohn

Düsseldorf, December 21, 1833

Circular for the composer, etc., and member too, etc. FMB: The aforementioned will be departing from here on Tuesday (the 24th) early in the morning in a special coach, is thinking of arriving at your place in Bonn toward noon or a bit later and thus requests that the necessary gingerbread horses with raisins be held in readiness for him.

FMB

P.S. Further and more precise details in person. I have received the port and am bringing some four-part things along.

To the Esteemed Musical Arts Committee

Düsseldorf, January 9, 1834

A careful perusal of the *Seasons* has so strongly confirmed what I asserted last night, though without certitude—namely that it would be impossible to put together a satisfactory performance of this work next Thursday—that I must entreat the esteemed Comité to put off the projected performance and perhaps advise the public thereof in a few words.

Felix Mendelssohn Bartholdy

To Julius Rietz

Düsseldorf, March 10, 1834

Dear Julius,

I shall not hesitate to provide you with a direct answer to Paul's letter, having now taken the necessary steps, in order to tell you everything as accurately as possible.

I can now assure you confidentially that your appointment at the theater here is a certainty. The greater Theater Association has come into being (early this morning the decision was made), and it will become a reality right away for the coming winter, with Immermann at the head, though with the stage entrusted to a theater director for the coming season; thus his influence on the choice of someone to fill the post of music director will remain unchanged, and so it is as good as assured for you. You don't even have a single competitor, and the Lord Mayor, to whom I conveyed Spontini's letter of refusal among other things, as well as Immermann, has given me written notice that they intend to bring up and conclude the matter at the next committee meeting. This meeting cannot take place this week, and so I am writing you before it is definite, since you need an answer immediately. The salary that they wish to grant you for the first year is to be sure less substantial than I had hoped, namely four hundred florins, but you must take into account that Düsseldorf is not a large city and that the theater is still in its beginnings, and that when all is said and done three *months* of the year will probably *remain completely free for you*, since there are no concerts here during the summer, that you will not have so much to do that there will be no time left over to give lessons, and for yourself, and that this is only stipulated for the first year. You can live *well* here on such a sum.

Since the theater, as I said, is closed during the summer, you will not, in any case, be able to assume your post and responsibilities before next September, and therefore I advise you—should the post offered to you be otherwise agreeable, as Paul writes, and on account of which you wish a definitive answer from me—not to turn it down. Around here engagements are almost always made for *months*, and since Paul writes that it would be in a city nearby here, I am convinced that you will be able to arrange matters so as to remain there from the end of next month until September, and then assume your duties here.

It would be best then if you could come here for a few days on your trip there so that we could discuss it more thoroughly in person and confer on the details. You will like it here, I am convinced; it grows more agreeable to me with each day, and you will find splendid associates and the opportunity of making a great impact.

It goes without saying that you must *not* mention in your correspondence with the other theater, with which I am not familiar, that we are expecting you here. But you will still be able to arrange matters easily so that the months in between will not be wasted as a result, and so that you will be able to be here by September. But that of course must be quite firmly established, so that I can build and expand on it. I entreat you to send me an answer very soon, and hope that you will find it possible to answer with a definitive yes, since a stage which is being created under such auspicious conditions and life here will both no doubt have their charms for you. I need hardly tell you what heartfelt pleasure it would give me to see and have you here, and to be able to work together with such a congenial, like-minded musician. If possible do stop by here soon, for then you will like it so much that you will certainly be happy to stay with us and live here officially in September. Yours as ever,

Felix Mendelssohn Bartholdy

P.S. The painter Schirmer, who plays the cello, desires urgently to know whether you might want to give him lessons too, or whether perhaps you might be too impatient with a beginner?

To Joseph von Fuchsius

Düsseldorf, July 5, 1834

Most Esteemed Herr Lord Mayor,
Your Excellency
is entreated by me to convey my sincere and heartfelt thanks to the esteemed Committee for the 1833 Lower

Rhine Music Festival, which has given me the most uncommon pleasure in the splendid gift which was sent to me last week. The memory of the music festival is among the most precious of my musical life, and shall not leave me, and as my stay here becomes more pleasant and fruitful with each passing day, it recalls to me again and again that festival which first brought me here for an extended period of time. In addition to these two reasons for my thinking so strongly and gratefully of the 1833 festival, the generosity of the committee provides a third, and I do not know whether I should be happiest for the beauty of the gift itself or for the friendliness with which it was given me and the kind words which accompanied the ring. I beseech Your Excellency to convey to the members my thanks for such a great display of friendship, and to continue to grant me the honor whereby I remain Your Excellency's most faithful

Felix Mendelssohn Bartholdy

To Julius Schubring

Düsseldorf, July 15, 1834

Dear Schubring,
It is now almost a year that I have owed you a letter. I shall not even attempt to begin by asking for forgiveness, for my wrong is too great and I'd never finish. How it has happened I myself cannot comprehend. For last autumn, when I was just getting settled here, I received your letter with the notes for *St. Paul*, which were the best suggestions I had yet received, and I began to ruminate on the matter the same morning, took up the Bible amidst the disorder of my room, and soon became

so engrossed that I could hardly force myself to finish the other projects which I absolutely had to complete first. At the time I wanted to write to you at once and thank you most kindly; then I thought that it would be nicer if I could tell you that I had already started on it, and when in the spring I actually did begin, some compositional problems came up that bothered me greatly. But today I simply cannot leave things in the abstract, but must write you and ask you how you and your family are doing. For I know that your family has grown in the meantime; that was hardly right of you not to notify me with a note or a postcard, and to let me find out thirdhand. Although I admit that I well deserved it, still, a minister such as yourself is hardly allowed to take vengeance or hold a grudge. But please don't do so now, and let me hear something from you again. Your notes for *St. Paul* were splendid, and I have used all of them without exception; it is strange (and good) that while composing, at all of the places where for some reason or other I had previously wanted to rearrange a phrase or change it, little by little things came back into the same order in which I find them in the Bible; that remains, after all, the best way. I have finished more than half of the first part, and am thinking that it will be completed by the fall, and then perhaps the whole thing in February. But how are you getting along in Dessau? I would prefer it if you could answer "just as ever." I hope you have retained your cheerfulness and joy in life and are playing the piano, and love Seb. Bach and remain as always. Such worries should not even occur to me, but here one is surrounded by such disagreeable specimens, priests who take every joy of their own and others and pour salt on it, desiccate it—prosaic fault finders who dismiss a concert as sin, a

stroll as distracting and pernicious, a theater as something of a sink of corruption, and all of spring with its
tree blossoms and beautiful weather as a Slough of
Despond. You will have heard of the Elberfeld style.
But it takes on an even worse form here and can make
one properly distressed. The worst part is the arrogance
with which such people regard others, which admits no
other possibility of anything good—I liked Mlle. Wein-
hold, whom you recommended to me, quite well at first,
but then after a while not at all; she has no real talent
for the theater, but has very prestigious engagements
for next winter in the Hague and Amsterdam as a
concert singer, *in felix meritis,* for which she will be well
suited, I believe.—Tell me though, you once wrote me
in a letter about Marx's last visit to Dessau that you
wanted to tell me something about him, but then you
didn't do so. What was it? He has broken off his
engagement, which I regret, and his compositions, some
of which he has now published, displeased me, to my
distress, so greatly that I have lost confidence in his
talent. But of course that is something which has often
put me in a bad mood of late. Recently I happened to
read in a journal a critique of a theological pamphlet
by Beetschneider, signed by Baur—is that our Baur?
And does he often write publicly? Musical matters here
are proceeding slowly but things are all right. This
summer we performed a mass by Beethoven, one by
Cherubini, two cantatas by Sebastian Bach, my *Ave Maria*
and *Verleih uns Frieden (Grant Us Thy Peace)* in the church,
and next month we'll do Handel's *Te Deum* (Dettinger).
Of course, much remains to be desired, but at least the
pieces are being heard, and little by little that makes
the performance and the performers better. What is
Seelmann doing? Has he composed anything new? And

how is your Graf holding up? Hauser in Leipzig has transcribed a score for a cantata in E minor by Seb. Bach from the manuscript parts; it is one of the strongest ones by him that I know of. If I can find the opportunity I shall send you a copy. But now I am out of paper and letter. Farewell, my friend, give my many regards to your wife, and write me. Your

Felix MB

To Joseph von Fuchsius

Düsseldorf, October 12, 1834

Your Excellency,
I must ask you, much as it grieves me to do so, to kindly relieve me of my duties as director of church music until circumstances allow for the appointment of a different organist to the one who rendered his services for today's mass at the Maximilianskirche. His incompetence makes impossible any successful performance, and it is thus so unpleasant for me to see the efforts of the other performers and of myself go entirely to waste that I hope you will graciously grant my request. With utmost respect your most faithful

Felix Mendelssohn Bartholdy

To Fanny Hensel

Düsseldorf, November 14, 1834

Dear Fenchel,
Be happy this day and in the year which lies ahead of you and remain true to me. I wanted to send you this year again some piece or other under which I could

write November 14, but these weeks of a director's life have swallowed up everything and I am only slowly returning to normal again. In recent days I have sketched the overture for *St. Paul*, and thought of finishing it at least, but work is far behind schedule. If only we could at least be together in the evening now, for when the candles are lighted I always wish I were at home even more than in the morning, and here they come now. And then, the time from the 30th of October through the 14th of November and the 11th of December up through Christmas and New Year's is not exactly the best time to be far from home, even if the evenings weren't long.[1] But then we can be diligent and go traveling again next summer and visit each other; today I only wish that it were possible already.

So what are you doing this evening? Making music and entertaining company? Or reading the newspaper aloud (in which I am told Hensel's school has been very highly praised and in many respects favorably compared with the one here). Or perhaps none of you are at home. I hope you are, and picture a pretty sight. I have spent the day monotonously enough, in that I had to sit for Hildebrandt all morning long—he is now finishing my portrait. At noon I was at the Bendemanns' and will go to see them later on as well, since Madame Bendemann's birthday is also today. The poor woman is spending it dejected, for tomorrow she is traveling to Berlin with her husband, and must be having a hard time with separating herself from the children. But in my opinion they are doing the right thing by going back, at least recently I sat and listened to Herr Bendemann explain the reasons to me so convincingly that

1. *30th of October*, etc.: dates of birthdays in the family.

I had to acknowledge he was right and was amazed that he spoke in such animated fashion about the matter, which I would not have expected from him. Eduard is a splendid and delightful person and such a good son that his mother's bad mood seems quite natural to me. But you, birthday child, our judgments about paintings are not in agreement this time, for Stilke's has always been one of the most repugnant to me; when a work of art tries to portray misery artificially, such as starving in the desert, then I have no sympathy for the picture at all or for the people, no matter how well executed it is, and it isn't even that. The whole thing seems to me nothing other than a variation on Lessing's *Königspaar (Royal Couple)*, this time with dead horses. The mood of the work is prosaic, and even if he decks it out in bright colors twenty times over it doesn't help. So I don't even agree when you speak of the violin revolution since Paganini in connection with Lafont, for I know of no such revolutions in art, at least in any case not among these people, and I think the very same things about Lafont would even have displeased you if you had heard him before Paganini's appearance—and you would not praise his good sides less for having heard the other. I have just read a few new French musical journals here in which they are always talking of a *révolution du goût* and a musical upheaval which supposedly has been taking place in the last several years, in which I am supposed to be playing quite a role—such things make me feel quite nauseated. At such times I always think that one should be diligent and work hard, above all hate no one and leave the future to God, finish the oratorio by March, compose a symphony in E minor and a piano concerto and set out traveling again, and visit Leipziger Str. No. 3, but if possible meet somewhere else. And with this song and dance we are back to Hofisen. I see that on the last page I slipped into quite a sullen tone, oh please pardon me, birthday child. But the day after tomorrow I have to conduct *Oberon* again, and hound the Düsseldorf orchestra like nothing else, and yesterday was the second concert: *Sinfonie* by Bürgmüller (the younger), aria by Mlle. Deutler, cello concerto by Julius Rietz (there was the elegy by Romberg, cf. Paul), then in the second half: overture to *Medea* by Cherubini, three songs with piano by Wöringen, *Bächlein, lass dein Rauschen sein* by Curschmann, *Leise zieht durch* by me, and *Herz mein Herz* by Beethoven, then my E-flat rondo (Rietz conducted very well), and finally a damned duet by Mercadante.—Aren't we *fashionable?* And it was so packed, and all the ladies so elegant! No one was eating bread and butter or apples! Afterward there was even a court soirée with all Their Excellencies and their fancy speech!—Now I have slipped back into a grumbling tone which is not very appropriate to birthdays. That subject I strike up once more, and wish you much luck and a good year in 1835. Farewell, my good cantor, and good cheer to you and the parents and siblings and everyone. Your

Felix MB

Beckchen, I remain liberal, despite the old dragon. Fragment.

To Friedrich Kistner

Düsseldorf, January 3, 1835

Most Esteemed Sir,
Please accept my sincere thanks for the kindness you

have shown on my behalf, and which you expressed in the letter I received yesterday. As much as it would please me to be active on behalf of music in your city too, to the best of my abilities, and as thankful as I am for your gracious communication in this regard, it is unfortunately impossible for me to accept an offer of this nature, even if it were under the most advantageous of circumstances. That is, I am in no way in a position to speak on music properly for even a half hour, let alone throughout an entire colloquium, and I don't think I could learn to do so even if my entire well-being depended on it. Not once have I ever been able to follow an entire colloquium satisfactorily, and always came away feeling more unmusical than I did when I went in, so that little by little I set myself the goal of being a practical musician and not a theoretical one. I have sacrificed my independence to that goal here, since I could easily live anywhere, in larger cities and ones more preferable to me, whether employed or not; since it occurred to me that I would learn a few practical things here and then be able to make use of some abilities which until then I had lacked. This is also the reason that I could in no case accept your offer, by which otherwise I feel so honored—for me the only motive for holding any sort of post lies in its sphere of influence, and as gladly as I would set aside my personal pleasure and well-being and all other considerations, so it is impossible to set aside, particularly with regard to this point, all of the plans and resolutions which I have made for my continued progress in music. I hope that you will approve of my convictions when you put yourself in my position, and will not fail to recognize that although I cannot avail myself of your generosity at this moment, I am nonetheless grateful for it, and

shall always remain indebted to you for the interest you
have shown in me and my musical career in this matter.
With deepest respect I remain yours faithfully,
Felix Mendelssohn Bartholdy

To Abraham Mendelssohn Bartholdy

Düsseldorf, January 15, 1835

Dear Father,

I have just received new offers from Leipzig to take up
a post there before this year is out, and since the matter
thus concerns my immediate future I am permitting
myself to ask for your advice, or rather decision, as to
what I should do. You would perhaps prefer it if I were
to decide for myself, and attempt to act independently
in such matters—but that I can turn to you and follow
your advice convinces me that it would be well to do so,
and I certainly realize that such a step can hardly harm
me later on. In short: I consider it my greatest blessing
that I can write this very letter, and would not like to
pass up the opportunity, even were I to win a measure
of independence thereby. My obligations here end with
the first of July; by then my oratorio, and I hope a new
symphony and a piano concerto as well, will be finished,
and the main purpose of my stay here, to be able to do
my own work in peace, will have been fulfilled. The
main question which thus arises is whether I should
again accept a position (for in this case I would very
likely remain there for the rest of my life), or remain
free for the next few years, which I can still count
among my youthful years, and make the art trip I had
planned.—In favor of the latter is the fact that I would
also be able to find a position later without any further

trouble, as I can well see here that I am not afraid of lacking for offers after the trip, and that I really do discern an impulse to be heard and seen out in the great wide world, and to hear and see, before I tie myself down and little by little am forced to let the world come to me. *On the other hand*, there is the fact that in so doing nothing further is gained than pleasure and perhaps fame in the end, and the fact that I understand quite well that two such years are more taxing and wearing than four calm ones in a steady position, and finally the main thing, that I would compose less, and make less inward progress, even if the years seemed faster and more brilliant on the outside.—To present both of these questions to you would have been my intention even without the offer from Leipzig, but since I would like to have your answer before answering Leipzig, I have had to write them to you in haste, and beg you to write me back quite soon. If both are all the same to you I shall of course have to make the decision by myself, but under no circumstances could I do so without first asking you about it, for as I said, my preference is to be able to follow your advice.

I would only want to stay here if I were to receive a good opera libretto or some other big project, for nowhere else is it so pleasant and easy to work in peace as it is here. But as far as musical performances here go, things are not all that spectacular: they are too inept, and good intentions alone are not enough. In Leipzig they offered me the directorship of the subscription concerts (at the Gewandhaus) and the Sing-Akademie, and moreover I would only need to spend the winter half of the year there, and could spend the summer months as I chose, which is what I desired; in return they offer 400 thalers, and would probably pay

600, and have promised the directorship of St. Thomas' School, with 1,000 thalers. Finally Bärmann in Munich has already exchanged several letters with me trying to persuade me to come to Munich, for the director there wants to offer me 1,800–2,000 florins to accept the post at the theater; financially this would be for the best, but it would be at a theater of which I am somewhat leery. Speaking for Leipzig is its proximity to all of you; and finally, speaking for remaining here is that they all appear to wish it strongly and would certainly be unhappy to see my resignation. But these are all considerations that first come into play after you have answered my aforementioned questions, therefore I beg you once again for a very timely reply. As I was pondering this morning what I should write to Leipzig and it occurred to me that I could ask you about it first, I suddenly felt quite cheerful. Farewell, dear Father, the mail is leaving; a thousand thanks for your lovely and friendly New Year's letter. Your

Felix Mendelssohn Bartholdy

The publisher Friedrich Kistner's private initiative to obtain Mendelssohn as musical editor in Leipzig was followed by the offer to direct the famed Leipzig Gewandhaus, presented to Mendelssohn by Schleinitz and Rochlitz on behalf of the "concerts management." The whole thing was so ingeniously maneuvered—for Kistner too was a board member of the concerts management—that Mendelssohn was only able to put up a diplomatic resistance in his letter to the Leipzig attorney Schleinitz, and then immediately offered a cautious acceptance to Rochlitz, a renowned musical authority. For the directorship of the Gewandhaus concerts was one of the most important musical posts in central Europe.

To Heinrich Konrad Schleinitz

Düsseldorf, January 26, 1835

Esteemed Sir,

Please accept my sincere thanks for your gracious note and the friendly disposition toward me which it bespeaks. That it would be a pleasure for me to find such an extensive circle of influence in your city as you describe you can well imagine, since it is my only desire to further the cause of music down the path which seems right to me, and with that I would gladly accept a calling which would place the means of doing so within my reach. But I would not be pleased if such a declaration caused me to give offense to anyone else, and I would not wish to occupy a post from which I had had to force out a predecessor; first, I consider it unjust, and in addition such a quarrel would no doubt bring nothing but harm to music. So before I can give you a definitive answer I must ask you to clarify a few matters which I cannot quite discern from your letter, namely: On behalf of whom would such an appointment be made? With whom would I be dealing, a society, or individuals, or a board? And would I be offending some other musician by accepting? This last matter I bid you to answer me quite candidly, and put yourself in my position, in that I would never either directly or indirectly wish to force someone else from his position. It is another matter when such a post is to be vacated anyway. Furthermore, it is not clear to me from your letter how the director of the Sing-Akademie could be engaged with the summer half of the year free to himself, for you know how indispensable continuous

practicing is to precisely this type of institution, and
how therefore nothing could be accomplished in half a
year which would not be lost in the next. Or is there
another director there, who would take over the directorship during the summer in my absence? Finally I
confess to you that with regard to pecuniary matters I
would at least not wish to jeopardize my current position,
but of course this too could probably be arranged, since
you write of a benefit concert, and we would no doubt
be able to come to an agreement on this matter.

But all of these are questions for later; the main point
on which I desire an answer from you is: whether the
position of which you write to me is vacant or whether
my reply to you will contribute to its becoming vacant?
In the latter case I would refrain from making any
asseveration and prefer to remain here, and I hope you
would approve of my views on this matter. In the
former case, on the other hand, I strongly request that
you answer my aforementioned questions, but in particular that you let me know to whom I would be
responsible, with whom I would be dealing, in this post.

But please do not misunderstand these reservations,
and do not think that I am any less grateful to you for
the great kindness you show me. But before I can say
for certain that I would want to give up a position such
as the one I hold here—which holds a number of
attractions for me and from which they would not like
to release me—I consider it necessary to understand
clearly what I will be taking on in return and whether
I will come sufficiently closer to the goals of my musical
life in so doing that I can reconcile myself to the change
and the serious disruptions it entails. I am being quite
candid with you, and hope you will not take it amiss;
in any case I ask that you gratify me with a reply very

soon, and believe me that I am and shall always remain thankful to you for your entire lovely letter, as well as for all of the honor it does me. With deepest respect, yours faithfully,

Felix Mendelssohn Bartholdy

To Friedrich Rochlitz

Düsseldorf, April 16, 1835

Esteemed Privy Councillor,

Once again I have occasion to thank you, and most deeply and sincerely at that, this time for the friendly note which you enclosed with the letter from the directors of your concert series. You know well how gratifying it would be to me to live in your city and work at an institution such as the one there, and you know how pleased I was to see your handwriting accompanying such lovely prospects right from the start. I am still convinced that it is largely to your generosity that I owe this joy and all of the confidence placed in me by the directors, by which I am so honored. Therefore I hope you will permit me to implore you to remain so gracious and kind to me, and help to clear away the difficulties which still stand in the way of my coming, which I shall describe in greater detail in a letter to the gentlemen of the board. For if it is possible at all, then you will surely know best. If sometime, then, I really could enjoy the pleasure of discussing and choosing the music for the concerts with you, as you suggest— then I should want to thank you in person, more properly than I can do now in writing. Farewell and remain kindly disposed toward me, who with deepest respect remain your most faithful,

Felix Mendelssohn Bartholdy

P.S. I have not yet received the communication from the ministry which you mentioned in your letter, but did not want to delay my reply any longer.

To Rudolf Schramm

Düsseldorf, May 5, 1835

Esteemed President,

In the wake of our recent discussion I am allowing myself to remind you of the request I made at that time, and to entreat you to convey its purport to the Musical Arts Committee at its next meeting, while expressing my sincere and heartful gratitude to its honorable members for all of the kindness and generosity they have displayed toward me during the entirety of my stay here. If I find it necessary to resign my present post at the conclusion of the second year, it is solely from considerations pertaining to the musical path which lies before me. That is, it is my desire to be of as much service to the course of good music as lies within my power. But I have had to convince myself that I am not in the position of being able to fulfill the post here as well as another with other qualities would be; for whatever advantage I might perhaps have over someone else in musical capability I lack in routine, in the calm working through of difficulties, which is of greater importance to this particular position. In the long run it would have given rise to tensions, and it is my only wish that I be the first to recognize this, before anyone else does. Yet I can rest assured that during the time I have been associated with the Committee for Music I have worked to the best of my abilities, and I believe I can say that in some respects progress and improvement have been unmistakable. I am convinced that this progress will be greatly magnified under the musical direction of another, if the committee persists in its beneficent activity to that end, and grants to another musician, who does not lack for the aforementioned qualities, the same confidence and participation, for which I now wish to convey my sincere thanks, and the pleasant memory of which I shall always guard. In asking you to kindly deliver my thanks to the committee I remain, with deepest respect, Your Excellency's most faithful

Felix Mendelssohn Bartholdy

THE LEIPZIG YEARS

The post Mendelssohn found in Leipzig was an ideal one for him; the best orchestra in Germany was entrusted to his care, he had sufficient time to compose, and was able to meet his obligations abroad as well. Finally, and in contrast to Berlin, he found a circle of people from all sorts of professions that appealed to him in this city of book publishing. He felt at home here, especially after his marriage to Cécile Jeanrenaud from Frankfurt, which took place without extensive consultation with his mother and sisters.

Naturally Berlin, something of a sore point for him, sometimes forced itself on the by now famous composer. There was much official correspondence, and the entire family even relocated there, but despite all of the esteem in which Mendelssohn held Kaiser Friedrich Wilhelm IV no satisfactory solution was ever found. The young Mendelssohn couple moved back to Leipzig together with their three children.

Though Mendelssohn's life had always been a hectic one, the pace of his last years in Leipzig became almost breathtaking. The preparation of the Gewandhaus concerts, including even reading the proofs for the printed programs, the conductor's campaign to improve the social standing of his orchestra musicians, the engagement of such soloists as Clara Novello, Clara Wieck, and Henriette Schröder-Devrient (always in consultation with the gentlemen from concerts management), the correspondence with his composer colleagues (Louis Spohr, whom Mendelssohn regarded very highly, Robert Franz, and Niels W. Gade)—it was all difficult to manage without assistants.

Here one may observe that he typically avoided written judgments about compositions, preferring to deliver them orally; usually his comments pertained only to the technical side of performances he had conducted. All of these letters are in the composer's own hand, and he dictated to his wife only at his bedside when ill, then still signing them.

In addition to this "official" correspondence he continued to exchange letters with his friends. Next to Klingermann, the Leipzig attorney Heinrich Konrad Schleinitz became one of his closest; Schleinitz was also a member of the board of directors for the Gewandhaus and had a say in concerts management. Mendelssohn, of course, often wrote to his publishers and had to thank German and foreign musical societies, choral groups, and musical-arts academies for the honorary memberships he was granted.

His ties to Leipziger Strasse 3 in Berlin remained close, although as time went on the household became emptier. As in years past, detailed reports were provided; following the death of his mother in December 1842 they were addressed only to Fanny and his brother Paul. The latter grew ever closer to his famous brother, as confidant in all legal matters and as custodian of the family estate, especially since travel between Berlin and Leipzig was greatly improved and quickened by a newly opened railroad line.

But only until everything fell apart in 1847. Mendelssohn, severely shaken by the death of his sister Fanny, sought refuge in Switzerland with his family and that of his brother. Rested and full of new plans for a trip to Vienna, he died unexpectedly in Leipzig following a brief illness. All Europe mourned his death.

To Abraham Mendelssohn Bartholdy

Leipzig, September 10, 1835

Dear parents,

First, my heartfelt thanks for your lovely letter, which made me very happy. Please, dear Father, do continue sending along a few lines to me; you well know what a joy it is to me, and please write as often and as much as possible, so that we can hold as good a conversation as is possible from twenty miles apart. I intend to continue writing regularly every week, even if only briefly, i.e., except when I have to write or answer more often. Doubtless not much of interest will arise, but there will always be subject matter and time enough to make for a few signs of life. How nice that right at the start of our correspondence this time a coincidence has arisen which continues to give me pleasure: namely, the day before I received the letter I had taken lodgings and thus followed to the letter the advice I was to receive only later. For although they are exceedingly expensive, they are also most charming and comfortable, so that every morning I am happy to have them, which even justifies the cost in that they put me in a good mood for composing and make me feel assiduous and domesticated, so that in the three days in which I have lived there so far I have already gotten some work accomplished. I was so weary and exhausted from searching for accommodations that I was thinking of moving to an inn because I most certainly did not want to impose on Hauser for more than a week; but each and every flat was worse and seemed more unfriendly than the last. I saw only the staircase in some of them before turning quickly around, and was asked to pay thirty thalers per month for a room and bedroom on the third floor—for the impending fair gives people strange ideas about prices. Then at last I found these lodgings on the second floor, which consist of two large, elegant rooms with morning sunlight, and are located in the best part of town. Of course it costs twenty thalers per month, but as said I would gladly part with them, for it is altogether delightful, with very friendly neighbors, large, solidly closing windows, very elegant curtains, albescent wallpaper, a red sofa, and a large stove. So I am always pleased when I come in from the outside, and I don't like to go back out. Believe it or not, by the way, I arise every morning at seven and am working by eight after finishing my breakfast in the sunshine. Hauser had been coming to my bedside every morning with his viola and woke me with the most awfully gentle tones he could coax out of the instrument, so that I became accustomed to getting up early, and plan to continue this custom thanks to the barber who comes at seven. I am pleased far beyond all expectation with my reception here; if it keeps up the winter will be a very pleasant one indeed. I can hear my overtures being played outdoors by complete string orchestras from the large garden by the kitchen and in the morning at the fountains, and even these orchestras cannot be compared with my orchestra in Düsseldorf—they play so cleanly and in unison and musically, so that I certainly look forward to much joy from the Concert Orchestra, which is supposed to be the elite of Leipzig. Next week there is an interim rehearsal at which I am supposed to be ceremoniously introduced to the orchestra by the directors (Rochlitz will want to deliver a very long speech, I suspect), so then we shall see. A tentative repertoire has also been chosen, and it pleases me well; I thought it was nice of them that they insisted that I should *not* play in the first concert, and not offer my new overture until the second one, although I had said I was prepared to do both in the first concert. They insisted, however, that I was their director and that anything else was extra, and that they mustn't toss off everything in the very first concert as if the pieces were just clever trifles. Thus my *Melusine* will not come until the second concert, and my concerto and *Calm Sea* won't be until the third one. The first (on October 4) will begin with Weber's *Beherrscher der Geister*, then comes an *Aria in blanco*, then a double concerto for two local violinists, then a quintet from *Ali Baba* which has never been performed here before, and in the second half a Beethoven symphony to conclude the concert.[1] Moscheles will probably be in attendance, since he will be giving a concert here shortly afterward. He will meet his mother here and stay for several days before returning to Hamburg, as he has informed me in a very friendly letter he sent here. I asked him to give you some English currency which he is still holding for me, dear Father; it ought to be about sixteen pounds, or a little more, and I ask you to deposit it with my funds. This brings me to the subject of a letter of credit for here, about which I forgot to ask you before leaving. You told me that you could give me one for Frege; from what I have heard here I would do well to become a customer of that house, provided that they are not more expensive than others. But in any case I ask you to send me some such letter very soon, since after prepaying the rent I have only fifteen thalers left over, which will certainly evaporate soon into necessities, trousers, boots, etc. I took my latchkey along by mistake, but have entrusted it to Albert Magnus, who passed through here yesterday, and looked me up between one express mail coach and the next. I hope he will deliver it to you in good order, dear Mother; we reminisced about old times traveling, and he told me some tales from Paris and London that I found interesting. Hiller has prepared the piano reduction of *La Juive*,[2] and according to everything Magnus told me about him, and unfortunately in keeping with everything I see and hear of him, he has jumped on the

1. *Ali Baba*: opera by Luigi Cherubini.
2. *La Juive*: Opera by Jacques Fromenthal Halévy (1835).

great Parisian bandwagon altogether and will probably take things as far as Halévy and Meyerbeer and Herold, becoming universally prized in ten years, and despised in ten more. Chopin and Berlioz want to come here, it is said. Yesterday evening I heard Taubert playing *Lieder ohne Worte (Songs Without Words)* at a social; upon my honor it is just completely crazy to excerpt someone as he does me. He tears me to pieces, adding on all sorts of rubbish of his own. I have bought Cramer's two books of etudes for you, dear Father, and am waiting until Fanny passes through to give them to her so that you too can hear them right away. Once again there are some very pretty ones among them; he has given all of them titles, which in a few cases are so silly and naive that I had to laugh out loud.—Mme. Franck passed through with her sons and tried to persuade me in person, as she had before in writing, to continue the lessons with her son here; but since he has not practiced in the slightest during the whole time since Düsseldorf I declined, saying that first he would have to show some diligence, without which the separation from his family would be all naught. The mother tried to insist, but when I asked her to let her son decide for himself he immediately opted to stay in Breslau, and we parted on completely good terms. I have hereupon happily delivered myself of my letter to Hermann, fulfilled my obligations, and the matter is taken care of.—Dear Mother, I am enclosing three pretty announcements for the anthology; the two together appeared in yesterday's paper here, which I bought for that reason, it costs one penny and that much the advertisements are worth; the other one I had given to me. I hope that they are respectable. Now I am closing, and must be off to St. Thomas' School, where they want to put on some

Seb. Bach for me. Farewell, farewell, dear parents, and remain true to me. Your

Felix MB

To Heinrich Konrad Schleinitz

Berlin, November 25, 1835

My dear Herr Schleinitz,

I ask you to write me in a few words when I am expected back in Leipzig. If it were possible that I would not be needed there until late Monday evening I would prefer it so; I could, however, also arrive Sunday evening. Before then I would not like to take leave of my family. You would also be doing me a great favor if you could put together the repertoire for the next concert without me and have the notice printed; then I would still be able to hold the rehearsals for it myself, since up until now none have been scheduled before Tuesday. I had added Spohr's *Weihe der Töne* for the following concert— but do everything as you see fit. Herr David is here and will arrive together with me in L. Please send me a prompt answer to this. My family is so composed and calm that it is a consolation and an example for me; but I myself can hardly see how I shall carry on with my life. I must try to go on as he would have wanted us to if he were still with us, and hope only that God may grant me sufficient strength and resolve to do so. Farewell. Yours,

Felix Mendelssohn Bartholdy

To Benjamin Mendelssohn

Berlin, November 26, 1835

My dear Benni,
On behalf of my family I am compelled to communicate to you the painful loss which we have suffered. We have lost our father; he departed from us without sickness and suffering, gently and peacefully, on the morning of the 19th at ten-thirty, after having spent the previous evening with Mother and my siblings most cheerfully and happily, as was customary in recent days. Thus his long-held wish for a quick and painless end has been granted by God, and may the latter grant us strength and composure to carry on our lives in the wake of such an irreplaceable loss. Mother and my siblings are as physically well and composed as can be expected; Mother in particular is a consolation and an example for us all. She sends her regards to you and has charged me with telling you that even in the last days Father took such a lively interest in your book, and was gladdened by your dignified appearance therein and hoped it would provide the entire family with much happiness. The loss we have all suffered cannot even be comprehended in the first few days. Farewell, dear Benni, and regards to your wife from all of us. Your
                    Felix Mendelssohn Bartholdy

To Friedrich Schneider

Leipzig, March 21, 1836

Esteemed Kapellmeister,
I have only now gotten around to returning to you the parts which you were so kind as to send to us for the subscription concert here, and to thanking you gratefully for them. Unfortunately we did not have an opportunity to hear the second symphony performed, which you enclosed along with the one in B minor, and since there was no full score, I was not able to become acquainted with it myself. On the other hand I think you would have been very pleased by the performance of the B minor symphony had you been in attendance; it was precise and lively and the audience applauded repeatedly, in particular after the Andante, which the orchestra rendered best of all. In the first movement I might have wished for a few better horn players; thereafter they too did their best and acquitted themselves without mistakes, although to be sure not very beautifully. The last movement and the Scherzo on the other hand went almost completely impeccably. Please accept once again my thanks for sending this work and for the pleasure that you have given everyone by so doing.

Your new oratorio will probably not have a chance to be heard in Leipzig very soon, though, for at the moment the amateur singers appear to be lacking in spirit and initiative—and to have your choruses performed by the Thomas Choir alone would seem ill-advised to me, since to me it seems intrinsically calculated for female voices. It had not once been possible to perform a single larger choral work all winter, and I almost fear that this deficit will not soon be made up.

Pardon me, esteemed Kapellmeister, for the haste of these lines, but I am so overwhelmed with all sorts of business lately that soon I might not be able to get around to writing at all. But I didn't want to allow the music to be returned without conveying my thanks and best regards to you. Farewell and think kindly of your faithful

Felix Mendelssohn Bartholdy

To Fanny Hensel

Leipzig, March 28, 1836

Dear Fanny,

I need hardly tell you how happy your lovely visit here made me and how nice it was of you to come; you know what delight you have brought me, but I still want to put down in a few short words how much I thank you for it, and have it in writing. Of course I had wanted to write that same day, and it is wrong of me not to have, but I am so overwhelmed with work that is now becoming so urgent that I have had to summon all my strength. You sent a lovely layer cake to our group, it is true, and even wrote a nice letter; Schleinitz had invited us to Schlemmer's farewell party on Friday at noontime, and then the cake and the songs arrived just in the nick of time and we were most delighted. They wanted to write you such a wonderfully nice letter that in the end I think they still haven't done it at all; you are supposed to receive a gold certificate as a member of the Leipzig club. Moreover there were great discussions about how much cake the Schuncks and Mathilde

Clarus should have—David claimed each should get one bite and no more, and what has become of it now I don't even know, since I can't get out very often; in any case I thank you most fervently for my portion of sugar cake and even more for the pretty song in F major with the variation, and the even prettier one in C major. Some other time I should describe to you in full detail what pleasure you afforded the Leipzig Friends of Music by your playing, and how often and intently it is still being discussed. But for today no more than that I shall never forget your lovely visit and that you shall always have my most heartfelt gratitude for it.

If only I hadn't grumbled at you so the last evening and morning! It is strange that as long as we were together I hardly thought of it, but when I found myself sitting alone in the coach it weighed heavily upon my heart, and I should like to have given myself a thrashing. I know well that you will forgive me for it, but I have not been able to quite pardon myself yet.

Anyway that's how I was and am, but hope however that I shall become better. In spite of the cold and the wind everything is continually turning green, spring will soon be here, and then I must be off again. But remain true to me, and think of your Leipzig visit from time to time with a measure of the delight that it has afforded me. And for this I thank you too, Hensel, and my regards to you, and kiss Sebastian for me, and may you both be granted whatever your hearts desire. Your

Felix MB

To Heinrich Konrad Schleinitz

Frankfurt, June 30, 1836

Dear silent Schleinitz,

Can such a thing be plausible? Isn't your own hair standing on end? That I, the worst correspondent in the kingdom, am writing for the second time already, and you, one of the best, have yet to write one at all. What important questions I posed in my letter from Cologne just to force you to reply, but you continue calmly putting it off—over fifty days already—and by the time it occurs to you it will surely be too late. I have just received an entire letter on upcoming concert matters from Councillor Dörrien, which you would certainly have received if you had not remained silent so long; but I don't really want to assert that or in the end you shall not write me at all. Seriously, are you still alive? I repeat herewith my entire letter from Cologne.

And Henriette Grabau arrived and David arrived and still no one writes me half a line, I who wait with daily apprehension here in beautiful Frankfurt for word to arrive. My address is c/o Herr M. J. Herz. But you know that already. Oh Schleinitz! This is atrocious beyond all atrocity; I am writing this entire letter *con fuoco*.

I am still at work preparing the manuscript of my oratorio for publication and would give much to have it done with already. But in a week it will be finished; then I plan to do absolutely nothing for a week. Eat cherries, draw, go walking with Schlemmer, lunch and dine with Hiller, conduct the Caecilienverein each Wednesday, read what Eckermann has to say about Goethe, visit a few pretty girls, bathe in the Main River in the morning, which flows beneath my window—these are to be my only occupations, as so far they have also tended to be. Toward the end of July I am thinking of leaving here and going to a seaside resort. And at the beginning of September, God willing, we shall see each other again.

How are things with the female choir from Prague, and with the tenor? Before we forget, the notice for the first subscription concert must be sent to the printer. The cellist Breuer, who played at the Düsseldorf Music Festival, and whom David got to know, would very much like to come to Leipzig. I have also written to Dörrien of this; the main issue is the pecuniary one—I didn't know what to tell him the salary for the position would amount to approximately. Then there is also the question of whether the change is desirable in the first place, or whether perhaps the orchestra ought to remain exactly as is during the coming winter? You know my opinion on the matter, and how much it seems to me that vocal works are the main thing for the time being. In addition to this cellist, who is an excellent orchestral player but less good as a soloist, by the way, I also found an altogether outstanding oboist and a similarly excellent hornist on my trip, both of whom would be happy to change their current positions. If you should perhaps hear of an orchestra in which there is an opening, please do me the favor of writing me to let me know, for they are absolutely *outstanding*. Perhaps Kistner may even know of a vacancy. No doubt instrumentalists are not in demand everywhere; but the tenor! That is my *denique censeo*.

They have offered to appoint me permanent director of the Caecilienverein, since unfortunately it does not seem that Schelble will be taking on the job. The

conditions would be most agreeable, and two years ago
I would have accepted with the greatest pleasure, but
now I can assure you that I was not sorry for a moment
that I had already given my word for the coming winter,
because my previous obligation has granted me nothing
but satisfaction and pleasure musically, and because I
feel truly grateful for it and am already looking forward
to the coming winter and the Leipzig Orchestra.—And
I don't fail to praise it loudly whenever the subject
comes up, either; Aloys Schmitt, the hypochondriac,
answered me recently that in Leipzig people are no
doubt the same as everywhere else, after all. No objec-
tions could be raised thereto.

They gave a *diner* for Rossini, which I must spend a
whole evening describing to you alone in a hotel sometime. You will laugh as you did at the way things turned
out in Düsseldorf. Meanwhile picture Rossini overflow-
ing with enthusiasm for Sebastian Bach, and for German
music, and for my *Melusine* and *Hebrides*, etc., etc.; a
spectacle for the gods themselves. But he patiently
insisted upon it and we swore eternal friendship (à la
Parisienne). He swore to me that I must visit him in
Italy, where I could obtain as much pretty music as I
wanted, and just as many pretty girls. For the Germans,
he said, all had overly large feet. I said I didn't think
so.—They played a serenade for him, which went badly,
and they came close to messing it up completely. When
later they appologized to him the rascal said that there
were two kinds of music: With the one everything
depends on the performance, and that type had always
been loathsome to him—but the other kind was the
language of the heart, and that was *his* favorite music,
and that was the kind they had just played for him.
Whereupon they were all delighted by how charming

he was. If he had told them that they should do it better they would have said he was an arrogant wretch. What is your opinion? Should one remain an honest man?

You would do me a great favor by having the fugue in B minor for piano copied from the green composition book I gave to you when I left and sending it to me by stagecoach. It begins like this:

It would be very nice if I could have the copy here as soon as possible. It would also be nice, now that I think of it, if you would perhaps instead write me a few lines and report to me whether you are still alive?

Were I to speak of giving my regards now the letter would become twice as long. Even so my regards above all to your dear wife, and please ask her in my name to see to it that you write me very soon, and say hello to the Schuncks, whose relatives here are very lovely people, to whom I am often indebted for the pleasant company they have provided me with (tomorrow evening, for example, we are playing trios there, Schlemmer on the piano, Benecke on the bass, and I on the violin), and give my regards to the Claruses, to whom I myself wrote several days ago, and to David, Henriette Grabau, Weiss, Carus, Porsche, and Limburger. How is my piano doing? I have often wished I could have it here. And now farewell and remain true to me. Yours,

Felix MB

To Lea Mendelssohn Bartholdy

Frankfurt, July 24, 1836

Dear Mother,

A thousand thanks for your lovely, friendly letter, and for telling me for certain that sometimes you would have liked to write but stopped yourself because there was no letter from me there—truly it shall not happen again. You cannot have any idea how happy you make me every time you write, and when I on the other hand was forced to respond with only my dull, dry notes to let you know I'm alive I preferred to put it off until better days, and thus arose the long lapses about which you were angry with me. But it shouldn't happen again. Now I am preparing for my departure to the Hague, which is set for the day after tomorrow. Schadow will be coming along, and will pick me up here today or tomorrow; thus my address for the next three weeks is *poste restante* in the Hague. But I shall hardly be able to stand it there for much longer than three weeks—I don't know what I would give to be able to stay here in Frankfurt the whole time, with the nice girl about whom I already wrote last time, and with her charming family. I have spent the first truly merry hours of this year there and felt freer and happier than I have felt for a long time. The older people, the Souchays, are a bit too upstandingly Frankfurt-like for me, and weren't quite to my liking at first; but the younger Souchays and Beneckes (whom Paul also knows) and Madame Jeanrenaud, a daughter of the house with her own altogether delightful daughters—these are the kind of people I like and who are good for me, and moreover they all live in the same house, as we did at Leipziger Strasse No. 3, and the place is swarming with pretty children, and Schlemmer, a cousin, is passing through the house and causing not a little uproar, and this whole family life and the many pretty, happy people warm my heart greatly, and I have been counting the hours until I can be there. Beneckes and Schlemmer have only been gone for two weeks now, the former to Switzerland and Schlemmer back to Leipzig; but the Souchays and Jeanrenauds are still here and really the main attraction anyway. You can well imagine that I have been there as often as possible lately, and how I could thank them for all the kindness they have shown me I don't know, nor how I shall take to Scheveningen after such a while. To be sure, I am still constantly in a downcast and sad mood here, almost always when I was not there. But in my piano reduction I had one of the most tedious tasks I have ever had to undertake, and I was often beside myself over the tiresome and imperceptible progress I was making despite my best intentions. But as of yesterday, though, the entire work (all the way up to the final chorus) is out of the stable, or rather into the printer's, and so I hope that soon I shall be finished with this work, which has now occupied me for over two years. How glad I shall then be if something therein pleases you and if you think that Father would have found it agreeable, as you told me. A week ago today Alexander and his three boys got me out of bed, and I spent the whole day with him and his family, accompanied them to the watchtower in Mainz and then came back on foot. They are all the most charming, decent people, and pleased me exceedingly. This morning the door opened and four deputies of the Caecilienverein, clad in black, walked in and handed me a traveling kit of such elegance and splendor as I have never seen before, at first for a moment I was only sorry that I couldn't show it to you. It has three compartments with every possible variety of razors, scissors, writing and washing and brushing implements made of silver and ivory and velvet, and with that special English solidity and cleanness that I like so well. On top are engraved the words "FMB Caecilia." Isn't that sweet? I still have to tell you that I have read the first books of Goethe's *Dichtung und Wahrheit* here with the most supreme pleasure. I hadn't picked it up since my boyhood days because then I didn't like it, but I cannot even tell you how much I like it now, and over and above that how refreshing I find all of the localities, with which I am now familiar. A single page of it puts all of the present miseries in literature and art out of my mind.

Now a thousand thanks for the financial matters about which you wrote to me, and for the gifts you offer me. And who would no sooner accept them than I! Of course some difficulties will no doubt arise between here and there, but you know how strongly the wish has made itself felt to me since last autumn, and I believe my entire good fortune or misery depends on it.—Dear Mother, do ask Fanny to forgive me for not writing much these days and for not being able to answer her lovely letter; she would greatly oblige me by sending me some news now and then even so. How happy I was to hear in detail from her about *St. Paul*, and her musical undertakings. Oh Fanny, write again, and don't be angry with me. And to you, dear Mother, farewell and think of your

Felix MB

To Lea Mendelssohn Bartholdy

Frankfurt, September 9, 1836

Dear Mother,
At this moment, as I walk back into my room, the only thing I can do is write you that I have just become engaged to Caecilie Jeanrenaud. My head is spinning from what I have experienced today, it is already far into the night, I don't know what else to say, but I had to write to you. How rich and happy my life is. Tomorrow, if at all possible, I shall write you in greater detail, and if possible my dear betrothed as well.

Your letter is lying right here, I opened it in order to make sure that you are all well, but have not yet been able to read it. I am also writing these lines to you, dear Fanny, to Mother and you. Farewell and stay close to me always.

Felix MB

P.S. The family tells me it would be desirable not to make it public for a while, therefore I ask you not to mention it to *anyone*.

To Louis Spohr

Leipzig, December 13, 1836

Esteemed Kapellmeister,
You would never believe how happy your letter and pretty song for my bride's album have made me. I cannot yet even begin to express to you how salutary it is for me to read a letter from you, or how much I

should like to thank you for it. But above all now for the pretty song, which is so perfectly suited to my fiancée's voice, and which will bring her so much joy. But then also for what you write me about your new overture and for the prospects of having and hearing it here soon. You tell me that my *Melusine* overture may have contributed to its genesis, and that is doubtless the dearest and greatest honor you could have done me, and makes me fond of my piece all over again. The gentlemen of the board for the subscription concerts, to whom I was able to convey your letter immediately after receiving it, have charged me with thanking you many times over on their behalf for the gracious offer of your overture, and to tell you how pleased and honored they feel by it, and to ask you to send it as soon as possible so that we can rehearse and perform it immediately upon receiving it. I am also to take this opportunity to repeat the request that whenever you have a new piece which might be suitable for the Leipzig subscription concerts you should not forget to entrust it to us as soon as possible for performance, for we shall arrange one as soon as is at all feasible, and certainly shall all work to the best of our abilities to achieve a worthy performance.

I am writing you in great haste and therefore beg your pardon, but I am leaving in a few hours for Frankfurt, and thus you can imagine that things are a bit hectic. Unfortunately the time allotted me is so short that I won't even be able to spend a full two weeks there, and even so will have to travel day and night en route there and back; thus I cannot accept your friendly offer to come through Cassel, as much as I should like to thank you in person for the lovely song, and as much as I should like to play duets quite a number of times with you. Perhaps I shall come again to Cassel during the course of the summer or fall, and how greatly that would please me you well know. You must have my *St. Paul* by now—at least, the piano reduction has been available here for about two weeks. I would ask you to address the package with the overture to Herr W. Härtel here, unfranked. And now there remain my fond greetings to your honored family, to Hauptmann, to Frau von Malsberg, and the request to pardon me for these hasty lines, written in the pleasant chaos of departure. Continue your generosity and kindness toward me and accept once again my sincere thanks and the admiration of your faithful

Felix Mendelssohn Bartholdy

To Lea Mendelssohn Bartholdy

Frankfurt, March 24, 1837

Dear Mother,

I must report to you our safe arrival here in great haste and with just a few brief words. You know that my wedding is set for next Tuesday, thus you can imagine how much there is to take care of and attend to in these last few days. Until yesterday the papers still were not in order, for the gentlemen from Frankfurt are even more narrow-minded and difficult than usual, but yesterday a letter from Schleinitz arrived providing all of the proper attestations, "that I am not yet married, that I am not a vagabond," and such rubbish, and now everything is set for Tuesday, God willing. We will be wed at eleven, and in the afternoon we are thinking of departing for Mainz, and then slowly on up the Rhine through Speyer, Worms, etc., to Strasbourg, a stretch with which I am not at all yet familiar. We have not yet made a proper itinerary, for if there is still snow and ice we want to spend most of our time in the cities, and if spring should arrive we'll no doubt also manage to come up with an itinerary. I am thinking of returning here toward the end of May, and remaining for a while, but that too is as yet undecided. My address here will remain the same all summer from now on: c/o M. J. Herz.

I had hoped to find here a report of your safe arrival, but in vain. Yet I imagine that you are all well and happy, that no untoward circumstances have prevented you from writing, and look forward to seeing your lovely handwriting each day.

Now, dear Mother, farewell, and give my regards to my sisters. I do not believe that I shall write you again as an unmarried man, but God willing things are as ever between us, and will always remain so. Think so. Think of me on Tuesday, and good-bye. Your

Felix MB

To Lea Mendelssohn Bartholdy

Strasbourg, April 9, 1837

Dear Mother,

I am writing you in great distress over the complete lack of news from you and my sisters; except for the lovely note we received on our wedding day we have had no news from any of you since your departure from Leipzig, and the note contained not a word about your and my sisters' health. I had hoped at the time to be able to assume that you were all well, but since then I checked daily but in vain for letters in Speyer, where

we stayed for over a week, and received all sorts of
other letters but not the ones I was hoping for. I am
becoming alarmed and implore you to write me immediately at the address of M. J. Herz and tell me what
this long silence is about. I am doubly apprehensive
because my sisters were sick recently, and am causing
myself much anxiety. Please come to my rescue soon.

For this is the only dark spot on these otherwise
altogether happy, blissful weeks. You cannot imagine
how good I feel, and how sweet life is with my dear
Cécile. We are enjoying it to the fullest, and one day
after the next flies past without any real schedule except
being happy; that one we follow carefully. It has been
a long time since I have immersed myself in the present
so cheerfully. We want to be back in Frankfurt by the
beginning of May—that much we are sure of—but of
nothing further. It depends largely on the weather,
which has again become so fiercely cold and wintry that
all of the peach and other blossoms have been killed by
the frost here in Loerach. The day before yesterday we
could not even begin our trip at all because it was
snowing all day, and then yesterday we still had to drive
here from Speyer through the deep snow. Should it
become warm and springlike again we will go to Freiburg the first nice day and remain there a week or
longer; if not we shall soon turn around and head back.
And yet how splendid was yesterday's trip through the
deep snow drifts, the countryside looks wonderfully
beautiful, and above all I was delighted by how France
suddenly made its appearance at the border with all its
different customs and people, with French speech and
food and manners. Such polite *douaniers*, and postilions
with their pleated hair and boots who paddle with their
arms while riding on horseback and crack their whips

when they ride through a village, and French signs with their big wide letters, and the yellow placards one can read from a hundred paces away, and fifty sous de guide—it all begins right at the border, and reminds me so oddly and strongly of Father and his favorite country that I kept talking about him to Cécile all the time, and thinking of him.

This morning I ran over to the cathedral and have never been so impressed by architecture in all my life. It is the most wonderful thing I have seen, and I am still full of rapture from simply strolling back and forth in front of and inside it, for first I wanted to just look around cursorily, and plan to become better acquainted with it little by little. The day after tomorrow I shall write Beckchen; then I shall provide you with a thorough report on all of our life and doings here and in Speyer. But this afternoon I have to go back to the cathedral, this evening to the theater with Cécile, and besides I am so besieged with letters requiring replies. Pardon me then for closing, I would like to write longer and more. Tell Fanny that at the cathedral I saw the beautiful stained-glass windows across from a Silbermann organ with thirty-two-foot pipes, which engenders my respect even to look at it, and doesn't make a bad impression at all—tomorrow I plan to become acquainted with it more intimately. And tell her that in Speyer I composed three organ preludes, among other things, which will be published soon, and I hope that one or even two of them will be particularly well received.

But above all please put my mind at ease with regard to all of your well-being, for even as I write all this I begin to feel so anxious again, and I would like to first see your or my sisters' handwriting on the address.

Allow me to hope that everything is well and as usual, and for a cheerful reunion. Your

Felix

Dear Mother,

I also wanted to ask you in a few brief words today to comfort my Felix and me soon with news, for we are anxious on account of his dear sisters. Please, please dear Mother, grant our wish and pardon my haste, the dinner bells are being sounded. As ever your loving daughter,

Cécile

To The Gesellschaft der Musikfreunde

Leipzig, October 12, 1837

To the Friends of Music Society of the Austrian Empire, I did not have the honor of receiving the communication and certificate whereby I am designated an honorary member of your organization until a few days ago after returning here from a long journey, and thus first of all must beg your forgiveness for the lateness of my thanks. The distinction which the society has conferred upon me is particularly precious, and obliges me all the more to convey my most enthusiastic gratitude in that I had scarcely believed that my musical works would have won friends even at such a great distance, and since it is all the more unexpected that one of the foremost societies in the German fatherland would have encouraged and recognized my efforts. For this encouragement and the great honor it does me I would very much like to express my appreciation, tell you how grateful I am for it, and with what esteem I shall always remain the esteemed Friends of Music Society of the Austrian Empire's most faithful

Felix Mendelssohn Bartholdy

To Ottilie von Goethe

Leipzig, December 1, 1837

Dear Ottilie,

Since I hear that it has now been decided that the Weimar court is *not* going to Berlin, and since Clara Novello is thinking of departing from here at the end of next week, I wanted to make inquiries to you on her behalf once more—whether you would advise her to stop in Weimar, whether she might be able to sing at the court there or during the entr'actes—and finally, how much of her time it would take and what (approximately) the honorarium would amount to? Pardon me for imposing on you once more; one gladly wagers on someone else's behalf what one would never ask for oneself. And I don't want Miss Novello to return to England with an unfavorable impression of German musical life. Thus my repeated questions and requests, above all for a reply as soon as possible. If you think that she would be able to make an appearance there during a stay of a week's time, I believe that she will come and will sing some splendid things for you. You would be very pleased.

One more request. If it happens that you are asked for your opinion, or mine, of a young conductor named Julius Rietz from Düsseldorf, or have the opportunity to say anything on his behalf, then I bid you to please do so. He is a most talented, accomplished, and circumspect musician, a friend of mine since our childhood days and very highly regarded (I have often mentioned his deceased brother to you, a friend of my youth); moreover he is an outstanding cellist, with the most gentle, pure tone, composes quite lovely pieces—his newer pieces in particular are first-rate—and thus his is certainly one of the few outstanding, true artist's souls which Germany possesses among its musicians. I write you this in order to ask you to do what you can on his behalf, should the opportunity arise as it well may.

As for Walter, who seems physically and spiritually better than ever lately, and is visibly progressing in his development, I hope to be able to tell you more than I can write—for according to your promise we shall soon see you here. Make it come true, and come soon.

Many, many thanks for the grammar book, which has been altogether a boon for my little St. Thomas' School pupils. And many regards to Ulrike from me, and to both of you from Cécile, who is as healthy and rosy-cheeked, thank goodness, as when you last saw her. Yours as ever,

Felix Mendelssohn Bartholdy

To Paul Mendelssohn Bartholdy

Leipzig, February 11, 1838

Dear Paul,

This letter is a request to stand godfather and a solemn invitation to you and Albertine to attend the baptism. You once let me know via Fanny that you wanted to come here for the baptism—half in jest—but now take it seriously and come! We discussed it back and forth this morning, but the end result was that we were unable to schedule anything until we knew when you were coming (for we no longer have the slightest doubt about whether); then the baptism will take place. So tell us. But don't come too late, so that Mme. Jeanrenaud, who must leave for Frankfurt soon, will still be here. What do you think of two weeks from now? Or perhaps three weeks at the latest?

Cécile, thank goodness, is so well that it is a joy in itself, and a good fortune for which I cannot be grateful enough. Clarus was just here, found no traces of fever, and now since the fourth day is already drawing to a close I look cheerfully forward, God willing, to her complete recuperation soon.

I am looking forward tremendously to seeing you again, my dear brother, and when you and Albertine have met Cécile, and everything has gone well, and if the weather stays warm, we can have you stay with us, which would be most lovely; but I can only suggest it if the weather is warm, for in cold weather the larger rooms on the north side, which are reserved for you, cannot be heated and are uncomfortable. But if it continues to thaw and spring comes, as indeed it seemed to a few days ago, then you must.

I just don't seem to be making any headway with writing—I hope to be able to speak to you soon, to see you, make music with you, go walking—that is better than a letter. But I still must thank you for your most recent lovely one, in which you enlightened ignorant me a little bit about paper management. What can I do about the fact that you are so musical and I can never return the favor in kind?

Farewell for today, dear Paul; write me soon and respond to our invitation and accept it! Cécile sends her very best regards to you and Albertine. Remain true to me. Your

Felix

To Karl Wilhelm August Porsche

Leipzig, March 29, 1838

Esteemed City Councillor,
The former clarinetist in our orchestra, Drobisch, approached me in writing yesterday and asked me to put in a good word with you, since he believes that you would then be more disposed to grant his wish. Namely, he mentions in his letter to me that after *nineteen* years of service in the orchestra he can scarcely maintain himself and his family on a pension of eight thalers and his small salary as a choir member, and that he has therefore already petitioned the city council for the vacant copyist's position at Windmühlentor, that this position is the object of his desire (as he puts it), and asks me to put in a good word to you for him. I can think of no better way of doing so than to simply tell you the story, as I have just done, and am convinced that you will certainly be glad to perform such a good service, if it accords with your views on the matter and if you are otherwise pleased with Drobisch, and be happy to help out a needy family owing to your well-known philanthropy. And if I can see an elderly musician and nineteen-year member of the orchestra assisted in this manner, you know that I shall thank you gratefully and first and foremost. Your faithful and devoted

Felix Mendelssohn Bartholdy

To Johann Verhulst

Leipzig, April 16, 1838

Esteemed Sir,
I have looked over the changes made in your overture
in B minor and find that the piece has been decidedly
improved by them; I am especially pleased that you
have so felicitously changed the modulation right at the
beginning and introduction to the middle movement
(which resembled the overture to *Der Freischütz*), and I
am convinced that your work will find many friends in
its present form. I hope it will also soon appear in print,
at least to me it seems completely worthy of being
published, and I am looking forward to this, as well as
to the new overture you have promised me for the
coming winter.
With deepest respect, your most faithful
F. Mendelssohn Bartholdy

To Clara Wieck

Leipzig, December 2, 1838

Esteemed Fräulein,
I would love it if you could play as soon as the next
concert, since this would be the perfect thing to round
it off nicely, as I recently discovered. But of course we
must not give up a single one of your pieces for it! May
I therefore schedule the last movement of the Chopin
concerto after the overtures and the Thalberg Caprice
at the end of the first half on Thursday? I would be
greatly obliged if you could give the bearer of this letter

a reply (if possible a yes) so that he can bring it back to me. And many thanks for this morning. As ever yours faithfully,

Felix Mendelssohn Bartholdy

To Sebastian Hensel

Berlin, February 7, 1839

Dear nephew,

I thank you so much for your letter and congratulations; I was very happy for both, for the letter was well written and in proper style, and the congratulations were surely heartfelt. Karl thanks you very much for his lovely chocolates; he is still too dumb to write himself, otherwise he would certainly do so. Cécile says hello to you and thanks you too for your nice presents. Do you also have such nice sled runs as we have here? If so you must have been quite thrilled. I find it lovely that you have seen an elephant; they are my favorite animals, so strong and powerful and yet so gentle and friendly and wise. Someday you too must become so.

Farewell and greetings to your father and your Aunt Minna. Your uncle

Felix

To Lea Mendelssohn Bartholdy

Leipzig, April 17, 1839

Dear Mother,

Albertine is back with all of you again and will no doubt have provided an accurate and detailed report on our merry life here. I hope she did not forget to ask you to excuse me for my long pause from writing, though, as indeed I asked her to do, and to describe to you how my days disappear into the widest variety of agreeable and disagreeable occupations and leave me with little free time as soon as the Easter Fair begins, and with it the visitors' days in Leipzig. I am now completely resolved once again to write home to you regularly at least every two weeks, and certainly plan to carry out this resolution throughout the summer. You all wanted to know our plans, but at present we have none and are making none at all, other than the ones of which you already know; we want to attend the Düsseldorf Music Festival, all three together (or four, if you count in Hanne), then to Frankfurt for the wedding, remain there a little while until about the middle of June, then to Bingen to sample some wine, then for about a week to Horchheim—and after that follow the advice of the weather, the pocketbook, *et cetera animalia*. Whether I shall travel to Vienna, or to Braunschweig, where they are preparing a music festival, or to Oxford, whither the newspapers are sending me to conduct an orchestra of two thousand persons, as I hear, and about which I have already received a number of inquiries from German musicians who want me to take them along, although I myself have yet to hear a single word on the subject from London, Oxford, or anyplace else, which is not unusual—I cannot yet tell you about any of this, since I would like to be known as a reliable man and still know nothing definite about any of these matters. Today I received a letter from Mary Sabilla, who claims to have visited you again—can it be true? Well, she will have a fine reception in Berlin, if neither Rellstab nor

Russia liked her, since both are important connoisseurs of art—so will the Crown Prince be obliged to make her his protégée?

Drouet should bring along this letter to you, dear Mother. He asked for a few lines of introduction to you, and since I know of few such complete virtuosos as he, and few musicians altogether who can afford me such indescribable pleasure as this magician with his silver-fluted tone, I ask you to do what you can to sweeten his stay. Unfortunately his stay here was soured by a half-empty concert he gave yesterday, and all sorts of annoyances; I hope from my heart that it will go better for him in Berlin, for no one is more deserving of an appreciative audience than he. If you can do anything to fill up his concert, please do so; incidentally I need hardly remind you, you remember, how often Father mentioned Drouet's name and sang his melodies, and how eighteen years ago Father was so completely delighted and taken by him, and that alone should assure him of a good reception from all of you. And when you hear how even after such a long time he plays just as beautifully, tenderly, and faultlessly as he did then, exactly as before, you will find it moving, as I did. Farewell, my dear, dear Mother. I intend to write once more before departing, and certainly hope to hear from you once more. Yours always,

Felix

To Lea Mendelssohn Bartholdy

Leipzig, October 2, 1839

Dear Mother,

At five o'clock this afternoon Cécile was delivered of a

daughter without too much difficulty and thank God in good health. Both are feeling well, and Cécile is just now complaining of hunger and eating beef broth and rolls. I am too dazed to write properly; it has been scarcely an hour and a half, and yet still today's mail is supposed to deliver the good tidings to you. Praise and thanks and glory to God that it all went well. I know you are happy with us and thank heaven with us. Tell all my siblings right away. More tomorrow. When it turned out it was a girl Cécile told me: Now even your mother will be happy with me, for this is what she wanted. I don't know what I am writing. More tomorrow. Your

Felix

To the Music-Publishing House of C. F. Peters

Leipzig, January 6, 1840

Your Excellencies
will receive herewith the corrected copy of the Prelude and Fugue in G Major by Seb. Bach. You will be amazed at the number of mistakes, but I am convinced that I have not yet found all of them, since unfortunately I am not in possession of the manuscript myself and also do not know where it is, and since my handwritten copy is not entirely correct either. In any case it is still more correct than the one which was used for the engraving, and in the doubtful places it is certainly plausible; most of the places which were corrected are beyond doubt, however. In particular there are a number of mistakes in the fugue which I would immediately have corrected at my own risk even without knowing the piece at all or owning a copy of it, and with regard to which old

Bach would have taken you to task quite severely: you have his subject entering with an extra eighth note once on page 7, twice on page 8, and even three times on page 9, and give it altogether dreadful middle voices and harmonies underneath, especially in the last two systems. If you can do anything by way of apology to the honorable fellow I would be obliged. Respectfully, your faithful

Felix Mendelssohn Bartholdy

To Wolf Graf Baudissin

Leipzig, Sunday, March 22, 1840

Esteemed Count,

Liszt, Hiller, and I would like to play Bach's Triple Concerto in D Minor with orchestral accompaniment in a (private) concert at the Gewandhaus which I have arranged. It happens, however, that the parts, which were here earlier, are no longer in Leipzig, and hence my request to you, if you could send me yours tomorrow (Monday) on the train (naturally if there are duplicates then the duplicates as well—the more the better). I hope that you will receive this letter by tonight; in that case it would be best for me if you could have them entrusted to the conductor before six o'clock tomorrow morning with instructions to bring them to me imme-diately after the first train arrives. If that is impossible for you, there would still be enough time if they came on the second train, but *then* the conductor would have to bring them *to the Gewandhaus, not* to the apartment, for our performance is to begin at six in the evening, and the train will not arrive until six-thirty.

Dare I make so bold as to request that you yourself

do us the honor of attending on such short notice? But the performance was not set until late yesterday evening; we plan to play several of my overtures and Psalms, the Schubert symphony, and lastly the concerto, should by virtue of your generosity we receive the parts. If only you yourself would come!

Please excuse these very hasty lines. The mail is leaving, and I am forced to write in the middle of a large number of people.

With deepest respect, Your Excellency's most faithful
Felix Mendelssohn Bartholdy

To Fanny Hensel

July 13, 1840

Once more I am writing you from Berlin, dearest Fanny, but this time without my better half. I received your lovely letter right in the middle of the nastiest troubles pertaining to the Book Publishers' Fair—no doubt you have read of them in the papers—but what they did not tell about was that Mühlenfels, Benni, and Rosa were staying with us, a horde of other out-of-town visitors were coming and going all day long, and that I was made quite dizzy in the head with rehearsals and learning my music. This is a symphony for *chorus* and orchestra in B major; when and where shall I play it for you? Our summer plans are still not fixed; in the next several days I absolutely must write to England to find out if I will be traveling there in mid-August or not.—I actually hope and wish the latter, but as I stated I shall not decide for certain until I am in Leipzig. Until that time we shall surely remain in Leipzig, and our only absence from there might be a week in Dresden, but that amounts to more or less the same thing now thanks to the railroad, and in any case I hope that we shall see other again on your[1] return trip. Until the middle of August any letters addressed to Leipzig will reach me here. Now write soon and say that—and when—you are coming. Pardon these confused lines. Traveling all night, evenings spent in revelry, and the whole Schwerin Music Festival are all buzzing in my head.

Kiss and give my most heartfelt regards to Sebastian and Hensel and be true to your

Felix

To Paul Mendelssohn Bartholdy

Leipzig, November 20, 1840

Dear Paul,

Your wonderful letter gave me the greatest pleasure, and I would have answered it at once in order to give you the information you requested about the *Lobgesang (Hymn of Praise)* had I myself known anything definite about it. Now I hear from Uncle that you are expected in Berlin again around this time, and thus I shall at least state what I can say for certain on the matter, and what I cannot. In the first place, I would very strongly wish that you keep your promise and come here too; I would so much like to hear what you have to say about it, especially since I have by now grown fond of the piece, and would like to see if you like it. I also believe that it will be given a good performance by our orchestra. But in spite of all this, if you would be able to spend

---

1. *Euer* (plural).

a little less time here for this performance than for any of the others I would ask you to come to one of the others. For after all, the most important thing about our days in Leipzig is the lovely, relaxed time spent together with Albertine and Cécile and you and me, and even one extra day gained is pure profit. If both can be combined, a proper household and the concert, then that would be loveliest of all. Whether the piece will be performed, aside from this month, during the course of the winter is not yet certain; but it is very likely probable. But I could not say at all when. Even the day of the upcoming performance has not been settled yet, at this point it is supposed to be a week from Monday, the 30th, and I think it will remain so unless something extraordinary comes up. You know that the concert is for the benefit of the elderly and sick musicians, and that the *Lobgesang* is to make up the second half of it; in the first will probably come Weber's *Jubel-Ouvertüre*, then Kreutzer's Rhine Song, *Sie sollen ihn nicht haben (They Shall Not Have It)*, by the chorus, then an aria by Mademoiselle Schloss, then Beethoven's *Choral Fantasy* including a performance by Herr Kufferath. As for the aforementioned Rhine Song I could write you such a letter of complaints as you wrote me about the state of taste in Hamburg and Liszt's coffee hour. You have no idea how they are applauding it here, and how revolting such journalistic enthusiasm is to me. And moreover to cause such an uproar about it so that the others don't get what is due them! That is worth some real uproar, and some complaining in itself. And when a piece itself is nothing then not a single note ought to be sung, in order not to ruin what one already has. Little boys and fearful people shout about such things, but real men make no production out of what they already have, and instead just have it, and so be it. It annoys me that among other things they recently printed in the papers that in addition to the four compositions which Leipzig has produced (Verhulst, Schmidt from Leipzig and Schmidt from Weimar, and Schumann)[1] there was one other by me which had come to light— my whole name in print, and I cannot punish anyone for slander precisely because I maintain public silence. At the same time the Härtels have informed me that if I should desire to compose it for them they would feel confident enough to print six thousand copies in two months. Well, Paul, that just won't do.—How greatly your opinions about Listz interested me, although I cannot concur with you completely. Have you heard him often or only that one time? The people from Hamburg are *not* planning on my baton at their music festival; at least it did not seem at all to me as if Herr Grund were kindly disposed toward me, and I have heard things to that effect before. But now adieu! A thousand, thousand regards to Albertine, and until we see each other very, very soon. Your

Felix

To Louise Härtel

Leipzig, December 8, 1840

We the undersigned wedded couple do discharge our obligation and legal duty to attest that only by means of urgent compunction and not without judicial remon-

1. Conradin Kreutzer's patriotic *Rhein lied* ("They shall not have it, the free German Rhine") was also set to music by the four composers mentioned.

stration could Herr Raymund Härtel (of the firm of Breitkopf and Härtel) be detained for several hours in the forehouse at Lurgenstein's Garden. May this attestation serve as a legally binding alibi for him in the eyes of the lonely half of his marriage, and contribute toward mediating any possible legal quarrels which may arise in consequence. Such is the wish of

Cécile Mendelssohn Bartholdy
Felix Mendelssohn Bartholdy

"The passions are easily kindled by such statements."

To Wilhelmine Schröder-Devrient

Leipzig, February 18, 1841

Most Esteemed Madam,

Pardon me for imposing on you with a letter and query pertaining to your generous, only half-intimated promise. But the rumor has been spreading among many of our local friends of music and in the concert directorship that it is possible that we might be able to welcome you here again next Thursday, and ever since I have hardly had a free moment from all of the questions, requests, and petitions being put before me for an answer. Even the directorship has charged me to ask you urgently to inform us in a few words very soon if you are going to grant our requests, so that we can arrange the concert schedule around it, and should it have become impossible for you to do so, as indeed I hope it has not, then I would ask you for a reply all the sooner, in that it would then be very difficult for us to come up with another program having once led the public astray in this hope.

Hopefully until we meet again. As ever yours faithfully, with deepest respect,

Felix Mendelssohn Bartholdy

To Paul Mendelssohn Bartholdy

Leipzig, June 15, 1841, evening

My dear Paul,

Since in the Berlin affair you have been a confidant in all our joys and sufferings I can hardly fail to report to you (God willing) on the recent caviling which is now coming to a definitive close, just so that you will not be angry with me for not fixing the day of our return. The letter from Minister Eichhorn was delivered last week, but of all the things in Massow's report to the king it touched only upon the matter of salary. Otherwise it reaffirmed that I would hereby be placed at the head of the music department of the Academy and the only point remaining was to create a satisfactory function for me, to which end I should submit ideas to the minister as soon as feasible. I had told Massow as well as Kortum, and both had agreed, that it would be impossible to appoint me to be the head, as mentioned; there was not a single word of reference to the Kapellmeister title, which was the principal point of Massow's report. Whereupon I wrote to Herr v. Massow, outlined this to him, told him that ever since our last conversation I had firmly made up my mind to come, provided his proposals were adhered to, but that this was not clear from the ministerial communiqué in several respects, in particular the Kapellmeister title, and would he please tell me if any difficulties had arisen or how it had happened that no mention was made of this. Where-

upon M. replied to me today that he had remarked to
Kortum that I was to be bound only to the conditions
which he had agreed upon with the king, with my
approval, sending along Kortum's reply, which says
hereto: "Since the Supreme Order pertaining to Herr
Mendelssohn did not contain an express authorization
of Your Excellency's preconditions, nothing in particular could be said about the desired title in the communication from Herr M. The minister was of the
opinion that the matter could be taken care of easily at
a later date. In consequence of Your Excellency's honorable communication a special petition has been made
to confer the title of *Kapellmeister Allerhöchsten Orts*, and
thus it may be hoped that Herr Mendelssohn will be
appeased in this respect as well."

Since you think me a hairsplitter I would be happy
to give up the "desired title" and the "appeasement"—
but as I have been saying from the start: The manner
in which the matter has been dealt with is not such as
to engender my full confidence, and it is not right to
portray something as coveted which was offered to
someone who was in no way involved. My decision
remains practically as it was: provided the conditions
set forth in Massow's report are fulfilled, i.e., provided
that for the present I am granted the title of Kapellmeister (I would like to take another occasion to present
to them in writing the impossibility of dealing with the
present head of the Academy), then I will come; if not,
I won't. That is not spite but fairness. June is being
wasted over it, and I foresee that it may go on until the
end of July, and thus I shall lose the coming summer,
which I should like to have spent traveling. But it
doesn't matter; for that is a personal affair and was not
expressly mentioned in the letter. Thus I would still be

coming for August unless something changes. But I solemnly oblige you not to take another single step in this matter, in particular not to say anything regarding all this to Kortum; this would really look like pressuring and even the appearance of that must be avoided. I wanted to share it with you for the reasons above, and had to, but please grant my request.

Everyone is well here; the Davids arrived yesterday happy and in good health. A thousand regards to Albertine and everyone at Leipziger Strasse. Your

Felix

To Woldemar Frege

Berlin, August 28, 1841

Dear Herr Doctor,

Please accept my sincere thanks for your lovely, friendly note, by means of which I learned of your arrival and residence in Heringsdorf. May God grant that the baths bear you good fruit and revive and strengthen you at least physically, even if nothing can be done for the time being to relieve the sorrows of the spirit. That the baths tire you and at the same time excite the nerves, as you write, seems only natural to me, for things were exactly the same with me when I was in Scheveningen; it cost me much effort even to write a letter, and at times eating seemed almost too much trouble, and only sleep was comfortable. But the good, truly curative results made their appearance even after the first two weeks at the baths, and so I hope and wish with all my heart that this may happen in your case as well. But try to occupy yourself professionally again as soon as possible, even if at the beginning you find it intolerable;

for after all, the only possible human consolation is to be found in ceaseless, continued work.

For this reason it also pleased me greatly to learn that your wife is again keeping herself occupied with music, that you have taken a piano, and therefore I have taken the liberty of sending along several musical items, some handwritten, some printed, in the accompanying package, which I hope that you will receive cordially and play or sing through from time to time. My sister writes me that singing is becoming difficult or impossible for her. How could I imagine that!

Our life here is rather solitary, i.e., we are often at parties, but even so. But it is nicest when we are alone with our family in the evenings, and those are really the only moments in which I am entirely happy about being in Berlin. For two weeks now I have been taking the waters, and like you I am horribly weary of it; I feel as idle as a sloth. But it suits me exceedingly well, and in the few hours of work I have set for myself I have made great progress on all sorts of new things. I have also turned to painting again, and am living quite a mechanical, relaxed existence. The less I see of Berlin and Berliners, the happier I am. The few musicians with whom I am on close terms are either long gone or dead, and in a few cases unhappy fate has willed that they must die right at this moment. Thus during my brief stay here two of the best have passed away, one of whom you certainly know by name: Curschmann, the most lovable and affable of all of them here. It was announced yesterday and has sorely grieved me.

I am quite charmed that you found proper lodgings there through my sister, since I often hear complaints about shortages of the same there. I hope your mother will also recuperate little by little, even though the difficult test for her, as for all of you, will not come until after your return to Leipzig. Meanwhile, as I stated, if only the body can be strong and steady, the spirit will then soon follow suit. That you will be able to use the railroad from here on you no doubt already know. Forgive me for touching on one more tedious point, but I can't help it; could you let me know how much money I owe you? It really must be set right, otherwise you will swear off ever traveling with musicians again, thinking them incorrigible; but don't think so, and put my mind at ease on this matter.—In all seriousness, please do so, for soon we shall both forget about it. Now excuse me for rambling on so much; give my warmest regards to your esteemed family and think kindly of your most faithful

Felix Mendelssohn Bartholdy

To Lea Mendelssohn Bartholdy

Interlaken, August 18, 1842

My dearest Mother,

Do you still remember how twenty years ago we were staying in the pretty inn here beneath the big walnut trees (I drew one of them then, and the paper was almost washed clean because Paul poured a glass of water on it), and with the lovely young landlady? When I was here ten years ago she didn't want to put me up because I looked too shabby from the long trip on foot, and I believe that was the only annoyance I suffered on that trip. Now we are again staying here as people of consequence, who arrive in a coach with Friedrich up in the driving seat; the Jungfrau, with her silver horns, is still just as delicate and graceful, and stands out sharply against the sky, looking

fresh as ever, but the landlady on the other hand has
grown quite old and I only recognized her by her deport-
ment. I also drew walnut trees again, much better than
last time, but still far worse than I know they ought to be,
and the post office in Unterseen brings us our letters from
the same building it did then, and many new houses have
been built, and the Aar gurgles and glides past as swiftly
and quietly through the greenery as it did then—*time is,
time was, time is passed.* Actually I don't really have much
else to write you about, other than that we are all well and
think of you daily and hourly. To describe Switzerland is
of course altogether impossible, and instead of a diary,
like last time, I am drawing away with a vengeance, and
sit all day long in front of a mountain attempting to ren-
der it (not until the picture has been ruined do I leave
off), and each day must turn out at least one landscape.
But he who had not seen the Gemmi knows nothing of
Switzerland, my dear Dirichlet, which is what everyone
says about each new thing he see in this indescribably
beautiful country. It is strange that this time it seems to
me as do the best of books, which change along with you,
showing a new side with each successive change, and yet
still always remain just as wonderful and elevated. Thus
this time I have a completely different impression than
last time, as I see everything with Cécile; before I wanted
to go running off to every jagged mountain and green
pasture I saw, but this time I want to stay put and remain
everywhere for months. I would not want to guarantee
that I wouldn't set out some fine spring with kith and kin
to come here, and not find my way back up north again
until all of the leaves have fallen. Such at least are the
daily thoughts and castles in the sky I build for myself; I
would be all too happy to have some little country house
in Lausanne or Vevey, or here, or maybe in Lucerne; it

would be nice if there were a small vineyard and pasture and cattle as well, etc., etc., etc.—In the vineyard several days we plan to go up to the Oberland, and I am looking forward to seeing the full moon in Lauterbrunnen, then coming back here, then by way of Furka and Grimsel to Lake Lucerne and the Rigi, and then away from this country of countries and back to Germany, where things aren't really so bad either. All in all, life pleases me most exceedingly some days.—Some pretty news I am writing, dear Mother! Forgive me, but I have nothing better, and also know that Albertine wrote extensively about everything a few days ago. When I see you there should be a story without end to tell. Twice a week we receive reports from Frankfurt about the little children, who are doing just as one might wish, thank God, according to the most recent letters. You will be delighted with them, dearest Mother, when we come to Berlin again in September. If only I knew whether it will be for good or for just a few weeks; how happy I should be write you the former! But the whole affair has been so topsy-turvy recently that I no longer can tell up from down, and am becoming quite perplexed and confused whenever I try to think about what I ought to do. When I return things will no doubt work out; but do not be angry with me for the long period of uncertainty, I can't help it. And now enough for today, good evening, dearest Mother (for it is time for tea and a game of merils), a thousand heartfelt greetings to Fanny and Beckchen, and to Hansel and Dirichlet, and to Sebastian and Walter—I shall bring along something nice for all of them. Until we meet again soon and happily! Yours always,

Felix

To Heinrich Konrad Schleinitz

Berlin, October 17, 1842

Dearest friend,

I will be returning to Leipzig with my wife and child shortly, by November 7 at the latest, and will conduct the subscription concerts as in the past; but I cannot accept the appointment by the King of Saxony because my position here is to continue, at least in part, and because I have not been released. This is the result of an almost two-hour discussion the king held with me yesterday, and in which he expressed himself to me in such a way that I feel my admiration and love for him compounded, so that it would be *impossible* for me to break off the relationship forthwith. He told me at length about all of the plans he has, going into the most minute detail, then he told me that if I were not to come back he would abandon the project at once, since he could hardly even begin it without me, and he added that until work is completed I could travel wherever I liked, to Leipzig to conduct the concerts, or to Italy to see some pretty countryside.—I chose the former. But as I stated, to enter the service of the King of Saxony now is the one thing I cannot do. But return I can, and am looking forward to it enormously and utterly. The rest in person! Until then! I must still wait here for a few decisions pertaining to the external arrangements for the coming weeks, but as I stated I am thinking of being there by the 7th at the latest. The musicians will postpone their concert until my arrival, I trust? And will there be an Atonement Day week in November, or will the concerts continue every Thursday? But until then. *How is David's wife doing?* Write me in a few words, but *once* she is out of danger. Yours always,

Felix MB

Be so good to inform the concert directorship on my behalf of my impending return.

To Friedrich Wilhelm IV, King of Prussia

Leipzig, December 4, 1842

Most Serene and Powerful King,
Most Gracious Lord and Sovereign,
Your Majesty
has obliged me to the deepest, most fervent thanks by the Supreme Cabinet Order of November 22 and the new distinction which Your Majesty has conferred upon me by the appointment as director general of music. May I only succeed in earning through my accomplishments at least a portion of the many high honors with which Your Majesty has distinguished me! Would that I were able to express in my words of thanks how deeply I feel Your Majesty's generosity, and will feel it as long as I live! With feelings of sincere gratitude I remain until death Your Majesty's most obedient

Felix Mendelssohn Bartholdy

To Niels Wilhelm Gade

Leipzig, January 13, 1843

Esteemed Sir,
We have just held the first rehearsal of your Symphony in C Minor yesterday, and though I do not know you

personally I cannot resist the impulse to address you directly, in order to tell you what extraordinary pleasure you have given me through your outstanding work, and how grateful I am to you from my heart for the great pleasure that it has afforded me. Not in a long time has any piece made a more vivid, beautiful impression on me, and just as I found myself more amazed by every measure of it and yet felt more at home, so too I found myself compelled to express to you today my thanks for so much joy, to tell you how highly I prize your splendid talent, and how eager this symphony—the only thing I know by you as yet—makes me for everything that preceded and will follow it! And since I hear that you are still so young, I can very well look forward to what will follow, in addition to that which I welcome with solid hopes in such a beautiful work, for which I now wish to thank you, as well as for the pleasure I experienced yesterday.

We shall hold several more rehearsals of the symphony and not perform it for three to four weeks. The parts are still so replete with mistakes that we must have them all gone over carefully, and shall need to have several copied out again, and then it should not go off like a new piece, but like one with which the entire orchestra is familiar and loves. To be sure that was already the case yesterday, and we musicians were as one in this. However, it must also go off such that everyone can *hear* it. Herr Raymund Härtel told me that rumor has it that you yourself may come to visit in the winter. Would that it were so, and I were able to express or demonstrate my gratitude and great esteem to you more fully and clearly in person than with these empty written words! Whether or not we might desire to become acquainted at this time I bid you to always regard me as one who will follow all of your works with love and interest, and to whom a meeting with an artist such as yourself, and with a work of art such as your Symphony in C Minor, will always be the highest, most heartfelt joy.

So please accept once more my thanks, and permit me the complete esteem with which I remain yours faithfully,

Felix Mendelssohn Bartholdy

To Heinrich Konrad Schleinitz

Leipzig, March 29, 1843

It is impossible for me to go calmly to bed when I have parted from such a friend as you in anger. Thus I was just at your place in order to ask you if perhaps you thought the same way as I did—but I found no one at home there, not even the girl, and no light in the hallway by which to write anything. Forgive me if I have offended you, it was certainly not my intention, and so it is with you as well, as I know from long experience. Tomorrow I cannot come to see you until between twelve and one; but answer me only if that is *not* agreeable to you. So I hope to receive no answer. Your

Felix MB

To Heinrich Dörrien

Leipzig, April 20, 1843

Esteemed Government Councillor,
You have no doubt already heard that I intend to unveil

the monument to Sebastian Bach, which has been executed by the stonemason Hiller and the sculptor Knaur according to the specifications of Bendemann and Hübner. After the concert in the Gewandhaus is concluded, i.e., at around twelve-thirty, I was thinking of holding another short celebration with a portion of the chorus and orchestra on the plaza around the monument to commemorate its donation to the city, and thus I would above all like it if the concert directorship could be present. I thus ask you herewith to invite them humbly on my behalf to participate in the brief ceremony, and will see to it that the necessary seats will be reserved in the innermost circle adjacent to the monument. In the hope of not having made a fruitless request I am, with complete respect, your most faithful

Felix Mendelssohn Bartholdy

To Friedrich Fleischer

Leipzig, May 8, 1843

Esteemed City Councillor,

Enclosed I have taken the liberty of sending you the 115 thalers for the railing around the Bach monument, with the request to please be so kind as to pay the bill for me. But permit me to seize this opportunity to convey my heartfelt, most sincere thanks to you for the extreme goodwill and the kind readiness with which you have anticipated my wishes in the course of this entire affair, as well as for the highly tasteful decoration of the plaza, by which you have beautified and distinguished the monument! With complete respect, faithfully,

Felix Mendelssohn Bartholdy

To Heinrich Konrad Schleinitz

Berlin, February 6, 1844

Dear friend,

Your kind, dear remembrance of my birthday gave me the greatest pleasure; if only there had not been the news of your wife's indisposition! I hope, as in the case with all that is written, she will already have recovered by the time I first learned here that it was serious. May heaven grant it and may these lines find her completely recuperated and you completely at ease. But please tell me at once in a few words how things are going. You know what sympathy we all share with you in this. I myself of course have no doubt that by now everything is all right again, but tell me that it is, so that I can share your happiness. Forgive me also for not having written for so long. But the import of this whole letter and the reply to it should be one thing only: We must get together again soon. Everything of which you write to me can only be taken care of in person—I don't even want to begin to try to write about it, because it looks so far ahead, and therefore my thoughts have always turned to the day when I can finally came to Leipzig and be with you, even if only for a few days. The children's awful coughing spells kept getting in the way again and again; but thank God the situation seems to be improving little by little, and as soon as recovery is certain I will come to visit and we can discuss everything. I hope that will happen very soon—this all refers only to your question about my future and my return; for with respect to this year's concerts and my conducting them, even the matter of my symphony and *Walpurgis-*

nacht, I can already answer today, repeating the same thing I told you when I left. You disagreed with me, but since then I feel it *much more*, and I cannot depart from what I feel so strongly—do not be angry with me if it sounds blunt or unfriendly, for it is not meant to be. I can in no way participate in the subscription concerts in person, because my personal relationship to F. Hiller makes it impossible for me; therefore I cannot conduct the *last* piece, in fact I don't even want to speak my mind to you about the performance of my symphony, since it is already printed and available to everyone. The *Walpurgisnacht* is another matter, and no doubt I do not need to tell you from the start that I would prefer *not* to have it performed; but in no way would I want to oppose or stand in Hiller's way. Let him do whatever he thinks he will be able to answer for, to himself and to his art, and if Kistner wants to give him the score then I will *not* withhold it. Forgive me, forgive me that *I* am writing to you about the subscription concerts in such rage; but it is becoming hard for me not to lapse into a certain bitterness whenever I think of the whole miserable affair I have been involved in with Hiller. I don't want to be bitter, or to say one word too many, and yet it still comes out so odiously, no matter how I try to turn my eye and forget about it, for the whole thing is odious. For that very reason there is no cure but silence and distance. Fie upon it.

But something nicer. We must get together as soon as possible, that much is clear. Perhaps even next week? Is Gade still there? Is Rietz contented and cheerful? Couldn't you people succeed in bringing Servais once, when Rietz has played and another instrumentalist *after him*? He plays exquisitely, and would like to go to

Leipzig, as far as I know. Who is singing now in Miss Birch's absence?—But above all else write me a few words about your wife's condition, then the rest we can *speak* about with pleasure, God willing. Your

Felix

To Paul Mendelssohn Bartholdy

Soden, near Frankfurt, July 19, 1844

My dear brother,

And thus I am once more on German soil, having returned home happy and healthy and gay, I found all of my family in good health as wished! Cécile, praise God, is altogether changed from those awful days in Leipzig, and the country air and the relaxed life appear to suit her splendidly; the three eldest children are brown as Moors and exuberantly merry, and even little Felix is recovering visibly from his many ills. We are enjoying cheerful, pleasant days in this exquisite spot. And how are things with all of you? Cécile tells me that you have moved in with us; is it true? I wrote you even from England how happy that would make us! And what are the little daughters and Mama and Papa up to? Tell me about it soon, and at length (in fact *everything*).

My stay in England was wonderful; I have never been received anywhere with such universal kindness as I was this time, and played more music in the two months than I usually do in two years: my A minor symphony twice, the *Midsummer Night's Dream* three times, *St. Paul* twice, the trio twice, and on the last evening I was in London the *Walpurgisnacht* with an unbelievable ovation, in addition the four-hand variations as well, the octet twice, the D major and E minor quartets twice, various *Songs Without Words*, Bach's D minor concerto twice, Beethoven's G major concerto—and those are only a few of the pieces that were performed publicly, in addition to conducting all of the Philharmonic and other concerts, the countless socials, then the publication of *Israel in Egypt*, on which I was meanwhile working for the Handel Society and preparing from the manuscript, and the overture to *Athalie* as well.—You can form an impression of how colorful and hectic life was. My main purpose, which was to perform a service for the Philharmonic Society, was accomplished beyond all expectations; according to all reports they have not had a season like this one for many years. Of course it doesn't help with the nasty business with the radicals, which I had ample occasion to observe this time, and with which the society cannot continue to exist; the inwardly corroded ideas, musically *rotten boroughs*, etc. But all of this and everything else in person! Just one more thing, which made me sorry principally on your account: they had invited me to Dublin in order to make me a doctor at the university, and Morgan John O'Connell wanted to give me a letter to his uncle in prison—and I couldn't accept on account of the short time and the horrible commotion of such a five-day trip; I did not in any way overlook the thought that it would have pleased you, and gave up the idea with genuine regret. Klingemann wanted to write to you himself; it was the last thing he said to me when he took his leave of me in Gravesend, whither he had accompanied me. It is a wonderful thing to have such a friend, something one finds only once in life!

From tremendous excitement there to this quiet place —where food and drink and sleep are a person's principal occupations, and where a walk of ten minutes' length takes one up to the heights of the Taunus with a view across the Main and Rhine river valleys to Frankfurt, Worms, and Mainz. From there one can look out for days on end, needing nothing more, and accomplish as much or even more than over there with all of the hustle and bustle. And then too there is Cécile, who is happy to be with her mother and recuperationg daily, and the children going riding on donkeys, and the moon waxing in the clear sky. These are happy days. But you have your dear little daughter and we don't have to be jealous of one another.

I deposited 182 pounds at Hambro's and have withdrawn 32 of them; do write me to confirm this is right when you have a chance. Can you verify whether the King of Prussia is coming to the Rhine next month? You would do me a great favor if you could write me a few words with regard to this *as soon as possible*. If he does come here, then my plans would probably have to be altered; if he doesn't, then I shall come to Berlin in the middle of August. Could I reserve a tiny room with all of you at Leipziger Strasse?

From Beckchen I have a letter from Sorrento; they were planning to spend another month there and then begin the journey back. In a week I am going to Zweibrücken, but only for four days; I like it here altogether too well. But keep addressing mail to Frankfurt. I received your packet of letters with enclosures yesterday; please accept my thanks for sending it, and many more for having held on to it. And now a thousand regards from Cécile and Frau Jeanrenaud to you and Albertine, and until our next merry meeting, dear ones! Your

Felix

A thousand greetings to Fanny, and if you can find out anything about the mischief surrounding *Athalie* do share it with me. Naturally don't do anything in my name; the longer they want to postpone it the better it suits me. But I would just like to know whether they are still talking of *August*, for then I would have to be *punctual* about ending my vacation, which otherwise would probably not be so necessary, and very likely is not expected. But don't ask Herr von Massow about it. Pardon this cursed diplomacy. And adieu, without diplomacy.

To Paul Mendelssohn Bartholdy

Frankfurt, April 10, 1845

My dear brother,
You were doubtless right with respect to the beginning of your recent letter, we have both turned into Trappists! But we want to improve ourselves, at least I do, for you have already improved! But do continue on! Why in fact I was so silent I myself cannot comprehend; I had no reason at all to be. We are all doing quite splendidly, thank goodness; Cécile is in good spirits and the children all bring us the greatest joy. I was ill for quite some time, and the sniffling and coughing keep coming back, but since the onset of such uniquely splendid weather I have been taking long, long walks, and that is a good remedy, when one can take in the blue sky and the restless buds and the pointy branches and limbs. Oh, long live spring! But now first of all— have you heard directly from Klingemann that he has become engaged to Sophie Rosen in Detmold? To the daughter of our Rosen, who resembles him so much in

her good nature and charm, and moreover is so cheerful and pretty? A joy, is it not? I was jumping for joy around my room for five minutes after this unexpected letter dropped out of the sky several days ago. He wants to get married in May, and promises afterward to come to Frankfurt; if only he keeps his word! Last year she was in England with her brother; there she met Klingemann (and me as well), and then on his winter trip he passed through Detmold and saw her again. Then he went off to London, thought things over, wrote, and now he is a happy groom-to-be. Quite wonderful! She is blond, with smoothly parted hair, a proper rounded German face and blue eyes, very cultivated and yet very spontaneous and knows a lot and is very quiet (all of these details are given here really more for Albertine than for you)—in short, I grant my unconditional approval.

—We were not stranded by the floods, for our apartment lies in the highest part of the city; but it was really frightful for three days on end, with half of Frankfurt under water. They were using a rowboat in Frau Souchay's vestibule, and had to try to jump out of it onto the stairs; in neighboring houses even that didn't work, and they had to jump into the rowboat from the second floor—and in addition there were raging rapids. People have no idea what it is like in our part of the world, how in three short days it reduces houses, stone balustrades, and cobblestones to chaos, as if some badly behaved children had been playing with everything and ran off in the middle of their games. Now I remember again why I put off writing from one day to the next— because I wanted to send along your *Oedipus* to you, on which the copyist has been at work for many weeks now, and promises it from one day to the next. But he

is still not yet finished, though he swears "in a few days."
So in a few days I'll send it to you. A curious correspondence it was between His Excellency Müller and
me; in the first letter he demanded, rather peremptorily
in the name of the king, the composition of the *entire*
Aeschylean trilogy. Whereupon I proffered my reasons
for not yet having completed it, and named those things
which I had finished. Whereupon he wrote me that the
king was very pleased to hear this, and hoped to hear
the pieces in the summer, but only if I myself would
also come and conduct them. I am quite willing to do
so; whether it will come to pass is another question. In
any case I want to go to Berlin during the course of the
summer (perhaps toward the end) and "pay my respects." I promised Herr von Massow and Count Reden
to do so earlier, and now Minister Eichhorn as well,
who has also been corresponding with me, seeking my
advice about the music department of the Academy of
Arts. I am supposed to tell him whether he should
appoint me, or some other composer (and whom) to be
the head of that department, and I think that that could
be better aired in person than in writing; we have
already exchanged letters twice on the matter. Wouldn't
it be *charmant* if we could ride to Berlin together after
our meeting at the Rhine and then enjoy life there for
a few weeks. I am thinking about it quite a lot these
days! So now saddle up in June, as you say, and the
sooner the better. We can of course proceed to Dei-
desheim and Dürkheim and on up the Rhine to Freiburg
together; it can be done in four days after all, if one
wants, and even if all four of us siblings were to travel
to Berlin thereafter it would give us some time together
for once, and ought to make for a splendid celebration
indeed! May heaven grant it so! I still have a few things

to reply to from your previous letters, or rather to ask:
What is this sled run about which you are so crazy? Oh
please describe it to me in detail. Is it perhaps very
indecent? (But if Albertine should see these lines!) And
how did *you* like Jenny Lind? And have you heard
Ronge preach? Since I read his "Vindication" I have
not the slightest regard for his character, his knowledge
of art, or for the man in general. But alas! Have you
read *Eigensinn und Laune*, the novella by Tieck? That
outdoes everything, and so boring and so lascivious!
You see that I am reading diligently of late, and I have
even worked my way through Schlosser; you are right,
it isn't very nice. I have also composed a trio, which so
far I like. Moscheles is not even thinking of going to
Leipzig or to Germany at all, as Klingemann writes me
in the letter before this last one (when he was not yet
engaged—how lovely it all is).—Now I ask you to write
me in all *seriousness* more and in greater detail about
Mme. Heine; I didn't even know that she was ill, and
thought that the business in the fall was just
temporary. What is happening there? A cheerful good-
bye, my dear brother. Your

Felix

To Robert Franz

Leipzig, September 15, 1845

Esteemed Sir,
Do not be angry with me if I cannot quite produce a
judgment in "black and white" regarding the song which
you sent me. I don't know what I really ought to say
about it—or at least write. In your judgment you appear

to place more emphasis on the individuality of the woman who composed it, her talent as a whole, and that is also the right thing to do, and I should like to do so as well, but that is exactly what I did not discern clearly enough in the song in question. So it is doubly fitting that I shall be (in all likelihood) stopping in Halle sometime during the next week, and then we can discuss the matter more thoroughly in person. I would like it if I could arrange things such that I could hear something done by your orchestra there; no doubt there will be a good opportunity during the next week or two? I ask you to let me know in a reply of a few short words, and if nothing can be arranged I'll simply come and we can talk (or argue) at great length and to our hearts' content. With deepest respect,

Felix Mendelssohn Bartholdy

To Louis Spohr

Leipzig, February 14, 1846

Esteemed Kapellmeister,

Do not be angry with me for having been so bold as to dedicate the enclosed trio to you without consulting you in advance. Hauptmann assures me that you would receive it well nevertheless, and so I hope that he is not mistaken. I would like to have saved the honor for a somewhat longer piece; but then I should have had to put it off, as I so often have had to of late; nothing seemed good enough to me, and in fact neither does this trio. But I think that you will look more to good intentions, and for my part I no longer wished to delay expressing for once the heartfelt gratitude for so many, many pleasures, for so much instruction, for which I am indebted to you! Indeed such thanks as I feel and intend for you can never be expressed in external, written words; so please show favor toward these unsatisfactory ones too, kindly and indulgently!

Please allow me as well to take this opportunity to reaffirm my thanks for the manuscript pieces which you were so kind as to send us for the performance, and do pardon me that we were forced to keep several of them here longer than was my intention. The parts for the *Kreuzfahrer* had to be sent back to Berlin suddenly, from where they had been lent to us, and have only just now come back from there. I am looking forward beyond all measure to this performance; we have now thoroughly rehearsed the choruses, with over two hundred voices, in six rehearsals, and moreover will have an organ in addition to the orchestra, and so I hope that it will go well. Yesterday we had the pleasure of hearing the *Quartet Concerto* at the music fund-raising concert; David, Sachse, Gade, and Wittmann played it, and had practiced it according to your instructions with a piano beforehand, with the result that it went well and confidently and was together.[1] But I found your observation that it still presents some difficulties confirmed yesterday, and even the orchestral accompaniment was not entirely free of mistakes. Tomorrow I am sending all of it on to Vienna to the address given to me, and a week from today I hope to play the quintet, which we were able to begin practicing only quite superficially here with such a large crowd of musicians around, and which ought to be known well and thoroughly before being performed in public. To that end

---

1. Quartet Concerto: Concerto for String Quartet and Orchestra, by Louis Spohr. (The other pieces mentioned are also by Spohr.)

I am planning on coming up with a few free evenings in the course of the next week, and thank you in advance for the renewed pleasure it will afford me. In addition the serious-style concert overture is also on our program, and when a while ago we did the *Weihe der Töne* I wished you could have been here; for I have never heard the symphony performed so well, and I fancy that you too would have been happy with it. The orchestra played so utterly with the right spirit!

And now farewell, esteemed Kapellmeister, and preserve a fond recollection of your sincere and most deeply devoted

Felix Mendelssohn Bartholdy

To Paul Mendelssohn Bartholdy

Leipzig, July 9, 1846

My dear brother,
What a joy it was when your letter first arrived, and after all of the lovely and good tidings it contained even held out the possibility of your coming here "for twenty-four hours" before my trip to England. My plan was always, if at all possible, to come to Berlin beforehand for a few days, and if in any way it can be managed I shall still carry it out; but if it can't, I implore you urgently and heartily to carry out yours. Whether I am coming will be determined once and for all in the next two weeks, and if *by then* I have not notified you of my arrival then I *cannot* come—but I shall remain here for at least four weeks. I am in no way planning on *before* the 10th of August, so that I guard the hope of seeing you again beforehand! We must discuss a whole multitude of things (plans too, etc.).

Your reply to Hambro was completely in line with my intentions. Certainly I shall stay with Klingemann for a few days, but I shall certainly not neglect to convey my thanks for the most friendly offer, and therefore do not forget to open a credit with H. for me either.

I foresee completing my *Elijah* in ten to twelve days; the larger part of the second half is already in England, and the choruses are starting to learn it. A few weeks ago I was quite worried about it all, but now am slowly beginning to look forward to it.

Do not hold it against me if I come forth with two more requests, but I write so seldom nowadays that everything must be crowded together into one letter. The first request is: to make inquiries at Scholz and Kuhnert's whether they would take back the empty bottles of red wine, of which I have a multitude, and then could *immediately* send back to me some of them filled. They could of course answer me themselves so that you don't have to go to any more trouble, but they must answer at once, for almost no more red wine can be found. The second request is to have my wages redeemed using the accompanying voucher.

And now give my regards to Albertine and our sisters and the coming generations and little ones,[1] and know that the wonderful room in which no man can turn around is holding out its arms to receive you again and waiting for you, and would very much like to have you stay. So would we too. Your

Felix

---

1. *Generationen und Generatiönchen.*

To Konrad Philipp Lattner

Leipzig, March 11, 1847

Esteemed Sir,
My hearty thanks to you for sending along the first act of the opera *Sakontala* and your comedy *Jean Beck*. I have read both with great interest and can only regret that the variety of projects I have already started make it impossible for me to take on the composition of the opera. I would still ask you to send along the second act and to let me keep the first here until then, as you were so kind as to suggest—but a trip of some length on which I shall soon be setting forth prevents me from being able to provide any sort of fixed address during the coming months, and inasmuch as I am therefore returning the manuscript with this note I remain with deepest respect yours faithfully,

Felix Mendelssohn Bartholdy

To Rebecka Dirichlet

Frankfurt, May 19, 1847

My dearest Rebecka,
I don't know what I should write you, and yet I must write you, for all day today I am standing in for Felix, would like to console him and yet still cannot. Then we speak of Fanny, and reminisce together and ask God to help us bear the heavy blow he has dealt us, without grumbling or sinful thoughts. Ever since yesterday, when the awful news came to us, our spirits have crumbled and grown faint.

After Hensel you, dear Rebecka, have suffered the greatest loss. In day-to-day life with beloved Fanny her beautiful soul lay open to you; you knew her best and the signs of her love accompanied you everywhere. My thoughts flew out to you at once, oh would that I could be with you at this time to lament and cry with you, and would that we were not now so far apart!—How often since yesterday I have regretted not having been in Berlin with all of you more often and reproached myself eternally for having been preoccupied with trifling details.

For I have also lost my best friend. I know well that she loved me, that I could count on her as on solid rock, and that she would never have deserted me. But she is no longer among the living, and I shall never again see her beautiful eyes, God help us all.

Keep healthy, dear Rebecka, and remember me with love. Your

Cécile

God help us all—since yesterday I don't know what else to say and think—you, my dear sister. I have written to Paul and to Hensel, but today and yesterday and for many days to come I shall not know what to write except—God help us, God help us! Yesterday all day long I felt as if I had to travel to Berlin in order to see you, my dearest Beckchen, you and Hensel. But it is true that I would scarcely have endured the hours of travel very well, with the certainty that I would arrive too late, could bring no help or consolation, as flustered and exhausted as I am from the last few weeks and from the separation from my wife and children. But now *we* are again separated from one another, and ought to be together. *Ach*, if only we had not been apart!

It fills me with the most bitter regret. And the only thing that helps even a little is crying quite a lot, if only one could always do so. The children come in from time to time and they do me good with their happy faces. May God preserve your family's health, and give you a moment of consolation in them. *Ach*, dear sister, I cannot write or think of anything but Fanny. Things will never change as long as we are on earth here together. Your

F.

To Paul Mendelssohn Bartholdy

Frankfurt, May 24, 1847

My dearest brother,
After the letter I received from you today I am now counting the hours and days until I can see you. I cannot bear the company of others now, and don't know what to tell them, nor they what to ask—and I must now console Cécile, with whom I always enjoy every moment of speaking, and must pull myself together when I am with her so that she recovers from the terrible shock. And alone I couldn't travel to see you either, as you know. And so the news that you are coming is a joy to me, as far as there can be any joy for us now and for a long, long time. Do not postpone your trip, if at all possible, and occupy yourself much with your children, for theirs are the only faces, and their carefree words are the only words, which do one good.

And since we have learned today that we shall be able to see you here in the area again, we have resolved to travel to Badenweiler and wait for you and your family there, and to see if the place suits you in your recovery and me in mine (for I am also supposed to be drinking whey). We hope that it will not be too far from Frankfurt for you, since one can get there comfortably in a day from here, and since it is probably the quietest of all the places to stay that could be considered. But we still want to try beforehand to see if one can relax quietly and undisturbed in Baden-Baden, since it is not yet the season for the baths; if so, we shall expect you there, since it is a half day's journey closer to Frankfurt, and in accordance with what you write I would prefer to choose the *closest* spot.

I would not like to stay here at the inn any longer; it is doubly sad here because everything is so noisy, and now there is a railroad to Soden; F. Bernus lives there and is assembling all of Frankfurt around him, so that won't do either. Get off here at the Englischer Hof; I shall write to you *either* from Baden-Baden that, and where, you can find us in Baden-Baden, *or* if you do not find a letter from us at the Englisher Hof then we are in Badenweiler. We shall not fail to be there.

It seems to me as if I will only truly be able to believe everything once I have seen and spoken with you. Now I find myself thinking with every footstep I hear, with every letter to be opened, that it might undo what cannot be undone. Or rather I do not think so, but it seems that way to me, even though I am sure of the opposite, and it is all such a horrible business. You will probably not believe me, but I am counting the days and hours until I see you again. God preserve you and your family's health and courage to carry on with life. The pen cannot say it, nor the mouth. Come soon. Your

F.

To Paul Mendelssohn Bartholdy

Interlaken, August 24, 1847

Dear brother,

Yesterday, exactly four weeks after your departure, I received the news of your safe arrival with your letter of the 17th and another from Rebecka from the 15th, which the American, Mr. Richard, brought up to my room at once. We had started to worry in the last few days and finally I wanted to write you yesterday and ask you about Mother Dirichlet and your trip from Bielefeld to Berlin—then the replies came before I had even asked, and arrived praise God as hoped for, and put our minds at ease. But Albertine still tells me of a subsequent illness in Mannheim, and the indisposition of the little ones at the railway station, and finally her horrid fall in the cellar. Thank God that everything has turned out well; please accept our best wishes too. And hopefully not a single trace of all of it will remain in evidence when we see each other again, and you will have to explain how everything happened in greater detail to us as a matter of past history.

We are doing well here, thank heavens, and our life proceeds so comfortably and uniformly as during the first weeks you shared with us, inaugurating it. At the beginning of September the journey home will probably begin, and I am planning on being in Berlin during the second half of September. That Webern had to go to Frankfurt (no doubt the one on the Oder river) came as a complete surprise to me; the last news I had from Berlin was from him, and in it there was not a word of this. I find it quite disagreeable; is there a promotion involved? Or is his departure just a departure from the ideas and pace and people who were supposed to be united in Berlin in 1840? Had there been much discussion of a change in his status and good reputation beforehand? Is this transfer a consequence? As I said, I am very surprised by it, and unpleasantly surprised. And just what did you say *to* Beauvallon and to crown it off to the Duke of Praslin? Did you not think of Fanny as well during this last business and of the horror with which she would have viewed it? One must crawl back behind the shelter of one's own four walls and be happy to be able to be underneath a roof during such a storm of evil and wickedness. I have been leafing through a new book by Sue since you left, who relates everything together with the greatest precision. I have also met Herr Hansemann, who visited me because he thought it was you, and was very disappointed not to find you still in Interlaken. There has been no shortage of strangers of all sorts here, especially during the past weeks. Dr. Härtel too has also come, and I have spoken with him about the publication of the works of our dear sister as planned. There was no doubt that he would consider it an honor to be able to see such works published by his firm, as I said before; I have asked him to put together a precise accounting of the costs and to send it to me as soon as I arrive in Berlin, for not until then can it be agreed upon and discussed (with him or others.) Please tell Hensel all of this. I find it charming that the engraving can now be published. Whether we shall avail ourselves of Benni's apartment is still not yet certain; I doubt that we shall bring along the children, for they shouldn't be shuffled back and forth too much, and the sooner they can be ensconced in the continuity of their winter lodgings the better.

Cécile and I are hoping in any case to come to Berlin *before* proceeding to our winter lodgings—the two of us might perhaps stay in your guest room (behind the kitchen)? But I shall certainly write to you of all this once more in greater detail from Frankfurt. It will be difficult for me to break away from such a relaxing and orderly summer sojourn—but the summer itself is coming to an end, the mountains around us themselves were heavily covered with snow this morning (today is already the 26th), and thus if you answer this note address it to Frankfurt, where we shall in all probability be in several weeks' time. The best thing is that I can keep telling myself: Until we meet again soon. Your

Felix MB

Dear Albertine,
You will have seen from my last letter that the news of your arrival and good health has greatly cheered us; I thank you most heartily for your lovely letter. We shall soon follow, for since the cold has set in, the rain, and even the snow on the nearby mountains, one can no longer go on recklessly enjoying the calm life here. I must think of our empty apartment, maids, and of similar less idyllic matters. I am only very sorry that Felix absolutely doesn't want to have the children along in Berlin; I think it would cheer him up during the doubtless very difficult beginning. They are, thank God, all well, and Lilly still hasn't stopped talking of your fall into the cellar. I hope that these lines will find you as well as one might wish. Your

Cécile

To Friedrich Wilhelm IV, King of Prussia

Leipzig, October 17, 1847

Most Serene and Powerful King,
Most Gracious Lord and Sovereign,
Your Royal Majesty,
I am taking the liberty of laying with the utmost reverence the enclosed first copy of the score to my *Elijah* at your feet. It seems to me as if it were not only the deepest and innermost gratitude which makes this my duty, but as if I had no other means of proving to Your Majesty how continually I strive to be more and more worthy of all the generosity Your Majesty has shown me. May these strivings be visible in the present work.

It was my hope to find an opportunity to hand this work to Your Majesty myself while in Berlin. But having been detained here by illness I would not like to wait until the score is placed before the public, and am thus making so bold as to address these lines to Your Majesty.

With deepest reverence Your Majesty's most humble servant,

Felix Mendelssohn Bartholdy

CHRONOLOGY

1742

Moses Mendelssohn arrives in Berlin from Dessau

1762

June 22: Marriage of Moses Mendelssohn and Fromet Gugenheim in Berlin

1764

Oct. 24: Birth of daughter Brendel (Dorothea) in Berlin (married to Veit, later to Schlegel)

1770

Aug. 11: Birth of son Joseph in Berlin, later the founder of the banking house ("Uncle Joseph")

1776

Dec. 10: Birth of son Abraham in Berlin

1777

Mar. 26: Lea Salomon born in Berlin (granddaughter of Daniel Itzig)

1782

Jan. 7: Birth of son Nathan in Berlin (grandfather of Arnold Mendelssohn)

1786

Jan. 4: Death of Moses Mendelssohn in Berlin

1787

June 16: The widow Fromet Mendelssohn, her children, and her descendants are granted special protection as Jews (*General-schutzjudenpriveleg*) by the King of Prussia

1795

Joseph Mendelssohn founds the banking house, together with Moses Friedländer

1804

Dec. 26: Abraham Mendelssohn and Lea Salomon are married in Berlin and move to Hamburg, where Abraham directs the newly founded banking house Mendelssohn and Company

1805

Nov. 14: Birth of daughter Fanny in Hamburg

1809

Feb. 3: Birth of son Felix in Hamburg

1811

Apr. 11: Birth of daughter Rebecka in Hamburg; the family moves hastily from Hamburg to Berlin, taking up residence first at Neue Promenade 7, then at Markgrafenstrasse 48

1812

Oct. 30: Birth of son Paul in Berlin

1815

Felix receives his first musical instruction from his mother

1816

Mar. 21: Abraham M. has his children baptized as Lutherans in the Neue Kirche in Berlin; subsequently an extended trip to Paris with Felix

1817

Oct. 10: Cécile Jeanrenaud born in Lyon

1818

Felix appears in a public concert for the first time with the French-horn player Rudolf Gugel

1819

Felix begins studies with Karl Friedrich Zelter
Dec. 11: First surviving composition by Felix (song written for his father's birthday)

1820

Samuel Rösel gives Felix drawing lessons

Oct. 1: Fanny and Felix become members of the Berlin Sing-Akademie

Nov.: Felix finishes his operetta *Die Soldatenliebschaft (Soldiers' Loves)*

1821

Mar.: The operetta *Die beiden Pedagogen (The Two Pedagogues)* is completed

June 18: Premier of Carl Maria von Weber's *Der Freischütz* in Berlin

Oct.-Nov.: Zelter, his daughter, and Felix visit Goethe in Weimar

1822

Abraham Mendelssohn takes the surname "Bartholdy" and is baptized a Lutheran in Frankfurt, together with his wife Lea

May 1: Work on the operetta *Die beiden Neffen (The Two Nephews)* is started in Berlin

July-Oct.: Family travels to Switzerland

Oct. 18: The Piano Quartet No. 1, op. 1, is finished in Berlin.

1823

Mar.: String Quartet in E-Flat is finished in Berlin

Palm Sunday: Felix is confirmed in Berlin

Dec.: Felix's grandmother Bella Salomon gives him a manuscript copy of the score to Bach's *St. Matthew Passion*

1824

Mar.: Symphony No. 1 in C Minor, op. 11, is completed in Berlin

July: Felix and his father visit Bad Doberan

Nov.: Concerto for Two Pianos and Orchestra in A-Flat is completed in Berlin; Ignaz Moscheles befriends Felix

1825

Jan. 18: Piano Quartet No. 3, op. 3, is completed in Berlin

Mar.-Apr.: Felix and his father visit Paris, and, on the return trip
in May, Goethe in Weimar

Autumn: Abraham M. buys the von der Recke mansion in Berlin at
Leipziger Strasse 3

Oct. 20: Octet, op. 20, is completed in Berlin

1826

Aug.: Concert Overture to Shakespeare's *A Midsummer Night's
Dream*, op. 21, is completed in Berlin

1827

Feb. 20: Karl Loewe performs the *Midsummer Night's Dream* overture, op. 21, for the first time in Stettin

Apr. 29: The comic opera *The Wedding of Camacho*, op. 10, is performed at the Royal Theater in Berlin (only this one time)

Aug.-Oct.: Felix goes hiking through the Harz mountains, Thuringia, and southern Germany with Eduard Magnus and Louis
Heydemann

Oct.: String Quartet in A Minor, op. 13, is completed in Berlin

1827–28

Felix attends lectures by Hegel, Ritter, and Gans at the University
of Berlin

1828

Sept.: A cantata commemorating "Natural Scientist's Day" composed at the instigation of Alexander von Humboldt

Oct.: Felix travels to Brandenburg on the *Havel*

1829

Mar. 11: FMB directs the first re-performance of Bach's *St. Matthew Passion* at the Sing-Akademie

Apr. 10: Departure for England

June 24: FMB plays Beethoven's *Emperor* Concerto from memory in London (first performance in England)

End of July: Departure with friend Karl Klingemann for Scotland, begins work on Third Symphony (*Scottish*), op. 56, in Edinburgh

Sept.: String Quartet in E-Flat, op. 12, completed in London

Oct. 3: Fanny M. B. and Wilhelm Hensel are married in Berlin

Dec. 7: Return to Berlin

Dec. 26: Silver wedding celebration of parents; on the previous evening, performance of the Liederspiel *Die Heimkehr aus der Fremde (Returning Home from Foreign Lands)*, op. 89.

1830

Apr.: Fifth Symphony (*Reformation*) completed in Berlin

May: Felix starts out on his great *Bildungsreise*: Leipzig, Weimar, Munich

June 13: *Rondo capriccioso*, for piano, op. 14, completed in Munich

June 16: Birth of Sebastian Hensel in Berlin

August: FMB in Vienna

Autumn: Two string quartets, op. 12 and op. 13, are published in Leipzig

Oct.: FMB in Venice and Florence

Nov. 1: Arrival in Rome, where work on *Psalm 115*, op. 31, is completed Nov. 15

1830–31

Work on Fourth Symphony (*Italian*) is begun in Rome

1831

Apr.: Visits Naples and Pompeii

June-Aug.: Return via Rome and Milan to Switzerland

Sept.: In Munich, where Piano Concerto No. 1 in G Minor, op. 25, is completed

Nov.-Dec.: Travels to Paris via Stuttgart, Heidelberg, Frankfurt, Bonn, and Luttich, remaining there until Apr. 1832

1832

Mar. 22: Death of Goethe in Weimar

Apr. 23: FMB arrives in London

May: Marriage of sister Rebecka to the mathematician Peter Lejeune Dirichlet in Berlin

May 15: Death of K. F. Zelter in Berlin

June 20: Final version of the Concert Overture No. 2, or *Fingal's Cave*, op. 26, is completed in London

End of June: Return to Berlin

Autumn: First volume of the *Lieder ohne Wörte (Songs Without Words)* appears in London under the English title *Original Melodies*; in Leipzig the parts to the Octet, op. 20, are published

1833

Jan. 10: Die erste Walpurgisnacht (The First Walpurgisnacht), op. 60, is premiered in its original version at the Berlin Sing-Akademie under the direction of FMB

Jan. 22: K. F. Rungenhagen is chosen to succeed Zelter as the director of the Berlin Sing-Akademie with 149 votes to FMB's 88 votes

Mar. 13: Fourth Symphony (*Italian*), op. 90, is completed in Berlin

Apr. 14: FMB leaves Berlin to assume—after a stay in London—the directorship of the Lower Rhine Music Festival

May 20: FMB signs formal contract to direct the Musikverein, church concerts, and music festivals in Düsseldorf, and is named the city's musical director

June-Aug.: Together with his father in London

Sept. 27: FMB lives with the Schadows in Düsseldorf

Dec.: FMB publicly conducts—after twenty rehearsals—an opera for the first time, Mozart's *Don Giovanni*

1834

Whitsunday: FMB meets Chopin in Aachen at the Lower Rhine Music Festival

Aug.: First movement of the *St. Paul* Oratorio is completed in Düsseldorf

Aug.-Sept.: FMB in Berlin, returns to Düsseldorf via Leipzig and Cassel

Nov.: FMB has a falling out with Karl Immermann and resigns as conductor for the Düsseldorf opera

1835

Jan.: Management of the Leipzig Gewandhaus offers FMB the directorship of the Gewandhaus concerts

May 27: Marriage of brother Paul to Albertine Heine in Berlin

July 2: Farewell concert in Düsseldorf, with works by Handel and Beethoven

Aug.: FMB moves into an apartment in the Reichel's Garden section of Leipzig

Oct. 1: Conducts first concert at the Gewandhaus

Oct.: Visits Berlin; last meeting with his father

Nov. 19: Death of Abraham M. B. in Berlin

1836

Spring: St. Paul Oratorio, op. 36, is completed in Leipzig

Mar. 8: FMB is granted an honorary doctorate by the University
of Leipzig

May 22: St. Paul, op. 36, is premiered at the Lower Rhine Music
Festival under FMB's direction

June-Aug: Travels to Frankfurt, first meets Cécile Jeanrenaud;
short visit to Cologne

Sept. 9: Engagement to Cécile Jeanrenaud; return to Leipzig (end
of Sept.)

Christmas: Visits Frankfurt

1836–37

St. Paul Oratorio is published in Bonn

1837

Mar. 9: FMB appears as soloist for the first time in Leipzig,
playing Bach's Piano Concerto in D Minor

Mar. 28: Marriage in Frankfurt

Apr.-May: Honeymoon trip on the upper Rhine River as far as
Freiburg; *Psalm 42,* op. 42, several organ preludes, and the
String Quartet, op. 44, no. 2, are composed

Aug. 5: Piano Concerto No. 2 in D Minor, op. 40, is completed in
Horchheim

Aug.-Sept.: FMB travels from Düsseldorf via Rotterdam to London; participates in the Birmingham Music Festival

Oct. 1: The young Mendelssohn couple moves into an apartment
in the Lurgenstein's Garden section of Leipzig

1838

Jan.: String Quartet in E-Flat, op. 44, no 3, is completed in
Leipzig

Feb. 7: Birth of first child, Karl Wolfgang Paul, in Leipzig

Apr.: Mendelssohn family travels to Berlin, spending the summer there

July: String Quartet in D Major, op. 44, no. 1, is completed

Aug.: Return to Leipzig; contracts measles

Oct. 13: Sonata for Cello and Piano in B-Flat Major, op. 45, is completed in Leipzig

1839

Mar. 22: FMB conducts Schubert's Symphony in C Major (the *Great*), which had been discovered by Robert Schumann

May-Aug.: FMB directs the Lower Rhine Music Festival in Düsseldorf and spends the summer with his family in Frankfurt

June: The parts to the three String Quartets, op. 44, are published in Leipzig

Sept. 6–8: FMB directs the Braunschweig Music Festival

Sept. 23: Piano Trio in D Minor, op. 40, is completed

Oct. 2: Birth of second child, Marie, in Leipzig

1840

Mar.: Franz Liszt concertizes in Leipzig, and performs Bach's Concerto for Three Pianos and Orchestra together with FMB and Ferdinand Hiller

May-June: Mendelssohns in Berlin

Sept: Lobgesang (*Hymn of Praise*)(Second Symphony) is completed in Leipzig; negotiations pertaining to a "musical post" in Berlin

1841

Jan. 18: Birth of third child, Paul, in Leipzig

Apr. 4: FMB conducts a performance of Bach's *St. Matthew Passion* in the Thomaskirche in Leipzig

May: FMB conducts negotiations in Berlin for a new position and prepares to relocate from Leipzig

July 1: Named Royal Saxon Kapellmeister

Oct. 10: Music to Sophocles' *Antigone,* op. 55, is completed in Berlin

Oct. 13: Named Royal Prussian Kapellmeister; moves into apartment at Leipziger Strasse 112 in Berlin

Oct. 28: First stage performance of the music to *Antigone,* op. 55, at the New Palace in Potsdam before Friedrich Wilhelm IV, under the direction of the composer

Nov.: Guest conductor in Leipzig

1842

Jan. 20: Third Symphony (*Scottish*) is completed in Berlin

May: FMB and Julius Rietz direct the Lower Rhine Music Festival in Düsseldorf

May-July: Together with his wife, FMB visits London and is invited to visit Queen Victoria

Aug.-Sept.: Mendelssohns, including Paul and Albertine, travel to Switzerland; return to Berlin via Leipzig

Nov.: FMB returns to Leipzig

Dec. 12: Death of mother Lea in Berlin

1843

Feb. 2: First performance of *Die erste Walpurgisnacht* in its final form at the Gewandhaus in Leipzig

Late Feb.–early Mar.: Sisters Fanny and Rebecka visit FMB in Leipzig

Apr.: Music to Shakespeare's *Midsummer Night's Dream,* op. 61, is completed in Leipzig; *Variations sérieuses,* for piano, op. 54, are published in Vienna

Apr. 3: Leipzig Conservatory, founded by FMB, is opened

Apr. 13: FMB is made an honorary citizen of the city of Leipzig

Apr. 23: Bach monument at the Thomas Gate in Leipzig, donated by FMB, is unveiled

May 1: Birth of fourth child, Felix, in Leipzig

Oct. 14: Private performance of the music to *A Midsummer Night's Dream* before Friedrich Wilhelm IV in the New Palace in Potsdam, under the direction of FMB

Nov. 25: FMB conducts church music for the first time at the Berlin Cathedral

1844

Jan.-Mar.: *Die erste Walpurgisnacht,* op. 60, is published in Leipzig

Apr.-July: FMB travels again to London via Leipzig and Frankfurt, where his family remains behind

July 26–Aug. 1: FMB directs the Music Festival in Zweibrücken

Sept.: Piano reduction of the music to *A Midsummer Night's Dream,* op. 61, is published in Leipzig

Sept. 16: Violin Concerto in E Minor, op. 64, is completed in Bad Soden

Sept. 30: FMB again in Berlin

Nov. 30: FMB leaves Berlin and decides to remain in Frankfurt for the time being

1845

Mar.: Renewed negotiations pertaining to a professorial post for teaching musical composition in Berlin

Mar. 13: First performance of the Violin Concerto, op. 64, at the Gewandhaus in Leipzig, with Ferdinand David under the direction of Niels Wilhelm Gade

Apr.: Piano Trio in C Minor, op. 66, is composed in Frankfurt

June: Orchestral parts and piano reduction to the Violin Concerto, op. 64, are published in Leipzig

July: On vacation together with siblings in Frieburg (Breisgau); FMB decides to return to his post in Leipzig

Aug.: Mendelssohn family moves back to Leipzig, settling at
     Königsstrasse 3
Sept. 19: Birth of fifth child, Elisabeth (Lilly), in Leipzig
Nov. 1: First stage performance of the music to *Oedipus*, op. 93,
     before Friedrich Wilhelm IV at the New Palace in Potsdam,
     under the direction of FMB
Nov. 12: Music to Racine's *Athalie*, op. 74, is completed
Dec. 1: Private performance of the music for *Athalie*, op. 74, at the
     Royal Theater in Charlottenburg (Berlin) for Friedrich Wil-
     helm IV, under the direction of FMB

1846

Jan. 1: FMB conducts the premiere performance of Robert Schu-
     mann's Piano Concerto, op. 54, with Clara Schumann as
     soloist, at the Leipzig Gewandhaus
Feb. 14: FMB conducts Richard Wagner's overture to *Tannhäuser*
     in Leipzig
May 31–June 16: FMB directs the Twenty-eighth Lower Rhine
     Music Festival in Aachen and the German–Flemish Choral
     Festival in Cologne
July: *Elijah* Oratorio, op. 70, is completed in Leipzig
Aug.-Sept.: Ninth trip to England; rehearsals for *Elijah* in London
     (with Moscheles) and on Aug. 26 the premiere performance
     (in its first version) at the Twenty-second Birmingham Mu-
     sic Festival
Oct.: Moscheles comes to the Conservatory of Leipzig as professor
     of piano performance
Nov. 5: FMB conducts the premiere of Schumann's Symphony No.
     2 in C Major at the Gewandhaus

1847

Apr.-May: Last trip to England
Apr. 16: *Elijah*, op. 70, is given its first performance in its final
     version in London by FMB

May 12: Arrival in Frankfurt

May 14: Death of sister Fanny in Berlin

Late May–early Sept.: Vacation and rest in Switzerland together with Paul and Albertine M. B.

July-Oct.: Elijah, op. 70, is published in Bonn

Aug.-Sept.: String Quartet in F Minor, op. 80, is composed in Interlaken

Sept. 17: Family returns to Leipzig

Oct. 3: FMB hears his Violin Concerto, op. 64, performed at the Gewandhaus with Joseph Joachim as soloist

Oct. 8: FMB judges entrance auditions for the Conservatory

Oct. 28: Stroke

Nov. 3: Second stroke

Nov. 4: Death of Mendelssohn in Leipzig

Nov. 7: Memorial service at the Paulinerkirche in Leipzig

Nov. 8: Funeral at Trinity Cemetery in Berlin

Dec.: The score for *Elijah,* op. 70, is published in Bonn

1848

June: The score for the music to *A Midsummer Night's Dream,* op. 61, is published in Leipzig

1849

Mar.: The music to *Athalie* is published posthumously as op. 74 in Leipzig

1850

Feb.: String Quartet in F Minor is published posthumously as op. 80 in Leipzig

1851

The Liederspiel *Returning Home from Foreign Lands* is published posthumously as op. 89 in Leipzig

Mar.: Fourth Symphony (*Italian*) is published posthumously as op. 90 in Leipzig

May 16: Death of son Felix in Berlin

Sept.: Piano reduction and choral parts to the music to *Oedipus* are published posthumously as op. 93 in Leipzig

Dec.: The score for the music to *Antigone*, op. 55, is published in Leipzig

1852

May: The score for the music to *Oedipus*, op. 93, is published in Leipzig

1853

Death of Cécile M. B. in Frankfurt

1858

Dec. 1: Death of Rebecka Dirichlet in Göttingen

1861

Nov. 26: Death of Wilhelm Hensel in Berlin; Paul and Karl M. B. publish a selection of Mendelssohn's letters

1868

Mar.: Fifth Symphony (*Reformation*) is published posthumously as op. 107 in Berlin

1869

Eduard Devrient publishes his *Erinnerungen an FMB* (Memories of FMB)

1871

Aug. 5: Death of Cécile M. B.'s mother, Elisabeth Jeanrenaud, in Freiburg

1874

June 21: Death of brother Paul M. B. in Berlin; Ferdinand Hiller publishes his *Erinnerungen an FMB* (Memories of FMB)

1874–77

The (in fact incomplete) *Complete Works* of Mendelssohn are published in Leipzig under the supervision of Julius Rietz

1879

Nov.: String Quartet in E-Flat Major, dating to 1823, is published in Berlin (no opus no.)
Sebastian Hensel's *Die Familie Mendelssohn* is published

INDEX OF RECIPIENTS
OF LETTERS AND DATES

Numbers refer to the pages on which the letters begin

INDEX OF PERSONS MENTIONED

FMB = Felix Mendelssohn Bartholdy

INDEX OF WORKS

Works with opus numbers up to 72 were all prepared for publication by Mendelssohn himself, although he did not live to see opus 71 and opus 72 in print. Opus 73 to opus 121 appeared posthumously. A small number of occasional pieces appeared during the composer's lifetime without opus numbers. Many works, particularly from Mendelssohn's youth, have not yet been published.

The numbers refer to the pages on which individual works are mentioned.

Vocal Works

A. SACRED PIECES

1. For a cappella chorus

2. For solo voice or chorus with accompaniment

Psalm 19, for chorus, soloists, and piano accompaniment
Psalm 66, for female chorus, soloists, and piano accompaniment
Gloria, for soloists, chorus, and orchestra
Magnificat, for soloists, chorus, and orchestra
Salve Regina, for soprano and strings
Jesus meine Zuversicht, motet for chorus, soloist, and piano accompaniment
Te Deum, for eight-part chorus, soloists, and piano accompaniment
Tu es Petrus, for chorus and orchestra, op. 111
Ave maris stella, for soprano, orchestra, and organ
Hora est, for sixteen-part chorus, soloists, and organ
Three Sacred Pieces, for chorus and solo voices with organ, op. 23, 144, 200
O Beata, motet for female chorus and organ
Five cantatas for soloists, chorus, and orchestra:
    Christe, du Lamm Gottes
    O Haupt voll Blut und Wunden, 131
    Vom Himmel hoch, 145
    Wir glauben all
    Ach Gott, vom Himmel sieh darein
Psalm 115, for soloists, chorus, and orchestra, op. 31
Verleih uns Frieden (Grant Us Thy Peace), for chorus and orchestra, 200
Te Deum, for soloists, chorus, and organ
Responsorium et Hymnus, for tenor, male chorus, cello, and bass, op. 121
Two Sacred Songs, for voice and piano, op. 112
Three Motets, for female chorus and organ, op. 39
Psalm 42, for soloists, chorus, orchestra, and organ, op. 42
Three Sacred Songs, for alto, chorus, and organ
Psalm 95, for soloists, chorus, orchestra, and organ, op. 46, 130
Psalm 114, for eight-part chorus and orchestra, op. 51
Hymn, for alto, chorus, and orchestra, op. 96

Hear My Prayer, hymn for soprano, chorus, and organ

Herr Gott, dich loben wir, chorale for eight-part chorus, orchestra, and organ

Psalm 98, for eight-part chorus, orchestra, and organ, op. 91

Lauda Sion, for soloists, chorus, and orchestra, op. 74

3. Oratorios

St. Paul, op. 36, 198, 201, 203, 206, 223, 228, 232, 268

Elijah, op. 70, 277, 283

Christus (incomplete), op. 97

B. SECULAR WORKS

1. For unaccompanied chorus

Im Freien zu singen, six songs for mixed chorus, op. 41

Der erste Frühlingstag, six songs for mixed chorus, op. 48

Six Male Choruses, op. 50

Im Grünen, six songs for mixed chorus, op. 59

Wandersmann, four songs for male chorus, op. 75

Four Male Choruses, op. 76

Six Choruses, op. 88

Four Songs for Mixed Chorus, op. 100

Four Male Choruses, op. 120

Ersatz für Unbestand, for male chorus

Die Frauen und die Sänger, for mixed chorus

2. Solo songs and vocal duets with piano accompaniment

Twelve Songs, op. 8 (nos. 2, 3, and 12 by Fanny)

Twelve Songs, op. 9 (nos. 7, 10, and 12 by Fanny), 119

(Der Blumenkranz) The Garland

Six Songs, op. 19a, 181, 203

Charlotte and Werther

Seemanns Scheidelied

Weihnachtslied (Christmas Song)

Six Songs, op. 47